Studies in Art, Heritage, Law and the Market

Volume 13

Andrea Wallace, Law School, University of Exeter, Exeter, UK

Matthias Weller, Department of Law, University of Bonn, Bonn, Germany

The book series *Studies in Art, Heritage, Law and the Market* provides an international and interdisciplinary forum for volumes that

- investigate legal, economic, and policy developments related to arts, heritage, and intellectual property;
- critically assess how and for whom art and heritage values come about;
- promote novel forms of user engagement, participatory presentations, and digitalization of arts and heritage;
- examine the processes that transform cultural objects and practices into arts and heritage; and
- highlight new approaches in preservation and conservation science.

The series addresses a need for research and practice in the fields of art, culture, conservation, and heritage including a focus on legal and economic aspects. It deals with complex issues such as questions of authenticity and provenance; forgery and falsification; the illicit trade, restitution, and return of cultural objects; the changing roles of museums; the roles of experts and expertise; and the ethics of the art market.

Bart Zwegers · Renée Vulto
Editors

The Spillover Effect of Intangible Cultural Heritage

Exploring the Impact of Intangible Cultural Heritage on Conservation Practices

Springer

Editors
Bart Zwegers
Faculty of Arts and Social Sciences
Maastricht University
Maastricht, Limburg, The Netherlands

Renée Vulto
Department of History and Art History
Utrecht University
Utrecht, The Netherlands

ISSN 2524-7425 ISSN 2524-7433 (electronic)
Studies in Art, Heritage, Law and the Market
ISBN 978-3-032-25351-4 ISBN 978-3-032-25352-1 (eBook)
https://doi.org/10.1007/978-3-032-25352-1

This Springer imprint is published by the registered company Springer Nature Switzerland AG
The registered company address is: Gewerbestrasse 11, 6330 Cham, Switzerland

Contents

Introduction: The Spillover Effect of Intangible Cultural Heritage 1
Renée Vulto and Bart Zwegers

The Governance of Intangible Cultural Heritage

A Fiddle for Everyone? Municipal Level Decision Making and the UNESCO Process in Kaustinen, Finland 11
Outi Valo and Heidi Henriikka Mäkelä

The Governance of Intangible Cultural Heritage: Practices, Stakeholders, and Masterpieces in Zimbabwe 33
Jesmael Mataga

Rethinking Craftsmanship, Restoration and Reconstruction

The Relevance of Building Crafts for Cultural Heritage Conservation and the Quality of Life: Case Studies from Egypt 51
Ingy Waked, Koenraad van Balen, and Christian Ost

From CNC Machine to Chisel: Balancing (3D) Technology and Craftsmanship in the Restoration of Notre Dame, Dom Tower, and Grote Kerk 77
Liselore Tissen and Hendrik-Jan Tolboom

The Reconstruction of Kāṣthamaṇḍap: As Seen through its Intangible Ritual Practices 105
Binita Magaiya

New and Future Uses of Intangible Cultural Heritage

Reframing Museum Practice: The ICHC's Impact on Museums 121
Alix Ferrer-Yulfo

Learning from Intangible Cultural Heritage in Times of Climate Change 145
Bart Zwegers and Karim van Knippenberg

Introduction: The Spillover Effect of Intangible Cultural Heritage

Renée Vulto and Bart Zwegers

This volume critically examines how the concept of intangible cultural heritage has been developed, integrated, and contested since the 2003 UNESCO 'Convention for the Safeguarding of the Intangible Cultural Heritage', and how this has reshaped heritage management in the twenty-first century. The introduction of a framework for intangible cultural heritage (ICH) has not only expanded heritage ideas but also created a spillover effect on heritage policies and practices. Drawing on interdisciplinary case studies combining fields such as heritage studies, conservation, museology, economics, engineering, history, and music, and spanning contexts including Zimbabwe, Finland, Nepal, Egypt, France, and the Netherlands, the various chapters in this book explore evolving relationships between intangible and tangible heritage, authenticity and adaptation, and preservation and innovation.

In recent decades, the concept of cultural heritage has undergone profound shifts, reflecting changes in both international policy frameworks and scholarly thinking. For much of the twentieth century, the dominant notion of heritage—particularly as codified by UNESCO—centered around the preservation of tangible monuments, historic buildings, archaeological sites and collections of material artifacts. These sites and objects were often valued for their architectural, aesthetic or historical significance and treated as symbols of cultural identity. During the 1990s, UNESCO was increasingly criticized for its allegedly narrow understanding of heritage. The notion of monumentality that UNESCO asserted focused on the material, tangible qualities of objects. Inevitably favouring European heritage sites and largely ignoring forms of 'living' cultural heritage, such as crafts, cultural practices and traditions

R. Vulto
Department of History and Art History, Utrecht University, Utrecht, The Netherlands
e-mail: r.vulto@uu.nl

B. Zwegers (✉)
Department of History, Maastricht University, Maastricht, The Netherlands
e-mail: b.zwegers@maastrichtuniversity.nl

B. Zwegers and R. Vulto (eds.), *The Spillover Effect of Intangible Cultural Heritage*, Studies in Art, Heritage, Law and the Market 13,
https://doi.org/10.1007/978-3-032-25352-1_1

(Alivizatou 2022; Bendix et al. 2013; Labadi 2013). The criticism of this perspective not only came from scholars (cf. Hafstein 2018; Harrison 2012; Meskell 2013; Smith 2006), but also from non-Western UNESCO member states that addressed this omission and lobbied intensely for a more inclusive notion of World Heritage (Chakrabarti and Chakrabarti 2025; Frey and Steiner 2011). One of the outcomes of these debates was the 2003 'Convention for the Safeguarding of the Intangible Cultural Heritage' (ICOMOS 2003), which was hoped to offer a remedy to the imbalanced global spread of World Heritage by introducing a more dynamic and inclusive definition of the heritage concept.

The 2003 Convention thus represented a long-awaited attempt to recalibrate the heritage field, offering a framework designed to protect and promote intangible cultural expressions, practices, and knowledge systems. Importantly, the Convention introduced a more dynamic, inclusive, and community-centered understanding of heritage—one that emphasized continuity, collective memory, and the intergenerational transmission of knowledge and cultural practices. It sought to correct the imbalance in the global spread of officially recognized heritage, offering new opportunities for communities around the world to assert the value of their living traditions on an international stage.

The development of the 2003 Convention was neither sudden nor isolated; rather, it emerged from a broader theoretical and policy discourse that, over preceding decades, progressively expanded the conceptual boundaries of cultural heritage. As Lucas Lixinski notes in his work on intangible cultural heritage in international law, international efforts to safeguard intangible heritage can be traced back to several mid-twentieth-century instruments. These include the 1952 UNESCO Convention on copyright, the 1967 UNESCO initiative on the protection of folklore, and the 1973 convention concerning forms of Indigenous heritage (Lixinski 2013, pp. 30–31). However, the principles articulated in the Burra Charter (1979/2013) and the Nara Document on Authenticity (1994) were particularly instrumental in shaping the intellectual and normative foundations upon which the 2003 Convention was constructed. The Burra Charter introduced a value-based approach to heritage conservation, advocating for the recognition of diverse cultural values associated with heritage places, including social, spiritual, and associative meanings attributed by communities. Significantly, it emphasized the importance of community involvement in the conservation process and acknowledged that cultural significance encompasses both tangible and intangible dimensions. Building upon such developments, the Nara Declaration further challenged universalist interpretations of cultural heritage. The declaration asserted that conceptions of authenticity are culturally contingent and must be understood within the specific historical, social, and cultural contexts in which heritage is created and sustained. It extended the notion of authenticity beyond material fabric to encompass intangible attributes such as traditions, language, belief systems, and cultural knowledge. In doing so, the Nara Declaration emphasized the necessity of respecting cultural diversity in heritage identification and conservation processes, advocating for an inclusive and culturally sensitive approach.

These normative frameworks directly informed the formulation of the 2003 Convention, which represents the first legally binding international instrument dedicated to the safeguarding of intangible heritage. The convention defines intangible cultural heritage as the practices, knowledge, skills, and cultural spaces that communities and individuals recognize as part of their cultural identity. Passed down through generations, it evolves in response to the environment and history, fostering identity, continuity, and respect for cultural diversity and creativity (ICOMOS 2003, article 2). Central to the 2003 Convention is thus the principle of community participation, recognizing that the safeguarding of intangible heritage must be community-led and based on the consent and involvement of those who practice and transmit it (Alivizatou 2022).

The recognition of heritage communities within the framework of the 2003 Convention has also intersected with broader contemporary debates on community agency. Historically, heritage management systems—particularly within the context of international frameworks—were dominated by state authorities, expert institutions, and Western-centric epistemologies that privileged tangible monuments and sites while marginalizing Indigenous, local, and vernacular cultural expressions. The shift toward a community-centered safeguarding model represents a deliberate move to redistribute authority in heritage processes (Smith 2006). It acknowledges that communities themselves are best positioned to define the meanings, values, and appropriate safeguarding measures for their cultural heritage. This re-centering of community agency challenges entrenched hierarchies within heritage discourse and practice, opening space for culturally specific, locally situated, and often non-Western knowledge systems to inform heritage policy and conservation strategies. Moreover, it aligns with decolonizing agendas that seek to dismantle residual colonial structures within heritage management, advocating for the recognition of diverse ontologies and epistemologies. By foregrounding the voices, practices, and priorities of heritage communities, contemporary heritage governance begins to address historical imbalances and contributes to a more inclusive, equitable, and culturally pluralistic understanding of heritage in the global context (Bortolotto 2025).

It is no coincidence that the discursive changes in the broader heritage field ran parallel to the rise of critical heritage studies as an influential sub-discipline. Critical heritage studies reshaped thinking about intangible cultural heritage by challenging earlier, static understandings of heritage and emphasizing the power dynamics involved in defining, safeguarding, and representing heritage. Instead of treating heritage as a set of timeless cultural expressions to be preserved, critical scholars highlight that heritage is continually produced, negotiated, and contested within social, political, and economic contexts. This critical perspective draws attention to whose voices are included or excluded in heritage-making processes, how communities exercise agency, and how global frameworks can both empower and constrain local cultural practices. As a result, heritage is now more widely understood as a dynamic, lived, and often politicized process rather than a fixed cultural inventory. Moreover, critical heritage scholars challenged the dichotomy between tangible and intangible heritage, arguing that all heritage is socially constructed and subsequently intangible (Smith 2011; Smith and Akagawa 2008). These insights not only transformed heritage practices, but also sparked new academic research on intangible heritage.

Much of the academic research in the wake of the 2003 Convention has focused on defining the concept of intangible heritage (Fairchild Ruggles and Silverman 2009, p. 1), or on assessing whether it succeeded in broadening the heritage concept and facilitating a more even distribution of World Heritage designations (Blake and Lixinski 2020). Less attention, however, has been paid to the unintended and sometimes paradoxical effects of introducing intangible cultural heritage into conservation and heritage management discourse. This is a pity, because while the Convention's establishment marked a significant step forward, it also initiated a range of unforeseen consequences and complex debates. One of the central ideas behind this volume is the recognition that intangible heritage—far from existing in isolation—has actively reshaped how societies conceptualize, manage, and contest the meanings and uses of heritage spaces and practices.

A significant dimension of this shift lies in the way in which the Convention's flexible, less object-centered definition of heritage has been co-opted by a range of actors, including urban planners, developers and policymakers, to justify interventions in historic environments that might otherwise have faced resistance under stricter notions of authenticity and material integrity. By foregrounding intangible values—such as community narratives, cultural meanings, or social functions—stakeholders have sometimes used the concept of intangible cultural heritage to legitimize alterations to historic urban landscapes, leading to tensions between preservation, adaptation, and economic development. For example, proponents of the controversial Waldschlösschen bridge in Dresden—which would eventually cost the city its World Heritage status—legitimized the plan by referring to Dresden's bridge-building tradition (Zwegers 2022). Similarly, an initiative to reopen an eighteenth-century tin mine in Cornwall—which would have posed a significant threat to the valuable material remnants of the mining industry—was presented as a unique opportunity to revitalize the immaterial crafts, lifestyles and traditions associated with tin mining (Zwegers 2018). In this sense, the introduction of the ICH framework has not merely added to the existing heritage repertoire but has produced a spillover effect that influences heritage ideologies, policies, and conservation practices.

The chapters in this volume seek to examine these developments in detail, bringing together case studies, theoretical reflections, and analyses that explore how the conceptual underpinnings of intangible cultural heritage have been integrated, contested, and transformed in different contexts. The book offers a critical assessment of the consequences of the 2003 Convention for heritage management in the twenty-first century. Bringing together an interdisciplinary group of authors working in research fields such as heritage studies, heritage conservation, museology, economics, engineering, history, and music, the volume aims to foster an interdisciplinary conversation about the evolving relationships between intangible and tangible heritage, authenticity and adaptation, preservation and innovation. Apart from bringing together authors with various disciplinary backgrounds, the book sheds light on the impact of intangible cultural heritage in various national contexts—including Zimbabwe, Finland, Nepal, Egypt, France, and the Netherlands. The book is divided into three thematic parts, each addressing a key aspect of these debates.

The first section—'The Governance of Intangible Cultural Heritage'—examines how intangible cultural heritage is operationalized and negotiated within governance structures. It explores the complex processes by which communities, policymakers, and international organizations attempt to define, protect, and manage intangible heritage within formal frameworks. Outi Valo and Heidi Henriikka Mäkelä's chapter focuses on *Kaustinen fiddle playing* in Finland, a local musical tradition inscribed on UNESCO's Representative List of the Intangible Cultural Heritage of Humanity in 2021. The authors trace how this recognition influenced municipal decision-making, highlighting the interplay between global heritage conventions and local cultural politics. Jesmael Mataga's contribution turns to Zimbabwe, analyzing the country's experiences with the 2003 Convention through the case studies of *Mbende/Jerusarema dance* and the art of crafting and playing *Mbira/Sansi*. Mataga contextualizes these developments within Zimbabwe's postcolonial heritage politics.

Both chapters engage with the issues that arise with the interaction between different government levels: what is the effect on local intangible heritage practices when they are inscribed on an internationally recognized inventory? While the issue of listing has been raised and discussed before (Kirshenblatt-Gimblett 2004; Frey and Steiner 2011) both Valo and Mäkelä and Mataga dive into the spillover effect on local and regional levels. Valo and Mäkelä demonstrate how intangible heritage designations can elevate a local tradition of Kaustinen onto national and international platforms while simultaneously generating new tensions around resource allocation and cultural representation. Likewise, Mataga shows how national and local struggles in Zimbabwe over cultural authority, ancestral landscapes, and the institutionalization of Indigenous knowledge systems relate to the Convention's emphasis on community participation and living traditions. This is also a topic of Binita Magaya's chapter—represented in the second part of this volume—which engages with the tensions between different authorities and institutions in the reconstruction of Kāṣṭhamanḍap, a historic wooden pavilion in Nepal's Kathmandu Valley, after its collapse in the 2015 Gorkha earthquake.

The second part—'Rethinking Craftsmanship, Restoration and Reconstruction'—addresses the implications of intangible heritage recognition for conservation and restoration practices, especially in the face of technological innovation and disaster recovery. Ingy Waked, Koenraad van Balen and Christian Ost examine the role of traditional building crafts in Egypt, reflecting on how these practices contribute not only to heritage conservation but also to sustaining community livelihoods and quality of life. Through case studies of traditional craftsmanship sectors, the chapter highlights both the vulnerabilities and the vital importance of these intangible skills in maintaining historic urban environments. Liselore Tissen and Hendrik-Jan Tolboom investigate the integration of generative AI and 3D printing in the restoration of major European heritage sites such as the Dom Tower of Utrecht and Notre-Dame in Paris. Their comparative analysis sheds light on the ethical and practical dilemmas posed by digital technologies in heritage restoration, particularly the tension between mechanical precision and the human touch essential to traditional craftsmanship. The chapter questions how technological tools might alter public perceptions of authenticity and intangible value in restored monuments. As mentioned, Binita Magaiya's chapter recounts the reconstruction of Kāṣṭhamanḍap. The chapter demonstrates how ritual practices and esoteric philosophies—once dismissed as spiritual relics—were central to the rebuilding process, illustrating how intangible heritage can inform not only community identity but also practical conservation methodologies.

All three chapters investigate the tensions between traditional knowledges and craftsmanship and the availability of new technologies. Tissen and Tolboom, as well as Magaiya, describe how new technologies are or are not embraced in restoration projects. As such, their case studies touch upon the broader question of the relevance of craftsmanship and traditional knowledges considering present-day technologies that can potentially perform 'better' than past practices. The authors of both chapters can be said to argue that this idea should be approached from a critical perspective, showing in their analyses the significance of respectively the human touch and ritual practices. Bart Zwegers and Karim van Knippenberg as well, in the last chapter of this volume, engage critically with technological innovations. Their work on landscape management in the context of climate change shows that a trust in technological development has turned a blind eye to historical environmental knowledge and argue that intangible heritage practices can offer valuable knowledge for making our cities and landscapes 'waterproof' for the future.

The final section—'New and Future Uses of Intangible Cultural Heritage'—examines how intangible heritage is being mobilized in contemporary institutions and policy fields, addressing new forms of heritage activism and adaptation. Alix Ferrer-Yulfo explores the evolving relationship between museums and intangible cultural heritage since the adoption of the 2003 Convention. The chapter critically assesses the challenges museums face in moving beyond material collections to embrace community-based, performative, and living traditions. By tracing international museological debates and practical initiatives, the author highlights both the opportunities and tensions inherent in repositioning museums as active agents in safeguarding intangible heritage. In the concluding chapter, Zwegers and Knippenberg turn to the pressing issue of climate change. Their chapter focuses on the lessons that urban planners and hydrologists can learn from intangible cultural heritage and the cultural history of our landscape. It shows that intangible heritage can inform climate change adaptation and mitigation policies.

These two chapters raise the issue of expertise in relation to intangible heritage. As stated earlier, the 2003 Convention had a significant emancipatory function in aiming to acknowledge heritage beyond the material, giving agency to heritage communities however small and informal (Alivizatou 2022). Ferrer-Yulfo shows that this shift, giving voice to the community and the individual as experts of their heritage practices, has a predecessor in New Museology. The acknowledgement of the expertise of heritage communities also becomes apparent in Magaya's chapter, which shows how Kathmandu's local community took control in the restauration process of Kāṣṭhamanḍap. Similarly, Waked, Van Balen and Ost discuss the relevance of skills and knowledge of heritage communities for ensuring the sustainability of cultural heritage. And finally, Zwegers and van Knippenberg plead for giving a voice to intangible heritage in issues of climate change adaptation and mitigation policies. Ultimately, all these chapters show that, despite the efforts of UNESCO and national, regional and local NGO's, it is not yet evident that intangible heritage communities are unquestionably acknowledged for their knowledge and the cultural, societal, and economic value of their practices.

Collectively, the contributions in this volume underscore the often unexpected ways in which the concept of intangible cultural heritage has reconfigured the field of heritage studies and practice. The recognition of living traditions has not only diversified what counts as heritage but also transformed the discursive and institutional frameworks through which cultural value is negotiated. By investigating the spillover effects of the 2003 Convention—from local governance and technological innovation to museology and climate resilience—the case studies discussed in this volume offer new insights into the evolving landscape of heritage politics and conservation. In doing so, the authors invite scholars, policymakers, and practitioners to join them in a critical reflection on how the dynamic interplay between tangible and intangible, local and global, tradition and innovation will shape heritage practices of the future.

References

Alivizatou M (2022) Intangible heritage and participation. Routledge, Oxford

Bendix R, Eggert A, Peselmann A (eds) (2013) Heritage regimes and the state. Universitätsverlag, Göttingen

Blake J, Lixinski L (eds) (2020) The 2003 UNESCO intangible heritage convention: a commentary. Oxford University Press, Oxford

Bortolotto C (2025) Will heritage save us?: Intangible cultural heritage and the sustainable development turn. Cambridge University Press, Cambridge

Chakrabarti M, Chakrabarti G (eds) (2025) Intangible cultural heritage in a globalized world. Springer, Cham

Fairchild Ruggles D, Silverman H (eds) (2009) Intangible heritage embodies. Springer, New York

Frey B, Steiner L (2011) World heritage list: does it make sense? Int J Cult Policy 17:555–573

Hafstein V (2018) Making intangible heritage: El Condor Pasa and other stories from UNESCO. Indiana University Press, Bloomington

Harrison R (2012) Heritage: critical approaches. Routledge, London

ICOMOS (2003) Convention for the safeguarding of the intangible cultural heritage. ICOMOS, Paris. https://ich.unesco.org/en/convention

Kirshenblatt-Gimblett B (2004) Intangible heritage as metacultural production. Mus Int 56:52–65

Labadi S (2013) UNESCO, cultural heritage, and outstanding universal value: value-based analyses of the world heritage and intangible cultural heritage conventions. AltaMira Press, Lanham

Lixinski L (2013) Intangible cultural heritage in international law. Oxford University Press, Oxford

Meskell L (2013) UNESCO's world heritage convention at 40: challenging the economic and political order of international heritage conservation. Curr Anthr 54:483–494

Smith L (2006) Uses of heritage. Routledge, London

Smith L (2011) All heritage is intangible: critical heritage studies and museums. Reinwardt Academy, Amsterdam

Smith L, Akagawa N (eds) (2008) Intangible heritage. Routledge, London

Zwegers B (2018) Goldmine or bottomless pit. Exploiting Cornwall's mining heritage. J Herit Tour Serv Mark 4:15–22
Zwegers B (2022) Cultural heritage in transition. A multi-level perspective on world heritage in Germany and the United Kingdom, 1970–2020. Springer, Cham

Renée Vulto is an assistant professor of Intangible Cultural Heritage in the Cultural History department of Utrecht University. She has an educational background in musicology and literary studies and wrote her thesis on eighteenth-century Dutch revolutionary song culture. Renée teaches courses on media history, intangible heritage, and (post)colonial cultures in the BA programme History and the MA Cultural History and Heritage, and regularly engages with other student groups, interdisciplinary academic audiences, and a broader public.

Bart Zwegers is the curator academic heritage of Maastricht University and works as a lecturer at the Faculty of Arts and Social Sciences of Maastricht University. He has an educational background in arts and culture. Between 2018 and 2021 he was a lecturer in social and political history at Radboud University Nijmegen. In 2022 he published the monograph *Cultural Heritage in Transition. A Multilevel Perspective on World Heritage in Germany and the United Kingdom, 1970–2020* with Springer.

The Governance of Intangible Cultural Heritage

A Fiddle for Everyone? Municipal Level Decision Making and the UNESCO Process in Kaustinen, Finland

Outi Valo and Heidi Henriikka Mäkelä

1 Introduction

The chapter focuses on the Finnish musical phenomenon *Kaustinen fiddle playing and related practices and expressions* (hereafter referred as Kaustinen fiddle playing) which was inscribed to the UNESCO Representative List of the Intangible Cultural Heritage of Humanity in 2021, 8 years after Finland ratified the Intangible Cultural Heritage (ICH) convention. In our chapter, we utilize the discussions on Kaustinen fiddle playing as a case study to examine the impact of the UNESCO ICH convention and its listing mechanisms, by investigating the effects of the listing on local-level decision-making. Kaustinen is a small municipality in Western Finland with a population of approximately 4100 (see Fig. 1). The impacts of the UNESCO process on the local scale are analysed by examining the municipality's policy-making through local media texts and minutes of the Kaustinen Municipal Council (KMC) and Kaustinen Municipal Executive (KME).

In accordance with the Finnish municipal system, the Municipal Council is the highest decision-making body in Kaustinen. Elected through local elections every 4 years, the Municipal Council oversees the municipality's operations and finances. It is also responsible for the long-term objectives, finances, and preparing the municipality strategy. The Municipal Executive, which operates under the Municipal Council, manages the municipality's operations, administration, and finances (Suomi.fi 2024). Consequently, the Municipal Council is responsible for the most

O. Valo (✉)
Sibelius Academy doctoral programme and research centre, University of the Arts Helsinki, Helsinki, Finland
e-mail: outi.valo@kaustinen.fi

H. H. Mäkelä
Sibelius Academy, University of the Arts Helsinki, Helsinki, Finland
e-mail: heidi.makela@uniarts.fi

B. Zwegers and R. Vulto (eds.), *The Spillover Effect of Intangible Cultural Heritage*, Studies in Art, Heritage, Law and the Market 13,
https://doi.org/10.1007/978-3-032-25352-1_2

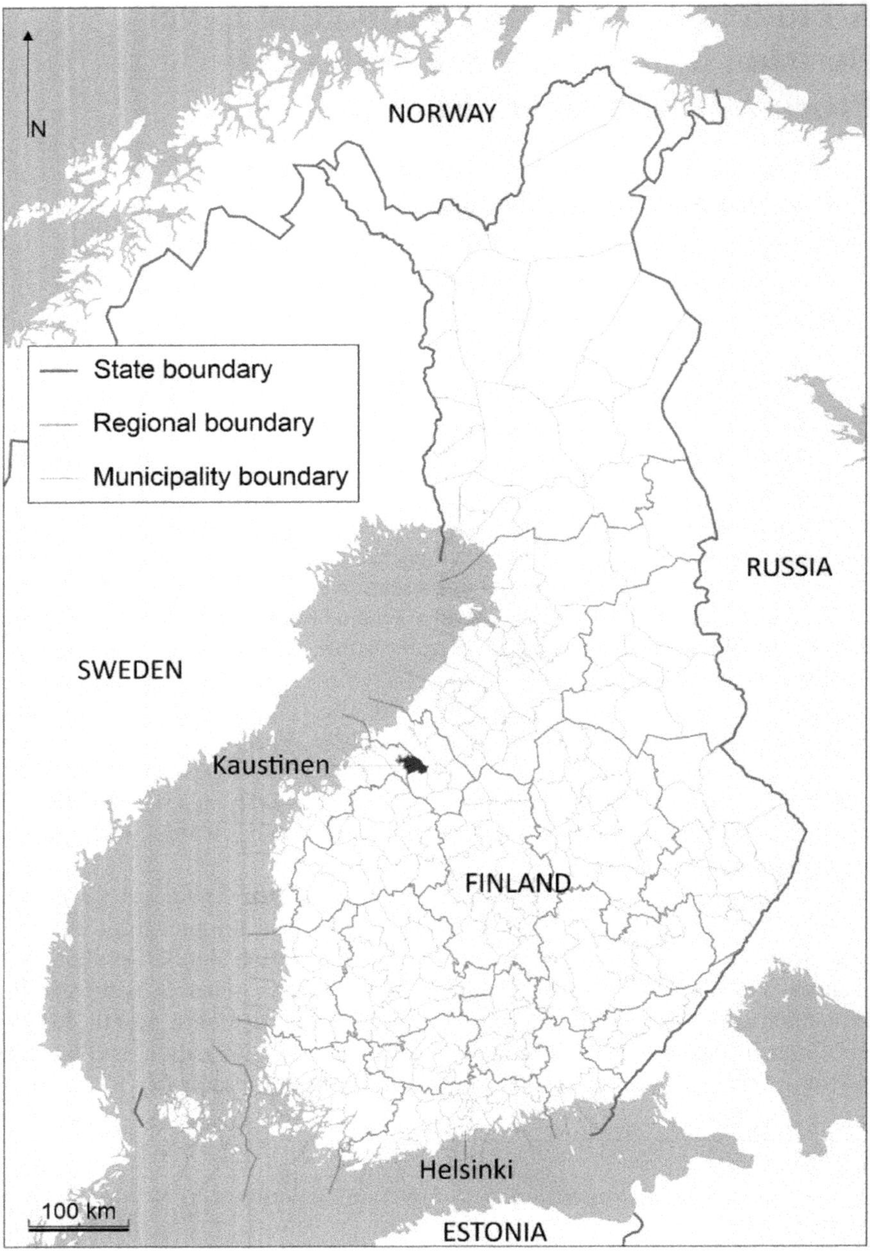

Fig. 1 The location of Kaustinen and Finnish regional and municipality borders (© Hannu Linkola CC BY 4.0)

significant decisions, while the Municipal Executive is tasked with implementing them. The political composition of the present Kaustinen Municipal Council (2021–2025) is as follows: the Centre Party (14 seats), the Finns Party (5 seats), the Social Democratic Party of Finland (1 seat), and the Greens (1 seat) (The Municipality of Kaustinen 2024a).[1] Of these parties, the Centre represents the centrist slightly conservative wing emphasising equal treatment of Finland's regions, the Finns Party the populist right-wing with anti-immigration themes, and the others the more liberal left-green wing (see e.g. Allianssi 2024).

In our chapter, we analyse the proceedings and discussions of these actors, with a particular focus on the status of heritage and cultural policy in the municipality's actions. By comparing the municipality's actions and the process of the Kaustinen fiddle playing UNESCO listing, we demonstrate the impact of the listing on the municipality's decision-making processes. We examine the way the concept of intangible cultural heritage was employed in the material, including the instances of its appearance in the discussions, the political parties involved, and the contexts in which it was referenced. Additionally, we analyse the manner in which politicians refer to the UNESCO status when making decisions related to culture and its funding.

We assert that speeches and initiatives related to intangible cultural heritage increased in the years of planning and achieving the inscription, as well as in the period following it, in comparison to the time before the UNESCO process commenced. The notion of heritage thus became more important for local politicians when it was noticed on a national and global level. Furthermore, all parties participated in the exploitation of the concept and the reputation it brought, and all adopted to some extent the language stemming from the ICH convention. However, the conservative and populist Finns Party sought to oppose the costs of heritage and to reduce municipal funding for it.

2 Theoretical Framework

We understand the concept of heritage as inherently 'cultural': it is a constantly changing process of social meaning-making in which certain types of material-discursive elements and practices of the past are chosen to represent identities, ethnicities, histories, and places to reshape and construct the present and the future (see e.g. Smith 2006, 2020). These processes may be rather exclusive, centred on professional practices, and reproduce normative values related to, e.g., nation, gender, and race (e.g. Mäkelä 2022). In particular, the UNESCO World Heritage Convention (adopted in 1972) and its inscriptions have been criticised for emphasising Western ideals of heritage by highlighting buildings and monuments made of stable materials

[1] In the previous Kaustinen Municipal Council (2017–2020) the Centre Party had one seat less and the Finns one more: the Centre Party (13 seats), the Finns Party (6 seats), the Social Democratic Party of Finland (1 seat), and the Greens (1 seat) (KMC 2017a).

such as stone, whereas for non-Western countries the skills required for reconstruction are more important than the building itself, and this has contributed to the renewal of non-Western models of heritage (Bortolotto 2010, pp. 106–107). Still, intangible cultural heritage, the UNESCO processes and the listings are innately tied to Western heritage administration and conceptualisations of heritage (Akagawa and Smith 2019; Hafstein 2018), and ICH is, as Barbara Kirshenblatt-Gimblett (2004) proposes, a form of 'metacultural production' in which the 'UNESCO machine' standardises and globalizes different kinds of local understandings of managing past-related phenomena.

In Finland, the UNESCO ICH Conventation implementation is supervised by the Finnish Heritage Agency (FHA), and despite of the very inclusive aspirations of the FHA, the ICH inventorying seem to generally produce rather a normative, nationalistic, and exclusive image of Finnishness (Mäkelä 2021, 2022). However, the spillover effects of the convention and especially the four UNESCO-inscribed elements of Finland (Kaustinen fiddle playing, sauna bathing, clinker boats building and glass-making tradition) have not yet been examined on local, regional, nor national level. Thus, our research is an opening step into this territory, as we examine the local effects of the listing particularly from the point of view of municipal decision-making.

Previous research has highlighted how nation states use global heritage conventions such as the World Heritage Convention for their own purposes, and this applies in many ways to the Convention for the Safeguarding of the ICH (Askew 2010, pp. 38–41; see also Beardslee 2016, p. 98). Anthropologist Marc Askew points to the potential impact of these uses at the local level, asking: "Are local meanings leached out or distorted in the process of being elevated to a global list?" (Askew 2010, p. 30). Furthermore, researcher Chiara Bortolotto has analyzed the local appropriations of the global convention, claiming that by using specific labels in the marketing of their products, local heritage stakeholders mobilize and display various kinds of evidence to prove their conformity with tradition and embeddedness in local culture (Bortolotto 2010, p. 110).

Our starting point is that the UNESCO listing is a strong tool and a metacultural mechanism that greatly influences not only the tradition in question itself but also the surrounding community and its social relations, politics, and everyday life. Many of those whose element has been inscribed into the ICH lists report that the effects of listing have been positive and empowering on a community level (Hafstein 2018, pp. 156–157). However, as Regina Bendix (2009, pp. 260–263) argues, heritagisations are tied to mechanisms of social and political control at different scales, and the "symbolic capital" inherent in the listed elements becomes quickly a desired tool in the power struggles of different kinds of governance systems. As we will show in this chapter, the symbolic capital embedded in the Kaustinen fiddle playing listing has inevitably become a significant actor in the Kaustinen area, and all political parties involved in the decision-making want to utilize this capital, simultaneously competing for power and control over it.

Furthermore, as we will show in the following subchapters, the municipal-level discussions on ICH—and, simultaneously, the spillover effects—are strongly tied to money and economy. Heritage is often represented as something that goes beyond the banalities of the everyday life, is "authentic" and "pristine", and thus, should not be "vulgarised by the economy" (Lixinski 2019, p. 55). However, the ICH listing mechanisms are inevitably linked to private law, economy, and commodification, not necessarily in a form of folklorised kitsch, but mainly through tourism and other activities that have economic dimensions (Lixinski 2019). In Kaustinen, the popular Kaustinen Folk Music Festival has been recognised as a force that impacts the area's local economy, tourism, business revenue, and employment (e.g. Jaskari 2023). We argue that the Kaustinen ICH inscription is a driving force in these sectors as well, nowadays being an even more significant pull factor than the Festival. However, the chapter does not concentrate on counting the economic effects of the listing. Instead, we focus on discussing how the listing has influenced values, beliefs, and understandings of heritage, and how these intermingle with the politics and economy of the municipality.

Because one of the important dimensions in this chapter is the powerplay between the Centre and the populist Finns Party, we also utilise the research done on contemporary populism, far-right movements and (music) heritage in Europe (e.g. De Cesari and Kaya 2019; Lähdesmäki 2020; Niklasson and Hølleland 2018; Helmersson 2020; Kaminsky 2012). These studies argue that heritage in these contexts is primarily a discursive political idea to which to refer to when one feels threatened by otherness (Kaya 2019). However, as we will show in this study, at the local level, heritage appeals to the Finns Party primarily because of the economic opportunities it offers, not precisely because of its potential to construct local identities.

3 The Politics of Kaustinen Fiddle Playing: From Peasant Music to an ICH Element

Kaustinen fiddle playing is described in the following way in the inscription on the Representative List of the ICH of Humanity:

> "Kaustinen folk music is a Finnish tradition where the fiddle (violin), although not the only instrument, is the main melodic instrument. [...] Based on playing by ear, it is characterized by syncopated and accented rhythms that are easy for people to dance to. The distinctive style and playing technique of Kaustinen folk music have existed for over 250 years, and there is a repertoire of several hundred tunes from the area. Kaustinen folk music is played in many contexts: in private, in organized groups, during public celebrations and ceremonies (including wedding parties), at concerts and public jam sessions, and at the annual Kaustinen Folk Music Festival. Performers often wear traditional costumes" (UNESCO 2024, p. 1).

Kaustinen fiddle playing has played a central role in the understandings what 'Finnish folk music' is since the Second World War, when the eyes of folk music collectors were focused on the western part of Finland instead of the eastern parts, which were considered too politically controversial due to the fragile relations between Finland and the Soviet Union (Valo 2022, pp. 100–122). The politically conservative peasant culture of the western parts of the country was seen as a good example of Finnish rural folk culture, and Kaustinen's particular style of fiddling was eagerly promoted (Valo and Mäkelä 2025). During the 1960s, Kaustinen became even more significant in the cultural politics of Finland, as the urban new wave folk music enthusiasts began to emphasise its remarkable folk culture. In this context, the brand new Kaustinen Folk Music Festival was established in 1968 (Ramnarine 2003, pp. 51–53). Since then, the festival has been a significant part of the Finnish folk music life, and today it is the largest folk music festival in the Nordic countries (Finland Festivals 2024). Moreover, the Finnish Folk Music Institute established in Kaustinen 1974 plays a significant role in the field of folk music, both at the regional level and nationally. Thus, the folklorist Kristin Kuutma's observation on how "UNESCO nomination does not drop into an empty space, but tops an already existing format of management and representation" (Kuutma 2019, p. 77) holds true for the Kaustinen fiddle playing as well.

Even before the UNESCO nomination, the Kaustinen Folk Music Festival and the folk music institutions of the area had a strong influence on the economy, tourism, and cultural life of the Kaustinen region (Ilmonen et al. 1995; Cantell 1993). However, economic difficulties of the Festival during the last decades have also complicated the cultural politics in the area: before 2011, the Finnish Folk Music Institute and the Kaustinen Folk Music Festival were managed by the same organization, the Folk Music Foundation (*Kansanmusiikkisäätiö*), but it went bankrupt in 2011. After that, the organisation was divided into two different associations, both of which rent premises from the Folk Art Centre (*Kansantaiteenkeskus*).[2] The Pro Kaustinen Association took care of the Kaustinen Folk Music Festival. The Municipality of Kaustinen took possession of the Finnish Folk Music Institute, the folk music group Tallari and the Folk Instrument Museum, which were part of the former foundation. In 2013 they were taken over by a new association, the Finnish Folk Music Institute (*Kansanmusiikki-instituutti ry*) (Finnish Folk Music Institute 2014).

In the early 2010s, a group of humanities professors proposed that the state of Finland should participate in the 2003 ICH convention. The planning of the proposal began at the meeting of the Creative Industries Network, where it was noted that it was embarrassing that there were no elements from Finland on the lists of intangible cultural heritage and that ratification had not taken place (Luovien alojen verkosto 2010; OKM Registry 2024). Even at that time the Kaustinen fiddle playing was brought forth as one of the best examples of Finnish heritage (OKM Registry 2024; see also Mäkelä and Valo 2025, pp 24).[3] The proposal itself came from the experts, but according to the report on the application process for Kaustinen fiddle playing, this

[2] The Folk Music Foundation used to own part of the stocks of the Folk Art Centre Ltd. (*Kaustisen Kansantaiteenkeskus Oy*), which were acquired by the Municipality of Kaustinen after the bankruptcy. Now the majority of the shares are owned by the Municipality of Kaustinen with 94% of the shares, but there are also other shareholders with smaller shares (The Municipality of Kaustinen 2024b).

[3] The Finnish inventorying process has three levels: (1) *The Wiki-Inventory of Living Heritage*, that is an open access inventory platform into which everyone (except commercial and political actors) can send their proposals, but the FHA administrates it; (2) *The National Inventory of Living Heritage* to which the Wiki-Inventory-involved communities can apply and that is coordinated by the FHA and a group of specialists; and (3) the international UNESCO lists into which the Ministry of Education and Culture nominates submissions for inscription (Finnish Heritage Agency 2024). Kaustinen fiddle playing has been one of the first submission on all these levels.

prompted the actors in Kaustinen to familiarise themselves with the 2003 Convention and its contents. The next application for the Europa Nostra award was made mainly through the expert work of the Finnish Folk Music Institute, but the submissions in the Finnish ICH inventorying processes were created together with the Kaustinen-based associations, the Finnish Folk Music Association and the Municipality of Kaustinen. In 2017, the local Kaustinen associations formed a 'UNESCO working group' (officially the Kaustinen fiddle playing ICH working group). This included the Kaustinen Youth Association (which maintains local folk dance groups in particular), *Kaustisen Näppärit* (which focuses on folk music education for children), *Kaustisen Pelimanniyhdistys* (a local association of folk musicians), Pro Kaustinen (which maintains the Kaustinen Folk Music Festival) and the Finnish Folk Music Institute (the main coordinator of the application, aiming to promote Finnish folk music and dance at the national level). In addition, the Municipality of Kaustinen was allowed to nominate its own representative to the working group as an observer (Oino 2020).

4 Research Process

The data of our chapter consists of the following materials (1) the minutes of the Municipal Council and the Municipal Executive (2016–2023) and (2) newspaper articles related to the meetings of the Municipal Council, published in the regional newspaper *Perhonjokilaakso*. The materials also include the budget plan for the year 2016 and the decisions related to the council members' initiatives from the year 2023. We have divided the materials into three time periods: (1) before the UNESCO inscription (years 2016–2017), (2) planning the file and application to UNESCO (years 2018–2020), and (3) after the inscription (years 2021–2023). During the research process, we carefully read all the materials side by side and traced chronological changes in the discourses. We have separated from the material all the speeches and decisions related to the funding of culture in Kaustinen, created headings for all three periods related to the central themes in the material and increased the examples from the material under each theme.

4.1 Before the UNESCO Inscription (2016–2017): Economic Problems and the 'Potato Cellar' Cultural Centre

The relationships between Kaustinen's decision-making, fiddle playing and the folk music festival were rather troublesome during the first period of our timeline. The 2011 bankruptcy of the former festival organizer Folk Music Foundation had given rise to dark clouds in the sky, as the Kaustinen municipality members had stood accused of being in charge of the bankruptcy in 2012. The council members were found innocent in 2013 by the district court and after complaints again by the court of appeal in 2014, but many of them were still somewhat bitter: "It felt unreasonable after the hours of work for the local culture" said one of the accused council members (Perhonjokilaakso 2016a).

The UNESCO process of the Kaustinen fiddle-playing tradition was still in its nascent stages during the initial period of our materials. In 2015, the Finnish Folk Music Institute had applied for the Europa Nostra award, which was inaugurated for ICH-related applications for the first time. While they received an honorary mention in the application process, they did not ultimately receive the award. In 2016, the Finnish Heritage Agency initiated the *Wiki-inventory for living heritage*, and Kaustinen fiddle playing became a part of it. In the 2016 budget discussions, both main parties proposed cuts to the cultural sector. The Centre Party proposed that 10,000 euros of the 70,000 euros allocated to the maintenance of the Folk Art Centre be transferred to one of the village schools so that it could keep the same number of teachers until the end of the school year. The Finns Party proposed that funding for Pro Kaustinen (20,000 euros) be removed. The Centre Party's proposal was accepted and the Finns Party's proposal was rejected in the vote (KMC 2015). Thus, the starting point for discussions on heritage were the cuts proposed by the two major parties in the Council.

In the year 2016, the planning for the 50th anniversary (2017) of the Kaustinen Folk Music Festival commenced. The festival organizer proposed an additional 50,000 euros for the anniversary celebrations from the Municipal Council. The proposal was not accepted easily. A member of the Finns Party wanted to move the funding for the festival organizer to be part of the funding provided to other cultural associations and reduce the funding for the Folk Art Centre from 70,000 euros to 50,000 euros (KMC 2016). In return, a member of the Centre Party emphasized that the following year marks the centenary of Finland and the fiftieth anniversary of the festival. Consequently, the municipality should make an effort to take care of the cultural centre it already has, the Centre Party argued, referring to the Folk Art Centre (Perhonjokilaakso 2016b) (see Fig. 2).

The cultural centre debate was related to the funding of the Folk Art Centre, and the debate influenced the municipal elections 2017 in Kaustinen: the result of the elections was a disappointment to the Finns Party, who had hoped for more favourable results due to the polls that preceded the elections. They identified numerous reasons for their defeat, which was in part attributed to the speeches related to culture (Perhonjokilaakso 2017a). Prior to the elections, there were discussions about the extent to which the municipality should support culture. This was precipitated by a candidate from the Finns Party who declared in the MTV3 channel TV news that municipal funds should be allocated to a wider range of activities than folk dance, and the building of the Folk Art Centre itself looked like a potato cellar (MTV3 News 2017). From the perspective of heritage debates, it is noteworthy that despite the perceived association of Kaustinen fiddle playing and other folk music and dance activities in the area with a white, middle-class, and even ultra-local identity, the far-right municipal elections candidates did not prioritize these elements in their political messages. This was probably due to the long and close history between the Centre Party and the

Fig. 2 The Kaustinen Folk Art Centre. Photo by Lauri Oino (2025) (© Archive of the Finnish Folk Music Institute)

Kaustinen Folk Music Festival; the Finns needed to separate them and not emphasize the same goals in local politics. In Sweden, for instance, the populist Sweden Democrats has, at least at the national level, promoted Swedish local folk music and advocated for increased state funding for it, rather than multicultural programs (Kaminsky 2012, pp. 81–83). This has caused resistance among the practitioners of traditional music in Sweden (Helmersson 2020).

Under the circumstances, the Centre Party emerged as the clear victor in the 2017 elections. As reported by the local newspaper, the discussions surrounding the allocation of funding for cultural initiatives are believed to have contributed to the observed increase in voter turnout. The Centre Party, in particular, has long been identified as a staunch supporter of cultural heritage, a position it has consistently espoused in Kaustinen since the 1960s (Valo 2022, pp. 183–188). At the end of 2017, discussions regarding the provision of financial support for cultural activities were once again brought to the fore. A member of the Finns Party proposed that the allocation to the folk music group Tallari be reduced from 22,000 euros to 6000 euros, with the remainder to be directed towards youth work. This proposal was defeated by a vote of 15–6, with the six members of the Finns Party unable to secure the support of the Centre Party. The Finns Party had hoped to facilitate the celebration of the 150th anniversary of Kaustinen by enabling all villages to engage in traditional cross-country skiing. Again, supporting sport rather than music was a way of highlighting differences between the Centre Party and the Finns in local politics. The Greens and Social Democratic Party proposed that the municipality should purchase the minority shares of the joint-stock company in order to increase the utilisation of the space at the Folk Art Centre (Perhonjokilaakso 2017b; KMC 2017b). In summary, the initial phase of the materials indicates that the discussions on cultural heritage were animated and occasionally contentious. However, the tendency of the Finns Party was to reduce the role of municipal funding, whereas the other parties mainly sought to reinforce the role of heritage in decision-making.

4.2 Planning the UNESCO Application (2018–2020): The Concept of Living Heritage Enters the Stage

During the second period, the Folk Music Institute and other partners planned and worked actively on the UNESCO application, which influenced the politics of the municipality. As our materials demonstrate, the idea of 'living heritage' was more commonly referred to, and the possible nomination was noted by the Municipal Council. The year 2018 marked the 150th anniversary of the Municipality of Kaustinen. The celebrations commenced in February with a series of discussions focusing on the municipality's strengths and the first topic of discussion was music. The discussion was open to all, and the former head of the local music upper secondary school moderated the discussion by saying that "there is enough vitality in tradition and music as long as they are properly utilized" (Perhonjokilaakso 2018a).

The nomination of the element to the *National Inventory of Living Heritage* was acknowledged in the discussion event. This was evidenced by the question, "The Kaustinen fiddle playing tradition is on the *National Inventory of Living Heritage.* Let's protect the tradition, but that tradition or thing should still be alive 50 years from now. How do we do it?" which was raised in the discussion event (Perhonjokilaakso 2018a). The newspaper article referenced here does not mention who asked the question, but the leader of the discussion event and the people who answered the question were all local cultural actors, not politicians. The responses included a discussion of the role of music in school education and ideas about how motivation for safeguarding can include the possibility of adding one's own layers to the heritage when it does not need to be identical from generation to generation. Additionally, the Folk Art Centre and its role were part of the discussions, and the council member from the Centre Party expressed the conviction that the municipality is making a genuine effort to make it a real cultural centre (Perhonjokilaakso 2018a).

In March 2018, the Municipal Council engaged in the development of the municipality's strategy. The strategy draft included several photographs from the Kaustinen Folk Music Festival. A member of the Finns Party proposed that the pictures be replaced with other topics, as they contained "too much music" (Perhonjokilaakso 2018b; KMC 2018a) which suggests that the atmosphere within the party was still not particularly heritage-positive. This stance seemed to include music-making as a practise of intangible cultural heritage, as well as material heritage such as the Folk Art Centre. Nevertheless, at this time, the concept of 'living heritage' gradually creeped into the discussions of the municipality. For instance, it was incorporated into the municipality's strategy as a result of the Centre Party's proposal to change six points in the strategy document, three of which included the concept:

During the debate, the following textual amendments to the strategy paper were proposed by the Centre group:

> "On p. 5 our objective is that;
>
> – Kaustinen is known nationally and internationally for its culture, living heritage, industry and natural resources.
>
> On p. 8 Implementation of the strategy, the following paragraphs were added to the programmes section:
>
> – Living heritage strategy and entrepreneurship strategy.
>
> p. 9 Accountability of the strategy;
>
> – Living cultural heritage strategy, education and culture performance area" (KMC 2018a).

As previously discussed in our article (Mäkelä and Valo 2025), similar discursive changes occurred in Finnish society at large during this period. These changes were reflected in the extensive coverage of ICH inventorying processes in the Finnish media. For instance, the Finnish state's broadcasting company YLE initiated new media campaigns related to sauna culture and the Finnish right to roam ('Everyone's rights' in Finnish), both of which were newly added elements to the *National Inventory of Living Heritage* (see Mäkelä and Linkola 2024). Overall, the late 2010s appear to mark a turning point in the discourse surrounding the concepts of living heritage (*elävä perintö*) and intangible cultural heritage (*aineeton kulttuuriperintö*). This indicates a rapid shift in the adoption of metacultural production related to ICH, with these concepts becoming prominent in national cultural politics.

The same rapid changes can be seen in Kaustinen as well: in June 2018, the Ministry of Education and Culture published a press release to announce that Finland is preparing to nominate two elements for inscription on UNESCO's List of Intangible Cultural Heritage. As only one element can be nominated per year, the preparations for the nomination of the Finnish tradition of sauna bathing was decided to be the first, with the Kaustinen fiddle playing tradition being the next element (Ministry of Education and Culture 2018). The forthcoming nomination was also mentioned in the budget report by the Municipality of Kaustinen, which was signed in the same month. In contrast, the earlier reports focused primarily on the municipal strategy, population, and employment rate. Furthermore, the Kaustinen fiddle playing and the people working for it was, for the first time in our materials, placed in alignment with 'the whole nation' and the national scale, which indicates that the nomination also changes the relation between the local and the national:

> "The secret of Kaustinen has always been that tradition is alive and well, not museumed but allowed to transform and evolve while preserving its essence. [The leading fiddle player in the area] and his team play a key role in this long-term effort to preserve, revitalise and export folk music as music for the whole nation. The Folk Music Institute has also been nominated as the first Finnish non-governmental organisation for UNESCO's intangible cultural heritage. These two recognitions support the development of the municipality's vitality and positively reinforce the Kaustinen brand" (KMC 2018b).

During the Kaustinen Folk Music Festival 2018 week, the municipality was commemorating its 150th anniversary and offered free admission to all festival attendees on the opening day of the festival. Additionally, the municipality had its own stage in front of the local high school, which was an old tractor with a trailer for the performers (Perhonjokilaakso 2018d). Tractors, in general, are used a lot in the Kaustinen fiddle playing imageries and promotion materials, as they indicate masculine rural work and nostalgic Finnish post-war landscape imageries and the building of the welfare society (Valo and Mäkelä 2025).

The news from June 2018 from the Ministry of Education and Culture regarding the nomination of Kaustinen fiddle playing (at that time known as Kaustinen folk fiddling tradition) for inscription on UNESCO's List of Intangible Cultural Heritage constituted a pivotal element of the opening ceremony of the festival. The interaction between the local and the national levels was evident in the speeches, indicating an enhancement of the profile of local tradition among political and national. As previous research demonstrates, this dynamic is a two-way relationship, particularly for local stakeholders who already possess specific resources: the local-national relations may facilitate new avenues and opportunities for sectors such as business and tourism at the local level (Jones 2018). This phenomenon was evident in our materials, where municipal stakeholders underscored Kaustinen's vitality in the opening ceremony where national policymakers were also present:

> "In his speech, [the Chairman of KMC], emphasized Kaustinen's deep cultural roots. When Kaustinen was founded in 1868, it had already established itself as a musical town. "The importance of music for the vitality and reputation of the municipality cannot be overemphasized," said the chairman. Juhani Kostet, Director General of the Finnish Heritage Agency, gave a presentation on Finland's progress towards ratification of the Convention on Intangible Cultural Heritage. The European Year of Cultural Heritage is currently being celebrated and Mr Kostet said that a lot has already been achieved. In Finland, the field of folk music and dance has been active in the process, so it is no wonder that the fiddle tradition in Kaustinen is one of the candidates for the UNESCO list. Minister of Economic Affairs Mika Lintilä said in his greeting that he supports both nominated candidates, i.e. sauna in addition to fiddling. Lintilä drew parallels between the fiddle playing tradition and the situation in Finland, saying that both must be able to reform" (Perhonjokilaakso 2018e).

Following the previous additions to the municipal strategy, the budget plan for 2019 also included the concept of living heritage: "Kaustinen is known nationally and internationally for its culture, living heritage, industry and natural resources" (KMC 2018d). It was also mentioned for the first time in the 2019 accounts in the context of the municipal education and culture services, which "supports local residents' access to the region's diverse cultural knowledge and living cultural heritage, not forgetting international and national cultural specialities" (KMC 2020a). After the Ministry's announcement that the Kaustinen fiddle playing would be the next nomination from Finland after the sauna file, the 'living heritage' was mentioned 3–4 times in each of the municipality's budget plans and final accounts until the end of the period covered by this article. The concept of 'intangible cultural heritage' was not mentioned (KMC 2019b, 2020b, 2021a, 2021b, 2022c, 2022d, 2023a). This indicates that 'living heritage' was easier to use in municipal decision-making than the concept of ICH applied in the 2003 Convention's basic text, perhaps because of its future-oriented and positive-sounding connotations.[4] The use of the concept of living heritage in Kaustinen may also reflect the Finnish Heritage Agency's eager promotion of the concept in Finnish media and cultural life.

The concept of 'living heritage' was not used only in relation to fiddle playing in the municipality's materials. In commemoration of the 150th anniversary of its foundation, Kaustinen published a database pertaining to its history and contemporary circumstances. The Municipal Council had established a separate celebration year committee, which expressed enthusiasm for the proposed initiative. One committee member stated that the project is "documenting and storing the living cultural heritage", while another member added that it aligns with the municipality's cultural education plan (Perhonjokilaakso 2018c). The concept soon became a key element of the region's tourism strategy, along with its diverse natural attractions (KME 2020).

Nevertheless, not all parties were satisfied with the proposed measures to strengthen the heritage sector of the area. In the end of the celebration year 2018, the Municipal Council was engaged in discussions regarding the potential hiring of a youth worker in response to the recommendations of several political parties. The Finns Party reiterated its stance on the necessity of further budgetary reductions within the cultural sector, and additionally proposed the exclusion of the violin-shaped sculpture designed for the city centre's roundabout from the proposed investments (see Fig. 3):

> "[The Finns Party suggested that] an amount equivalent to the salary of the youth worker would be taken from the grants of the Folk Art Centre, Pro Kaustinen and Finnish Folk Music Institute. The proposal was defeated by a vote of 15 to 6. The Centre Party's proposal to hire a youth worker from the education committee's budget through internal arrangements remained in force after the vote. The Finns Party also proposed that, to improve the municipal centre, i.e. to create a violin sculpture in the roundabout, the money be excluded from the investments and transferred to the construction of main sewers. This proposal did not go through, so the investment budget of EUR 70,000 for the sculpture remained in force" (Perhonjokilaakso 2018f; KMC 2018d).

In the previous years, the same party had proposed reductions in funding for the Tallari group, Folk Art Centre, Pro Kaustinen and Finnish Folk Music Institute. Despite the impact these cuts would have on the cultural sector, which employs a significant number of people in the area, the Finns Party did not prioritize this issue. Even though the Finnish Folk Music Institute's director introduced the ICH application process twice in years 2018–2019 in the council meetings (KMC 2018c, 2019a), the Finns Party reiterated their call for a reduction in funding for the cultural sector to half of the planned budget for the year 2020 in the Municipal Executive's meeting and a member of the Centre Party suggested that the funding for the Folk Art

[4] UNESCO considers the concepts of ICH and living heritage to be interchangeable. This observation is supported for instance by the organization's frequently asked questions website (https://ich.unesco.org/en/faq-01058). Furthermore, UNESCO has altered the name of the Intangible Cultural Heritage Section to "Living Heritage Entity" (UNESCO 2019). Within the Finnish context, the term "living" is more intuitively integrated into the language than "intangible," which is not as frequently encountered in other contexts.

Fig. 3 Sculpture *Jupet* at the roundabout in Kaustinen. The sculpture was designed by artist Jaakko Valo and executed by sculptor and blacksmith Samuli Alonen. Photo by Jaakko Valo (2020) (© Archive of the Finnish Folk Music Institute)

Centre should be changed to rent (KME 2019). The latter discussion did not continue, but the budget plan was returned to the agenda in the Municipal Council meeting, at which the Finns Party once again proposed reductions in funding for heritage sector. However, these proposals were unsuccessful in the voting (KMC 2019b). Kaustinen municipality's financial situation was not easy: in 2019 statistics, Kaustinen ranked fourth on the list of municipalities with the highest corporation debt per capita in Finland (Perhonjokilaakso 2019).

In the realm of national politics, the Finns Party has proposed reductions in the allocation of financial resources to the cultural sector, particularly regarding the funding of 'contemporary postmodern art'. This genre has been taken in contrast to the perceived cultural heritage of Finland (Lähdesmäki 2020). Furthermore, the Finns Party's national programme for media and cultural policy for 2020 emphasises that "Finnish culture must also be present in school life and curricula" (The Finns Party 2020). However, the Finns Party did not publish a specific election manifesto on culture, nor did it make any election promises on culture before the 2023 general election. The Centre Party, for its part, wanted to safeguard local cultural services (Jakonen and Renko 2023).

In Kaustinen, the comparison between postmodern art and heritage stands in a strange light, as the tradition of Kaustinen fiddle playing and related practices represents a compelling example of a non-postmodern, past-conscious, local, folksy, and even distinctly white heritage (Mäkelä 2022). As Niklasson and Hølleland (2018) point out in their study on Scandinavian populist parties and heritage politics, national and local heritages tend to be emphasized in the parties' rhetoric, but the rhetoric and budget proposals do not go hand in hand. The largest impact of this rhetoric is more discursive than economic: its main target is to place the notion of national belonging to the fore of political conversations (Niklasson and Hølleland 2018, pp. 136–137). In Kaustinen municipal politics the Finns Party seems to regard (music) heritage as not having intrinsic value, but, as we show in the following subchapter, the instrumental value, namely the economic gain, of the ICH nomination is eagerly utilised.

5 Inscription of the Element to the UNESCO List 2021–2023: A Fiddle for Everyone!

The inscription of the Kaustinen fiddle playing tradition on the UNESCO Representative List of the Intangible Cultural Heritage of Humanity was announced in December 2021, accompanied by a great deal of media attention and concerts, flag flying, and local celebrations in Kaustinen, despite the ongoing COVID-19 pandemic. At the municipal level, there was a noticeable shift in the heritage attitudes of all political parties, including the Finns Party, although the change was not immediate. In relation to the budget for 2022, the Finns proposed that the 25,000 euros for Pro Kaustinen should not be allocated but transferred to be distributed as a baby grant for children born in 2022 (KMC 2021b), and in February 2022 a Finns Party member suggested that the municipality should not reduce the credit guarantee commission, which also applied to the Folk Art Centre (KMC 2022a).

However, in March 2022, the municipality awarded a grant of 32,000 euros to the Finnish Folk Music Institute for the Kaustinen fiddle playing safeguarding programme without competing proposals from the Finns Party (KME 2022a). The Municipal Executive also elected two representatives to the UNESCO working group—one from the Centre Party and one from the Finns (KME 2022b). Subsequently, a further resolution was required due to the stipulation that only one representative from the municipality could be included on the UNESCO working group. Both parties had hoped to have their own candidate for the group, but following the vote, the Centre Party member received a greater number of votes and was consequently elected (KME 2022c).

In May 2022, a representative from the Finns Party proposed a collective initiative from the entire party, namely that the Municipality of Kaustinen would provide a ticket for its employees to the Folk Music Festival on a date of the recipient's choosing (Perhonjokilaakso 2022a; KMC 2022b). At the end of the year, however, members of the Finns Party proposed at the Municipal Executive meeting that the budget for Pro Kaustinen be cut again by 5000 euros (KME 2022d). This proposal was rejected in the vote, but in the Municipal Council a Finns Party member proposed that half of the Pro Kaustinen's funding be transferred to the separate UNESCO funding (Perhonjokilaakso 2022b; KMC 2022d). This indicates that the UNESCO brand was regarded as having a greater importance than the local festival organisation. Additionally, it implies that the symbolic capital embedded in the inscription was noticed and utilised rapidly.

In March 2023, the Municipal Executive proposed to the council that they should provide a loan of 250,000 euros to the Folk Art Centre Inc. A member of the Finns Party expressed a differing opinion. The financial situation was described as challenging due to the inability to organize events during the COVID-19 pandemic and the increased costs associated with maintaining the building, including higher electricity expenses (Perhonjokilaakso 2023a). The UNESCO card was also raised: "The Folk Art Centre will play an important role as part of the UNESCO recognition and its exploitation" (KME 2023). Moreover, in June 2023, a member of the Finns Party proposed an unexpected initiative. A local politician from the Finns Party suggested that all babies born in Kaustinen should be given a violin donated by the municipality. Additionally, they proposed the erection of a Finn horse statue at another roundabout in Kaustinen:

> "Two council initiatives were presented at the meeting. Both came from [a councillor of the Finns Party]. [The councillor] proposes that children born in Kaustinen after December 15, 2023 will receive a violin donated by the Municipality of Kaustinen. The initiative is based on the inclusion of the Kaustinen fiddle playing in the UNESCO list of intangible cultural heritage. As a second initiative, [the councillor] proposes that the Municipality of Kaustinen should start planning a statue of a Finnish horse at the roundabout on Highway 13, with its turf pointing towards the Nikula riding centre. The statue would honour those working in the field of equestrian sports and those who cherish Kaustinen's equestrian tradition" (Perhonjokilaakso 2023b; KMC 2023b).

The proposal to donate fiddles to new-born babies suggests that the symbolic capital embedded in the ICH nomination was now perceived as a resource for the future of the municipality. The Finns appeared to be willing to employ the UNESCO brand for economic reasons, while also placing emphasis on the tangible object itself rather than on the transmission process. In general, one might interpret that the fiddle-for-all-proposal also entailed an element of shock value and a desire to increase media attention. Furthermore, the proposal represented a form of differentiation from the Centre Party's suggestions.

However, the local heritage that the Finns Party was previously reluctant to support was now incorporated into the political discourse of all parties in Kaustinen. Furthermore, as evidenced by the aforementioned quotation, the politicians, including those affiliated with the Finns Party, appeared to adopt a novel linguistic register of 'heritage language'. Instead of engaging in discussions pertaining to matters such as sewers or finances, the Finns Party councillor employed expressions such as "to cherish Kaustinen's equestrian tradition". This was one of UNESCO's objectives, as stated in the decision of the Intergovernmental Committee, which noted that "at the local level, inscription might inspire greater interest in other elements of intangible cultural heritage" (UNESCO 2021). Even though the suggested initiatives were not implemented (KMC 2024), it appears that one of the spillover effects of the ICH inscription is that politicians alter the characteristics of the ICH language to befit other contexts, simultaneously representing local identities and pasts.

6 Concluding Remarks

As demonstrated in this chapter, the role of heritage underwent a significant transformation in Kaustinen during the period under investigation. Our materials indicate that the years 2016–2017 were characterized by a series of contradictory actions and budgetary cuts, particularly those proposed by the Finns Party. In contrast, the Centre Party consistently advocated for heritage-related funding throughout the research period. This is understandable, as the Centre Party has been the principal advocate in the area for local folk music activities since the 1960s (Valo 2022, pp. 183–188; Hill 2014, p. 401).

During the 2018–2020 period, the UNESCO application was already planned by the heritage sector of Kaustinen. However, the role of heritage was still subject to contradictory interpretations at the municipal level. The Finns Party in particular did not perceive the musical heritage as a matter of concern for them, and cuts for culture-sector funding were proposed eagerly. However, the discourse on ICH began to gradually alter the language used by politicians and the built environment of the village. The large violin-shaped sculpture in a roundabout is a tangible manifestation of heritage values and municipal decision-making that affects the community's everyday life and the lived environment.

During the last period (2021–2023), the discourse on heritage changed rather rapidly. The Kaustinen ICH inscription (2021) was eagerly appealed to at the municipal level. The Finns Party in particular, began to endorse the concept of living heritage and the potential for supporting local identity through it. Nevertheless, it appears that the Finns Party was not as enthusiastic about preserving the tangible structures (notably the Folk Art Centre) that are essential for the ICH infrastructure. It can be argued that the ICH listing represents a valuable discursive and rhetorical tool at the local level for all political agencies. However, the costs and tangible needs it requires are not accepted as easily.

The interest in ICH in the local decision making is one of the unforeseen implications of the notion of intangible cultural heritage, especially when considering different political parties and their collaboration. And if these spillover effects are visible at the local level, even greater effects can be expected at larger scales, such as in national policies or at the global level. Could ICH nominations become, for instance, a tool for populist parties to negotiate national belonging and identities at the national level, especially when their economic potential is recognised?

References

Akagawa N, Smith L (2019) The practices and policies of safeguarding. In: Akagawa N, Smith L (eds) Safeguarding intangible heritage. Routledge, London, pp 1–13

Allianssi (2024) Yleiskieliset puolue-esittelyt. https://nuorisoala.fi/palvelut/demokratiakasvatus-ja-osallisuus/yleiskieliset-puolue-esittelyt/

Askew M (2010) The magic list of global status: UNESCO, world heritage and the agenda of states. In: Long C, Labadi S (eds) Heritage and globalisation. Routledge, London, pp 19–44

Beardslee T (2016) Whom does heritage empower, and whom does it silence? Intangible cultural heritage at the Jemaa el Fnaa, Marrakech. Int J Herit Stud 22:89–101. https://doi.org/10.1080/13527258.2015.1037333

Bendix R (2009) Heritage between economy and politics: an assessment from the perspective of cultural anthropology. In: Smith L, Akagawa N (eds) Intangible heritage. Routledge, London, pp 253–269

Bortolotto C (2010) Globalising intangible cultural heritage? Between international arenas and local appropriations. In: Long C, Labadi S (eds) Heritage and globalisation. Routledge, London, pp 97–115

Cantell T (1993) Musiikkijuhlien yleisöt: Kaustinen, Kuhmo, Viitasaari. Taiteen keskustoimikunta, Helsinki

De Cesari C, Kaya A (eds) (2019) European memory in populism: representations of self and other. Routledge, London. https://doi.org/10.4324/9780429454813

Finland Festivals (2024) Kaustinen folk music festival. https://festivals.fi/festivaalit/kaustinen-folk-music-festival/

Finnish Folk Music Institute (2014) Toimintakertomus 2013. Finnish Folk Music Institute, Kaustinen

Finnish Heritage Agency (2024) Intangible cultural heritage: convention in Finland. https://www.aineetonkulttuuriperinto.fi/en/sopimus-suomessa

Hafstein V (2018) Making intangible heritage: El condor Pasa and other stories from UNESCO. Indiana University Press, Bloomington

Helmersson L (2020) Swedish folk music and dance—vibrant but contested. Nätverket: Etnologisk Tidskrift 22:25–42

Hill J (2014) Innovation and cultural activism through the reimagined pasts of Finnish music revivals. In: Bithell C, Hill J (eds) The Oxford handbook of music revival. Oxford University Press, Oxford, pp 393–417

Ilmonen K, Kaipainen J, Tohmo T (1995) Kunta ja musiikkijuhlat. Kunnallisalan kehittämissäätiö, Helsinki

Jakonen O, Renko V (2023) Cuporen kulttuuripoliittinen vaalikatsaus, osa 2: Millaista kulttuuripolitiikkaa puolueet tavoittelevat seuraavalla vaalikaudella? Cupore, Helsinki. https://www.cupore.fi/uutishuone/cuporen-kulttuuripoliittinen-vaalikatsaus-osa-2-millaista-kulttuuri politiikkaa-puolueet-tavoittelevat-seuraavalla-vaalikaudella/

Jaskari MME (2023) Rhythms of living cultural heritage: co-creating memorable tourism experiences. In: Rawal YS, Sinha R, Mukherjee SK, Batabyal D (eds) Advances in hospitality, tourism, and the services industry. IGI Global, Hershey, pp 180–195. https://doi.org/10.4018/978-1-6684-9957-3.ch014

Jones T (2018) International intangible cultural heritage policy in the neighbourhood: an assessment and case study of Indonesia. J Cult Geogr 35:362–387

Kaminsky D (2012) Keeping Sweden Swedish: folk music, right-wing nationalism, and the immigration debate. J Folk Res 49:73–100. https://doi.org/10.2979/jfolkrese.49.1.73

Kaustinen Municipal Council (2015) § 74. KMC minutes, 6/2015

Kaustinen Municipal Council (2016) § 68. KMC minutes, 6/2016

Kaustinen Municipal Council (2017a) § 27. KMC minutes, 3/2017

Kaustinen Municipal Council (2017b) § 83; § 84. KMC minutes, 6/2017

Kaustinen Municipal Council (2018a) § 6. KMC minutes, 1/2018

Kaustinen Municipal Council (2018b) § 38. KMC minutes, 3/2018

Kaustinen Municipal Council (2018c) § 51. KMC minutes, 4/2018

Kaustinen Municipal Council (2018d) § 72. KMC minutes, 6/2018

Kaustinen Municipal Council (2019a) § 8. KMC minutes, 5/2019

Kaustinen Municipal Council (2019b) § 63. KMC minutes, 4/2019

Kaustinen Municipal Council (2020a) § 22. KMC minutes, 2/2020

Kaustinen Municipal Council (2020b) § 55. KMC minutes, 4/2020
Kaustinen Municipal Council (2021a) § 21. KMC minutes, 2/2021
Kaustinen Municipal Council (2021b) § 99. KMC minutes, 7/2021
Kaustinen Municipal Council (2022a) § 8. KMC minutes, 1/2022
Kaustinen Municipal Council (2022b) § 19. KMC minutes, 2/2022
Kaustinen Municipal Council (2022c) § 25. KMC minutes, 3/2022
Kaustinen Municipal Council (2022d) § 55. KMC minutes, 6/2022
Kaustinen Municipal Council (2023a) § 35. KMC minutes, 4/2023
Kaustinen Municipal Council (2023b) § 40. KMC minutes, 4/2023
Kaustinen Municipal Council (2024) § 12. KMC minutes, 1/2024
Kaustinen Municipal Executive (2019) § 177. KME minutes, 18/2019
Kaustinen Municipal Executive (2020) § 190. KME minutes, 16/2020
Kaustinen Municipal Executive (2022a) § 45. KME minutes, 4/2022
Kaustinen Municipal Executive (2022b) § 46. KME minutes, 4/2022
Kaustinen Municipal Executive (2022c) § 79. KME Minutes, 7/2022
Kaustinen Municipal Executive (2022d) § 189. KME minutes, 18/2022
Kaustinen Municipal Executive (2023) § 64. KME minutes, 5/2023

Kaya A (2019) Populism as a neo-liberal form of governmentality: resorting to heritage, culture and past. In: Galani L, Mavrigaki E, Skordulis K (eds) Geographical literacy and European heritage: a challenging convention in the field of education. Solva-tech, Athens, pp 64–94

Kirshenblatt-Gimblett B (2004) Intangible heritage as metacultural production. Mus Int 56:52–65

Kuutma K (2019) Inside the UNESCO apparatus: from intangible representations to tangible effects. In: Akagawa N, Smith L (eds) Safeguarding intangible heritage. Routledge, London, pp 68–83

Lähdesmäki T (2020) European culture, history, and heritage as political tools in the rhetoric of the Finns party. In: De Cesari C, Kaya A (eds) European memory in populism: representations of self and other. Routledge, London, pp 191–209. https://doi.org/10.4324/9780429454813

Lixinski L (2019) Intangible heritage economics and the law: listing, commodification and market alienation. In: Akagawa N, Smith L (eds) Safeguarding intangible heritage. Routledge, London, pp 54–67

Luovien alojen verkosto (2010, April) 15. UNESCO—intangible cultural heritage expert meeting in Helsinki, 15.4.2010, the meeting was invited by Antti Huntus, coordinator of the creative industries network [meeting minutes]

Mäkelä H (2021) Digesting the Finnish Nature and Past: Food Pastness and the Naturalness of the National in the Wiki-Inventory for Living Heritage. Journal of Ethnology and Folkloristics 15(2):89–111. https://doi.org/10.2478/jef-2021-0019

Mäkelä H (2022) Visualizing Heritage, Ethnicity and Gender: Bodily Representations of Finnishness in the Photographs of the National Inventory of Living Heritage. In: Hoegaerts J, Liimatainen T, Hekanaho L, Peterson E (eds) Finnishness, Whiteness and Coloniality. Helsinki University Press, Helsinki, pp 41–71. https://doi.org/10.33134/HUP-17-3

Mäkelä H, Linkola H (2024) Nation-space and the transtemporal woodlands: The politics of the past in the heritagised narratives on forests in twenty-first century Finland." In: Bozoğlu G, Campbell G, Smith L, Whitehead C (eds) Routledge International Handbook of Heritage and Politics. Routledge, Oxon, pp 362–379.

Mäkelä H, Valo O (2025) Aineettoman kulttuuriperinnön käsite, käytäntö, politiikka ja tutkimus Suomessa. In: Mäkelä H, Valo O (eds) Aineeton kulttuuriperintö: käsite, käytäntö, politiikka. Suomalaisen Kirjallisuuden Seura, Helsinki, pp 15–56. https://doi.org/10.21435/tl.296

Ministry of Education and Culture (2018, June 1) Suomi käynnistää esitysten valmistelun Unescon aineettoman kulttuuriperinnön luetteloon [Press release]. https://okm.fi/-/suomi-kaynnistaa-esitysten-valmistelun-unescon-aineettoman-kulttuuriperinnon-luetteloon

MTV3 News (2017, March 28) Suomen perussuomalaisin kunta voitonvarmana vaaleihin: "Ei tarvita jytkyä, se on jo täällä". MTV3 News

Niklasson E, Hølleland H (2018) The Scandinavian far-right and the new politicisation of heritage. J Soc Archaeol 18:121–148. https://doi.org/10.1177/1469605318757340

Oino L (2020) Raportti kaustislaisen viulunsoiton hakemusprosessista Unescon ihmiskunnan aineettoman kulttuuriperinnön luetteloon. Kaustislaisen viulunsoiton aineettoman kulttuuriperinnön työryhmä, Kaustinen. https://kaustislainenviulunsoitto.wordpress.com/wp-content/uploads/2020/11/kaustislaisen-viulunsoiton-unesco-hakemusraportti-1.pdf

OKM Registry Ministry of Education and Culture, Finland (2024, November 21) The communication and a copy of the letter [email enquiry]. OKM Registry and Outi Valo

Perhonjokilaakso (2016a, October 20) Minulla olisi idea, saako sanoa. Perhonjokilaakso

Perhonjokilaakso (2016b, December 22) Kaustiselle talousarvio muutoksitta. Perhonjokilaakso

Perhonjokilaakso (2017a, April 13) Keskusta vahvistui Kaustisella: Paikallinen väri näkyi kuntavaalien tuloksessa. Perhonjokilaakso

Perhonjokilaakso (2017b, December 21) Kulttuurin tuki puhutti. Perhonjokilaakso

Perhonjokilaakso (2018a, February 1) Profiili on, nyt sitä rikastetaan. Perhonjokilaakso

Perhonjokilaakso (2018b, March 1) Kuvavalinnat kuntastrategiaan uusiksi. Perhonjokilaakso

Perhonjokilaakso (2018c, March 15) Arviiti korvaa historiakirjan. Perhonjokilaakso

Perhonjokilaakso (2018d, July 5) Kunta juhlii festivaaleilla. Perhonjokilaakso

Perhonjokilaakso (2018e, July 12) Kaustinen käynnistyi juhlavasti. Perhonjokilaakso

Perhonjokilaakso (2018f, December 20) Laskettelurinteen maat myytiin yrittäjälle. Perhonjokilaakso

Perhonjokilaakso (2019, June 6) Kunnanhallitus esittää musiikkilukion vanhaa osaa purettavaksi ja uutta peruskorjattavaksi. Perhonjokilaakso

Perhonjokilaakso (2022a, May 5) Keliberin kaavat nuijittiin yksimielisesti Kaustisen valtuustossa. Perhonjokilaakso

Perhonjokilaakso (2022b, December 15) Kevyttä väittelyä rahasta. Perhonjokilaakso

Perhonjokilaakso (2023a, March 28) Kansantaiteenkeskuksen laina etenee valtuustolle. Perhonjokilaakso

Perhonjokilaakso (2023b, June 20) Tilikauden tulos yli 2 miljoonaa ylijäämäinen, tytäryhtiöiden tilanne huolestuttaa. Perhonjokilaakso

Ramnarine T (2003) Ilmatar's inspirations: nationalism, globalization, and the changing soundscapes of Finnish folk music. University of Chicago Press, Chicago

Smith L (2006) Uses of heritage. Routledge, London

Smith L (2020) Emotional heritage: visitor engagement at museums and heritage sites. Routledge, London

Suomi.fi (2024) Municipalities and local government - Suomi.fi. https://www.suomi.fi/citizen/rights-and-obligations/digital-support-and-administrative-services/guide/how-finlands-public-administration-works/municipalities-and-local-government

The Finns Party (2020) Perussuomalainen media- ja kulttuuripolitiikka. https://www.perussuomalaiset.fi/tietoa-meista/puolueohjelma/

The Municipality of Kaustinen (2024a) Päätöksenteko. https://kaustinen.fi/paatoksenteko/

The Municipality of Kaustinen (2024b) Tytäryhtiöt. https://kaustinen.fi/yhteystiedot/tytaryhtiot/

UNESCO (2019) Intergovernmental Committee for the Safeguarding of intangible cultural heritage: 14COM item 5.B of the provisional agenda: report by the secretariat on its activities (January 2018 to June 2019). https://ich.unesco.org/en/14com

UNESCO (2021) Decision of the intergovernmental committee: 16.COM 8.B.13. https://ich.unesco.org/en/decisions/16.COM/8.B.13

UNESCO (2024) UNESCO - Kaustinen fiddle playing and related practices and expressions. https://ich.unesco.org/en/RL/kaustinen-fiddle-playing-and-related-practices-and-expressions-01683

Valo O (2022) Kansanmusiikin keruu ja kansallinen katse: Erkki Ala-Könnin tallennustyö toisen tasavallan Suomessa vuosina 1941–1974. Tampereen yliopisto, Tampereen. https://urn.fi/URN:ISBN:978-952-03-2318-9

Valo O, Mäkelä H (2025) Traktorilla Unescoon: Maaseudun representaatiot kaustislaiseen viulunsoittoon liittyvissä audiovisuaalisissa materiaaleissa. In: Mäkelä H, Valo O (eds) Aineeton kulttuuriperintö: käsite, käytäntö, politiikka. Suomalaisen Kirjallisuuden Seura, Helsinki, pp 95–133. https://doi.org/10.21435/tl.296

Outi Valo (PhD) works as an archivist-in-chief in Finnish Folk Music Institute, an UNESCO-accredited NGO situated in Kaustinen. She works also as a visiting researcher in the University of the Arts Helsinki where she is the responsible person in the research project 'Controversial folklore: involving communities in future archival research' until the end of 2028. Her research topics include folk music, archiving and documentation work, nationalism, heritagisation and the UNESCO process related to Kaustinen fiddle playing.

Heidi Henriikka Mäkelä (PhD, MMus) works as a lecturer in folk music at the Sibelius Academy, University of the Arts Helsinki. She is also a research fellow at the Finnish Literature Society. Her research interests include intangible cultural heritage (ICH), heritage, folklore, Finnish folk music, oral poetry, medievalism, and spirituality.

The Governance of Intangible Cultural Heritage: Practices, Stakeholders, and Masterpieces in Zimbabwe

Jesmael Mataga

1 Introduction

This chapter draws on developments related to the safeguarding of intangible cultural heritage (ICH) in Zimbabwe, reflecting on the implications of signing the 2003 Convention for the Safeguarding of Intangible Cultural Heritage (ICH) in Southern African contexts. The chapter draws on the activities around Zimbabwe's two elements on the Representative List of Intangible Cultural Heritage of Humanity, namely, *Mbende/Jerusarema* dance (submitted in 2005 and inscribed in 2008) and the *Art of Crafting and Playing Mbira/Sansi,* a traditional musical instrument (co-inscribed with Malawi in 2020). Building on the concept of heritage governmentality, this chapters offers a qualitative reflection, tracing the activities, structures, and developments related to the Convention since 2006, when Zimbabwe ratified the it.

The chapter shows how the 2003 ICH Convention facilitates the institutionalization, heritagization, and 'authorization' (Smith 2006) of Indigenous heritage. It also demonstrates that while the Convention recognizes and emphasizes the primary role of communities in their living traditions, it also prescribes and fosters new structures for heritage governance, and produces new discursive formats related to heritage (Manetsi 2022; Pyykkönen 2015). In this chapter, the influence of the 2003 Convention is also analyzed alongside the discursive forms of heritage in postcolonial Zimbabwe, where the link between intangibility and materiality reflected in the relationships between heritage places, and their value as sacred sites or ancestral landscapes has taken a central role in the production of official heritage.

J. Mataga (✉)
Sol Plaatje University, Kimberley, South Africa
e-mail: Jesmael.mataga@spu.ac.za

B. Zwegers and R. Vulto (eds.), *The Spillover Effect of Intangible Cultural Heritage*, Studies in Art, Heritage, Law and the Market 13,
https://doi.org/10.1007/978-3-032-25352-1_3

2 The 2003 ICH Convention: Safeguarding ICH Masterpieces in Zimbabwe

According to UNESCO, Africa has been one of the most active regions in ratifying and implementing the ICH Convention since its adoption in 2003. By 2025, all 54 African countries had either accepted, ratified, accessioned, or approved the Convention. South Africa has become the 184th State to join the 2003 ICH Convention, having deposited its instrument of ratification with UNESCO in January 2025 (UNESCO n.d.). This high level of acceptance of the Convention in Africa can be partly explained by the fact that it is perceived to offer space for the veneration of local cultures and traditions, which are a result of deep history and remain integral for many African societies. Africa's diverse living heritage plays a fundamental role in building strong cultural identities and ties, in what is a culturally and linguistically diverse continent.[1]

The 2003 ICH Convention provides two lists: the representative list of the intangible cultural heritage of humanity (article 16) and the list of intangible cultural heritage in need of urgent safeguarding (article 17). For the former, Zimbabwe's *Mbende/Jerusarema Traditional Dance*, (hereafter Mbende dance), (Fig. 1), was listed and inscribed in 2008 (Mataga and Chabata 2008). This is a popular dance mainly practiced by the Zezuru-Shona people (UNESCO 2008b). The second and most recent listing of Zimbabwean ICH is the *Art of crafting and playing Mbira/Sansi, in Malawi and Zimbabwe*, (Fig. 2), which was jointly listed with neighboring Malawi in 2020. The Mbende dance is characterized by acrobatic and sensual movements by both women and men, who are driven by a polyrhythmic drummer accompanied by men playing woodblock clappers and women handclapping, yodeling, and blowing whistles (Fig. 1). The dance is performed with an array of distinct costumes, musical instruments, and other accessories, which are produced by specialist craftspeople from the local communities, using local materials derived from the environment (Mataga 2008).

The dance and the craftsmanship related to the making of the instruments, associated regalia and condiments have been passed down through many generations. Mbende/Jerusarema remains one of the most important traditional performances in contemporary Zimbabwe and has managed to survive the colonial cultural and religious onslaught. It continues to be embedded in the social, political, and cultural fabric of Shona-speaking communities in the country (Mapira and Hood 2018; Mataga 2008; UNESCO 2008a, b; Asante 1985).

Inscribed in 2020, the art of crafting and playing Mbira/Sansi, the finger-plucking traditional musical instrument in Malawi and Zimbabwe, has persistently played a key role in the indigenous musical traditions of societies in parts of Africa. According to UNESCO, the Mbira/Sansi instrument consists of a wooden board with metal keys

[1] To support the implementation of the Convention, UNESCO has financially supported African state parties through over US$ 4.8 through its Intangible Cultural Heritage Fund. Two UNESCO Chairs on ICH and one Category 2 Centre have been put in place in selected African countries to support implementation (UNESCO n.d.).

Fig. 1 Members of a local traditional dance troupe performing the Mbende/Jerusarema Dance (© UNESCO Intangible Cultural Heritage)

attached on top, and the instrument is sometimes mounted on a calabash or wooden resonator. The metal keys are made from spoon handles, bicycle spokes or wire, and the keys are plucked using the thumbs or a combination of thumbs and fingers. The Mbira/Sansi produces a fluid percussive sound considered to be mystic, tranquil and enchanting. The instrument can be played on its own or with multiple instruments in a group (UNESCO 2020).[2]

Noteworthy in this nomination is the fact that living traditions in Africa are usually translational, in the sense that the practices oftentimes defy contemporary national political boundaries and are embedded in cross-boundary practices by groups who have deep historical and cultural connections. For instance, the Mbira is found in many communities in parts of Eastern and Southern Africa, and there are several varieties of this instrument, which is often played at religious ceremonies, rituals, and other social gatherings. The instrument, made by specialist crafters remains one of the most popular and well-documented traditional instruments in Southern Africa and has influenced many genres of music, both traditional and contemporary (Berliner 1993, 2020). The *Mbira Dzavadzimu* (Mbira of the ancestral spirits), has been played

[2] For more images of the Mbira/Sansi, see UNESCO's Art of crafting and playing Mbira/Sansi, the finger-plucking traditional musical instrument in Malawi and Zimbabwe, https://ich.unesco.org/en/RL/art-of-crafting-and-playing-mbira-sansi-the-finger-plucking-traditional-musical-instrument-in-malawi-and-zimbabwe-01541

Fig. 2 The Mbira/Sansi Musical Instrument, placed in a calabash decorated with cowrie shells (© Alex Weeks)

by the Shona people of Zimbabwe for thousands of years and is considered significant in Shona religious and spiritual culture (Berliner and Magaya 2020). This Mbira is considered a sacred instrument, played to invoke communication with ancestral spirits, hence its name *Mbira Dzavadzimu* (Tracey 1963). The musical instrument, in slightly varying forms, is found in many parts of Africa, but in Zimbabwe, it has risen to become a representation of traditional musical ingenuity and spiritual coherence (Uchiyama 2021). The instrument's persistent value and importance is reflected in how it continues to influence musical traditions and genres. It knows many practitioners and interested groups, including various online platforms[3] that continue the promotion and use of Mbira worldwide (Berliner and Magaya 2020; Berliner 1993, 2020). The instrument was recorded and studied in the 1920s by Hugh Tracey—an English ethnomusicologist who dedicated his life to collecting and archiving traditional local music from Southern and Central Africa, credited for popularizing the Mbira internationally (cf. Tracey 1963, 1970, 1972, 2021; Moon 2018).

[3] See for example *Mbiravolution*, a project founded in 2012 to promote the Mbira instruments and music. https://web.archive.org/web/20190824155712/, http://mbira.co.zw/. (Accessed 12 July 2024).

3 Heritage Keepers, Custodians, and Stakeholders in Zimbabwe

Ratification of the 2003 Convention places responsibility upon state parties to put into motion the structures, expertise, and systems for its implementation. These varied institutions range from government or state structures, non-governmental organizations (NGOs), to other heritage organizations, and particularly for this Convention, the local communities, custodians, and practitioners. Zimbabwe became a state party to the 2003 Convention in 2006. The Ministry of Education, Sport, Arts and Culture facilitated the formation of a National Intangible Cultural Heritage Committee (ICH Committee) to deal with the proclamation of masterpieces of the oral and intangible cultural heritage (UNESCO 2014, 2015). The ICH committee worked in collaboration with the National Commission for UNESCO in driving the implementation of the Convention, including raising awareness and building the capacity of institutions and communities. According to Stephen Chifunyise,[4] the Zimbabwean Standing Committee on Culture comprised representatives of government departments responsible for cultural aspects, arts and culture, parastatals and arts and culture experts, and representatives of arts and culture national associations. The Committee worked on nominations for the proclamation of selected practices on to the Convention's *Masterpieces of Oral and Intangible Heritage of Humanity*, and selected Mbende/ Jeresarema dance for nomination. A specialist committee was set up to compile the candidature file for Mbende/Jerusarema dance and the dance was listed in 2005 (Nhambura 2024; Chifunyise 2010; Mataga 2008).

As part of its preservation mechanisms, the Convention also places an obligation on state parties to draw up inventories of intangible cultural heritage within their territory, including tentative lists for the ICH Masterpieces list (UNESCO 2003). For Zimbabwe, beyond the two listed elements discussed above, and through the efforts of the various stakeholders and players, spearheaded by an ICH network inclusive of practitioners, tertiary institutions, and other stakeholders, a provisional inventory list was compiled, for possible future listing (see Table 1 below).

Drawn from the various aspects of deep-rooted living traditions of different cultural-linguistic groups across the country, the above list is only a small portion of the many practices that could qualify to be categorized as Intangible Cultural Heritage or be eligible for listing as Masterpieces. However, what this selection and prioritization points to is the fact that in one way these ways of working create "authorized" lists, demarcated by appointed institutions, in consultation with the traditional leaders of selected local communities (Smith 2006). What is also notable in this list is the linguistic and geo-cultural spread among the many linguistic-cultural groups, many of whom traverse the national (and in one case here international) political jurisdictions. This challenges the parameters through which UNESCO conventions operate

[4] 4 The late Stephen Chifunyise, was a playwright and cultural activist, and former government minister who played a pivotal role in cultural affairs in Zimbabwe and Southern Africa and was instrumental in the ratification and implementation of the 2003 Convention (see https://ich.unesco.org/en/news/in-memoriam-of-stephen-chifunyise-13229)

Table 1 Adapted from Ministry of Rural Development, Promotion and Preservation of National Culture and Heritage (2012), a provisional list of elements to be considered for possible nomination to the UNESCO ICH Masterpieces list

Element	Description
Chibarwe	*"Chibarwe",* also known as Sena, is a Bantu language, mainly found in Malawi and Mozambique, with a small number of speakers in Zimbabwe. The language is officially recognized as part of the minority Zimbabwean languages (Ministry of Rural Development, Promotion and Preservation of National Culture, and Heritage 2012).
Kuhlaisa Mavele	*Kuhlaisa mavele* is a traditional culinary practice of processing and preserving sorghum, using traditions/indigenous knowledge and practices (Ministry of Rural Development, Promotion and Preservation of National Culture, and Heritage 2012).
Bira	*Bira* is a ritual meant to bring back the spirits of the dead to reunite and take care of their family and descendants. It is widely practiced among most cultural and linguistic groups across Zimbabwe (Ministry of Rural Development, Promotion and Preservation of National Culture, and Heritage 2012).
Mangwingwindo Dance	The *Mangwingwindo* dance is a traditional ceremonial dance for the Korekore people who occupy the Hurungwe East in the Mashonaland West Province. It is performed as part of Korekore ceremonies and includes unique drumming and singing. This dance involves vigorous dancing and is held in the open outside the *banya* (a sacred hut) and is oftentimes performed as part of special rain dances (Ministry of Rural Development, Promotion and Preservation of National Culture, and Heritage 2012; Murimbika 2006).
Ngano	*Ngano* is folktale and is related to traditional didactic storytelling. This genre of storytelling has been practiced among many local groups and is a core part of the social and cultural makeup. *Ngano* are often told to children by grownups for didactic purposes (Hodza 1987). Among many groups traditional folktales are used preserve and pass on indigenous knowledge using words, idioms, proverbs, song and dance. (Chiparausha and Mavhunduse 2018; Makaudze 2013; Gudhlanga and Makaudze 2012)
Kutsungulwa kwegohona	*Gohona,* a mixture of indigenous fruits and herbs, is a component of traditional local knowledge and skills related to traditional treatments, particularly for conditions like cervical cancer. In some instances, it involves specific initiation ceremonies for learning and using these herbs. Research is exploring the potential of African medicinal plants, including those used in *Gohona,* for anticancer properties (Ministry of Rural Development, Promotion and Preservation of National Culture, and Heritage 2012).

(continued)

Table 1 (continued)

Element	Description
Komba	*Komba* refers to a traditional rite of passage, or initiation school, practiced by the VaRemba people—one of the minority Shona ethnic groups in Zimbabwe. The rite of passage is specifically for girls, marking their transition from girlhood to womanhood (Ministry of Rural Development, Promotion and Preservation of National Culture, and Heritage 2012; cf Shoko 2009).
Rain making ceremony (*Mukwererera*)	*Mukwerera* refers to the Shona practice of asking for rain through ancestor supplication, a ritual ceremony involving songs, rituals, and beer offerings to appease the spirits and bring rain. *Mukwerera*, also known as "*kukumbira mvura*" (asking for rain), is a crucial aspect of Shona religion and culture, particularly during times of drought or low rainfall. The ceremony is still being carried out by intermediaries through ancestor supplication where intermediaries, officials presided over rain-imploring ceremonies and petitioned God, via the ancestors on behalf of the community for rain (Chirikure et al. 2018, p. 46). The songs and rituals during *Mukwerera* are considered spiritual, as they are deemed to establish a transcendental relationship between living people and their ancestors (Ministry of Rural Development, Promotion and Preservation of National Culture, and Heritage 2012).
Vungayilabya kuaka dandala	This practice is related to the traditional craftsmanship, skills and knowhow of constructing a traditional granary which is used for storing grains, especially during the drier months. The food storehouses are a common feature in traditional Zimbabwean homesteads (Ministry of Rural Development, Promotion and Preservation of National Culture, and Heritage 2012).

and unsettles the idea of a "state party", which is linked to political boundaries demarcated during the colonial era. Cross-boundary living traditions such as the Mbira/Sansa and many others defy geopolitical demarcations and reiterate cross-boundary cultural affinities (Melis et al. 2022; Meskell and Brumann 2015). Therefore, the cross-national elements of ICH in African contexts such as the *Mbira/Sansa*, and many others, challenge and defy the normative demarcations and categories. Thus, for Mbira/Sansi, ascribing a "local" community may be reductionist as the instrument, and the music is not confined to one hemogenic cultural-linguistic group. The prevalence of the instrument is rather culturally ubiquitous, and its appropriation has gone beyond a singular ascription to a specific community.

Besides the formal institutions such as the government ministries and state departments, civil society organisations and networks play a pivotal role in domesticating the convention and implementing programmes and activities for enacting the convention, hence producing selected aspects of living heritage as "official" ICH. At the local community level, this officialization of ICH, is further validated by local traditional and community-based institutions, involving traditional chiefs who are widely acknowledged as the guardians of the nation's cultural traditions and practices. As heritage keepers, local chiefs play a significant role in safeguarding and promoting traditional knowledge, customs, and practices, which are unique to their communities. A central stakeholder is the local community or the practicing communities. In the case of the two masterpieces highlighted in this paper, these included local community gatekeepers such as traditional chiefs, village heads and other elders in the community political and religious hierarchies. In the case of Mbende/Jerusarema dance, it was mainly the activities of local traditional dance groups—many of whom had existed way before the ratification of the Convention and had occasionally worked either independently, or in association with existing cultural organizations.

In addition to the validation by local traditional structures, and various practicing communities such as musicians, dance groups and other cultural enthusiasts, the implementation? of the discourse of ICH also draws from involvement of other players such as non-governmental organizations (NGOs) and civic society. For Zimbabwe, this has included arts and culture organizations such as Nhimbe Trust. For instance, Nhimbe Trust, in addition to participating in activities related to the listed masterpieces, has done incredible work on documenting traditional dances from the spectrum of mainly minority cultural and linguistic groups (Nhimbe Trust 2022). The promotion of selected ICH practices and the listed elements has been facilitated through community inventorying projects and through platforms such as cultural festivals including the famous Harare International Festival of the Arts (HIFA), which has been one of Africa's largest international arts festivals. Another notable Festival is the Jikinya Dance Festival, facilitated by the National Arts Council of Zimbabwe (NACZ), a statutory body established for 'championing' the promotion and development of the arts sector by providing support, initiating arts programmes, and forging partnerships with key stakeholders in the arts and culture sector. This festival aims to promote and preserve Zimbabwe's traditional dances.[5] In the second largest city of Zimbabwe: Bulawayo, the Bulawayo Arts Festival (BAF), supported by the local city authority, focuses on the promotion of the arts in the city and surrounding areas. In the Manicaland province, the Matendera festival works to promote the arts and cultural activities of the area, centered around some of the most iconic heritage sites in the region (Chipangura et al. 2019).

One of the most visible institutions in the implementation of the Convention in Zimbabwe and within the Southern Africa region has been the Southern African Intangible Cultural Heritage Cooperation Platform (SAICH Platform). Its vision is "to be the regional hub of cooperation, networking, exchanges and support services for implementing activities and programmes in intangible cultural heritage (ICH), and its mission is "to build a vibrant sub-regional platform for the protection, preservation and promotion of the ICH that will grow into a regional UNESCO centre" (SAICH 2019; see also http://saich.org/home/). Formed in 2015, The SAICH Platform[6] is hosted by Chinhoyi University of Technology (CUT) in Zimbabwe, with the participation of countries in the SADC region (SAICH 2019). SAICH has become a

---

[5] National Arts Council of Zimbabwe. Jikinya Dance Festival. https://nacz.co.zw/jikinya-dance-festival/. (Accessed 12 January 2024).

[6] Included the Centre for Indigenous Knowledge and Living Heritage & Southern Africa Intangible Cultural Heritage (SAICH) Platform at CUT.

critical player in the implementation of the Convention and states its objectives[7] to be strengthening sub-regional cooperation and national capacities in Southern African countries for implementing the 2003 ICH Convention. It also aims to provide a space for discussion and exchange of information on the ICH Convention (SAICH 2019). The activities of organizations such as SAICH have been instrumental in the localization, intellectualization, identification, inventorying, promotion and eventual implementation of the convention (SAICH 2019; Mpofu-Hamadziripi et al. 2022). The activities of SAICH have included a survey on "Intangible Cultural Heritage in Tertiary Education Institutions in Southern Africa", a study that covered eight countries. The study mapped ICH-related education programmes, identified opportunities and interests in developing ICH-related programmes, and established a network of universities in the Southern Africa region in order to deepen reflection of ICH named the Southern Africa Intangible Cultural Heritage Academic Network (SAICHA-Net) (SAICH 2019).

4 Beyond the "Masterpieces": Balancing Intangible and Tangible Heritage

The 2003 Convention's rollout in Zimbabwe intersects with the local discursive formats related to the production of heritage, steeped in and influenced by Zimbabwe's push towards remaking heritage, and the fashioning of alternative cultural nationalisms in postcolonial Zimbabwe. A central aspect of the production of heritage in postcolonial Zimbabwe has been the foregrounding of the relationship between the physical and the intangible, as well as the natural and cultural heritage, amid a move towards reconnecting indigenous communities with heritage. Of note has been the recognition of the spiritual aspects of heritage formation in post-independence Zimbabwe. Notably, Zimbabwe has always had a deep-seated historical connection to spirituality, influenced by its deep-rooted traditions such as the *Mwari* local religion, or the community and family connections to *vadzimu* (departed ancestors), or *Mhodoros* (regional spirit mediums) (Ntoi 2006; Nyathi and Ndiweni 2005). A reading of the literature on Shona or Ndebele cosmologies from pre to post-colonial Zimbabwe underscores the critical role of spirituality, with ancestors considered to be the "guardians of the land" (Bourdillon 1982; Schoffeleers 1979; Daneel 1970). Thus, after 2006, ratification and steps towards the implementation of the convention played well into the ideals of reworking the spiritual aspects at heritage sites across the country (Chirikure 2020; Chirikure and Pwiti 2008; Fontein 2006; Ndoro 2005; Manyanga 1999). It would appear that what the ratification of the ICH convention worked to provide a further impetus for the veneration of living heritage as an integral part as well as the ICH and politics of identity and recognition in a multi-linguistic, multicultural society where the veneration of ICH plays into questions of identity and ethnic marginalization experienced by several minority

[7] See http://www.saich.org/home/

ethnic groups (Muchenje et al. 2023). For local groups, the Convention's emphasis on communities, and the recognition of their practices intersects with local ideas/ perspectives on heritage and the desire for veneration of local cultural practices.

In Zimbabwe, the activities related to the 2003 ICH Convention have had implications of discussions on the link between material heritage and nonmaterial aspects of cultural and natural heritage decried the implied division between ICH and immoveable heritage arguing that the two are connected and depend on each other (Munjeri 2004; Zulu et al. 2020). The process of the reworking of heritage in postcolonial Zimbabwe is reflected in the well-documented increasing claims by local communities to access and use rights at main archaeological sites and has become one of the biggest discussions on heritage management and practice in Zimbabwe. In validating such claims, local communities foreground their historical, ancestral, and spiritual connection to sacred sites and heritage places or objects. Commentary from Zimbabwe shows how the heritage management agencies had to deal with the increasing demands from local communities for access and use of archaeological sites for rituals and other religious activities (Chirikure 2020; Chirikure and Pwiti 2008, Fontein 2006; Ndoro 2005; Manyanga 1999; Pwiti and Mvenge 1996).

For local communities and specifically for several minority ethnic groups, heritage both tangible and intangible was seen as a conduit for reasserting identities in a diverse multicultural society (McGregor 2005; Fontein 2006). These developments in Zimbabwe highlight the futility of some of the binaries that get reproduced through the normative conventions and their instruments. The developments in Zimbabwe point to a desire and necessity of finding a balance between the tangible and intangible aspects of heritage. So pervasive is the connection between notions of tradition, culture, or religion, embedded within practices, rituals, and the proliferation of sacred sites, that Dawson Munjeri (1995, p. 1), the late African heritage professional and diplomat, declared that for Africa, the "Spirit of the people" is the "nerve of heritage". Further commenting on the 2003 Convention, Munjeri (2004, p. 13) suggested that "for Africa, the spirit of the site takes precedence over the substance" (Munjeri 2004, p. 14).

In the postcolonial Zimbabwean context, this connection between the physical and the spiritual manifests in the well-documented claims by local communities for access and use rights at main archaeological and other heritage sites across the country. The claims by communities, drawing from their historical, ancestral, and spiritual connection to sacred sites has been a persistent feature in heritage conversations and practice in postcolonial Zimbabwe (Fontein 2006; Ndoro 2005; Matenga 1998; Pwiti and Mvenge 1996). Thus, the institutionalization of ICH in Zimbabwe, underscores what several commentators, academics, and professionals on the heritage field have highlighted, i.e. the prospects of undoing the nature against culture; the material contrasted with the non-material and the tangible versus intangible heritage divide.

5 Conclusion

For Africa, the influence of UNESCO conventions on local heritage in Africa is reflected in the increasing ratification of conventions, and their concomitant working tools and other implementation protocols. What we glean from the Zimbabwean case is that at the local level, ratifying the convention throws into motion state-based systems, in collaboration with a myriad of other players and stakeholders, who get subsumed in processes that revise, alter, change and in some cases entrench notions of heritage (Smith and Akagawa 2009). Also, against the "Western", materialistic conceptions of heritage, the 2003 Convention, in Africa corroborates the link between the material and the intangible, giving impetus to the value and significance of living traditions, and the local custodians. The Zimbabwean case shows how implementation of the 2003 ICH Convention galvanized multiple stakeholders, into activities, and programs that benefit the identification and preservation of elements of ICH and produces new ways of working with indigenous heritage among communities who have always valued a holistic approach to heritage, an approach where the link between the tangible and the intangible has always been valued. While the Convention prioritizes communities, it may be that formal institutions take a bigger share in ratification, and implementation of the convention. Thus, the bigger question remains, within the context of the 2003 Convention, how can local communities and stakeholders collectively work in inclusive ways that balance the tension between the global prescripts, and the local values, perceptions, and approaches to heritage?

The commendable developments on the ICH Convention in Africa and the support from UNESCO talk to the ideals embedded in contemporary international heritage governance systems, namely, a desire to "democratize" heritage preservation by giving local communities more roles in preserving and promoting their heritage (Melis et al. 2022; Cameron 2015; Foucault 1991). Given that in many African contexts, indigenous heritage, and living traditions have always been preserved, through locally based, traditional management practices, the 2023 Convention partly draws on these systems but also ushers in a new language and new ways of approaching Indigenous heritage (Cameron 2015; Blake 2017). Heritage governmentality underscores how, endorsed by the nation state, heritage becomes an object claim and is controlled by institutional and non-institutional actors (Melis et al. 2022; Melis and Chambers 2021; Ortiz and Jiménez de Madariaga 2021; Eichler 2020; Akagawa and Smith 2019; Disko 2015; Cameron 2015; Meskell and Brumann 2015; Meskell 2015). The governmentality of heritage through international mechanisms brings together the various actors, including the state "who promotes it with an expectation of accumulating symbolic and economic capital as well as presumably procuring a political position, either internally, among geographic neighbors, or on a wider international scale" (Kuutuma 2015, p. 30).

In Africa, as elsewhere globally, the 2003 Convention has led to the recognition of the intangible dimension of cultural heritage. Yet as argued by Eichler "the ICH Convention may also not fundamentally disrupt structural inequalities embedded in institutionalized heritage practices" Eichler (2020, p. 793), cautions that ever since the adoption of the Convention, Indigenous and minority cultural rights have enjoyed increasing recognition, but at the same time, they have been exposed to public discourses and homogenizing language that might detrimentally affect communities' right to access and participation in the creation of intangible cultural heritage (Leblon 2023; Coombe 2013; Coombe et al. 2015). Part of the critique highlights how the ICH model, where practitioners are 'bearers' of reified, bounded heritage practices… neglects the lived realities of practitioners, ultimately safeguarding little and potentially exacerbating existing inequalities (Beardslee 2015, p. 89). For instance, there is notable inadequate integration of language revitalization with the safeguarding of cultural elements like dance and music within existing frameworks such as the ICH Convention of 2003 and national policies in Southern Africa. Furthermore the top-down implementation limits the effectiveness of current cultural policies. To address these issues, some have proposed an "indigenous humanistic' approach rooted in principles like *ubuntu/unhu* as a more effective community-based model for fostering cultural vitality and connecting language revitalization with other cultural expressions (Gwerevende and Mthombeni 2023).

In Africa, the increasing institutionalization of heritage, through the various Conventions, "creates a situation where a narrative template that has defined what heritage is and how it should be preserved" (Sinamai 2020, p. 57). Several African countries have recorded challenges related to the implementation of UNESCO conventions, citing capacity issues, complications related to communities' involvement in the heritage preservation practices, generally, (Abungu and Ndoro 2023; Baillie and Stig Sorensen 2021; Ndorom et al. 2018; Abungu 2015; Ndoro and Wijesuriya 2015). For the ICH Convention, the lack of a fuller understanding of the philosophical background of the ICH Convention, capacity issues and the contradictions of the advent, dissemination and binary use of the terms "intangible value" and "tangible value" have been acknowledged as affecting its implemantion in African context (Chami and Kajiru 2023; Gwerevende and Mthombeni 2023; Alivizatou 2012; Smith and Campbell 2017; Beardslee 2015). Thus, in Zimbabwe, ICH has on one hand been seen as a space for the veneration of previously marginalized cultures, but on the other hand has also presented a set of challenges and dissonancy (Muchenje et al. 2023; Mapira and Hood 2018; Katsamudanga 2003; Manyanga 1999). While the convention validates and revitalizes living traditions as Indigenous heritage and entrenches the role of communities in the processes of identification and transmission of ICH, it also creates new ways of working, prescribes new mechanisms or structures for heritage governance, and produces new discursive formats related to heritage.

References

Abungu GO (2015) UNESCO, the world heritage convention, and Africa: the practice and the practitioners. In: Logan W, Craith MN, Kockel U (eds) A companion to heritage studies. John Wiley and Sons, Chichester, pp 373–392

Abungu GO, Ndoro W (eds) (2023) Cultural heritage management in Africa: the heritage of the colonized. Routledge, Abingdon
Akagawa N, Smith L (2019) Practices and politics of safeguarding. In: Akagawa N, Smith L (eds) Safeguarding intangible heritage: practices and politics. Routledge, Abingdon, pp 1–14
Alivizatou M (2012) The paradoxes of intangible heritage. In: Stefano ML, Davis P, Corsane G (eds) Safeguarding intangible cultural heritage. The Boydell Press, Woodbridge, pp 9–22
Asante KW (1985) The Jerusarema dance of Zimbabwe. J Black Stud 15:381–403
Baillie B, Stig Sørensen ML (eds) (2021) African heritage challenges communities and sustainable development. Springer, Singapore
Beardslee T (2015) Whom does heritage empower, and whom does it silence? Intangible cultural heritage at the Jemaa el Fnaa, Marrakech. Int J Herit Stud 22:89–101
Berliner PF (1993) The soul of mbira: music and traditions of the Shona people of Zimbabwe. University of Chicago Press, Chicago
Berliner PF (2020) The art of mbira: musical inheritance and legacy. University of Chicago Press, Chicago
Berliner PF, Magaya C (2020) Mbira's restless dance: an archive of improvisation, 1 and 2. University of Chicago Press, Chicago
Blake J (2017) From traditional culture and folklore to intangible cultural heritage: evolution of a treaty. Santander Art Cult Law Rev 3:41–60
Bourdillon MFC (1982) The Shona peoples. Mambo Press, Gweru
Cameron C (2015) UNESCO and cultural heritage unexpected consequences. From folklore to intangible heritage. In: Logan W, Craith MN, Kockel U (eds) A companion to heritage studies. John Wiley and Sons, Chichester, pp 322–327
Chami MF, Kajiru EJ (2023) Assessment of 12 years (2011–2023) implementation of the 2003 UNESCO convention on safeguarding intangible cultural heritage (ICH) in Tanzania. Cogent Arts Humanit 10:1–15
Chifunyise S (2010) Zimbabwe's experience implementing the 2003 convention on intangible heritage. Archive and Public Culture, University of Cape Town. https://humanities.uct.ac.za/apc/zimbabwes-experience-implementing-2003-convention-intangible-heritage. Accessed 11 Jan 2024
Chipangura N, Nyamushosho RT, Pasipanodya TB (2019) Living site, living values: the Matendera festival as practice in community conservation and presentation. Int J Intangible Heritage, 14:16–31
Chiparausha B, Mavhunduse F (2018) The role of folktales in the preservation of indigenous knowledge among the Shona: a review based on Aaron C. Hodza's Ngano Dzamatambidzanwa. South Afr J Folk Stud 24:207–219
Chirikure S (2020) Great Zimbabwe: reclaiming a 'confiscated' past. Routledge, New York
Chirikure S, Nyamushosho RT, Chimhundu H, Dandara C, Pamburai HH, Manyanga M (2018) Concept and knowledge revision in the post-colony: mukwerera, the practice of asking for rain amongst the Shona of southern Africa. In: Manyanga M, Chirikure S (eds) Archives, objects, places and landscapes: multidisciplinary approaches to decolonised Zimbabwean pasts. Langaa RPCIG, Cameroon, pp 46–54
Chirikure S, Pwiti G (2008) Community involvement in archaeology and cultural heritage management: an assessment from case studies in southern Africa and elsewhere. Curr Anthr J 49:467–489
Coombe RJ (2013) Managing cultural heritage as neoliberal governmentality. In: Bendix RF, Eggert A, Peselmann A (eds) Heritage regimes and the state. Universitätsverlag Göttingen, Göttingen, pp 375–388
Coombe RJ, Lindsay and M. Weiss. (2015) Neoliberalism, heritage regimes, and cultural rights. In: Meskell L (ed) Global heritage: a reader. Wiley, Hoboken, pp 43–69
Daneel M (1970) God of the Matopo Hills. Mouton, The Hague
Disko S (2015) Indigenous peoples' rights and the world heritage convention. In: Logan W, Craith MN, Kockel U (eds) A companion to heritage studies. Wiley, Chichester, pp 355–372

Eichler J (2020) Intangible cultural heritage, inequalities and participation: who decides on heritage? Int J Hum Rights 25:793–814
Fontein J (2006) The silence of great Zimbabwe contested landscapes and the power of heritage. Routledge, New York
Foucault M (1991) 'Governmentality', trans. Rosi Braidotti and revised by Colin Gordon. In: Burchell G, Gordon C, Miller P (eds) The Foucault effect: studies in governmentality. University of Chicago Press, Chicago, pp 87–104
Gudhlanga ES, Makaudze G (2012) Useful or less serious literature? A critical appraisal of the role of ngano (folktales) among the Shona of Zimbabwe. Int J Asian Soc Sci Asian Econ Soc Soc 2:2291–2299
Gwerevende S, Mthombeni ZM (2023) Safeguarding intangible cultural heritage: exploring the synergies in the transmission of indigenous languages, dance and music practices in southern Africa. Int J Herit Stud 29:398–412
Hodza AC (1987) Shona folk tales. Mambo Press, Gweru
Katsamudanga S (2003) The dilemma of preserving intangible heritage in Zimbabwe. Papers from the 14th general assembly and scientific symposium of ICOMOS, Victoria Falls, October 2003. http://www.international.icomos.org/victoriafalls2003. Accessed 14 May 2024
Kuutuma K (2015) From folklore to intangible heritage. In: Logan W, Craith MN, Kockel U (eds) A companion to heritage studies. Wiley, Chichester, pp 31–54
Leblon A (2023) A policy of intangible cultural heritage between local constraints and international standards: 'the cultural space of the yaaral and the degal'. In: Bendix RF, Eggert A, Peselmann A (eds) Heritage regimes and the state. Universitätsverlag Göttingen, Göttingen, pp 97–120
Makaudze G (2013) It still makes sense!: Shona ngano (folktale) and the contemporary Zimbabwean socio-economic and cultural set up. Int J Dev Sustain 2:521–529
Manetsi T (2022) Heritage governance in post-colonial Africa. In: Abungu GO, Ndoro W (eds) Cultural heritage management in Africa. The heritage of the colonized. Routledge, London, pp 57–70
Manyanga M (1999) The antagonism of living realities: archaeology and religion. Zimbabwea 6:9–15
Mapira NN, Hood MM (2018) Performing authenticity and contesting heritage in the UNESCO-inscribed Jerusarema/Mbende dance of Zimbabwe. Interdiscip J Asia Pac Arts 1:1–11
Mataga J (2008) Beyond the dance: a look at Mbende (Jerusarema) traditional dance in Zimbabwe. Int J Intang Herit 3:96–102
Mataga J, Chabata FM (2008) Preservation of spiritual heritage in Zimbabwe: the case of Gomba/ Mazowe landscape. Zimbabwean Prehist 28:5–15
Matenga E (1998) The soapstone birds of great Zimbabwe: symbols of a nation. African Publishing Corp, Harare
McGregor J (2005) The social life of ruins: sites of memory and the politics of a Zimbabwean periphery. J Hist Geogr 31:316–337
Melis C, Chambers D (2021) The construction of intangible cultural heritage: a Foucauldian critique. Ann Tour Res 89:1–11
Melis C, Wise N, Badurina JĐ (2022) Geo-political complexities of governmentality and Balkanism: deconstructing UNESCO world intangible cultural heritage discourses. Polit Geogr 95:1–10
Meskell L (2015) Transacting UNESCO world heritage: gifts and exchanges on a global stage. Soc Anthropol 23:3–21
Meskell L, Brumann C (2015) UNESCO and new world orders. In: Meskell L (ed) Global heritage: a reader. Wiley, Singapore, pp 22–42
Ministry of Rural Development, Promotion and Preservation of National Culture and Heritage (2012) Zimbabwe national intangible heritage list and provisional list of elements. Ministry of Rural Development, Promotion, And Preservation of National Culture and Heritage Zimbabwe, Harare
Moon J (2018) Karimba: the shifting boundaries of a sacred tradition. Afr Music J Int Libr Afr Music 10:103–125

Mpofu-Hamadziripi N, Macheka L, Mapara J, Dembedza VP, Mushangazhike P (2022) Inventorying intangible cultural heritage assets affected by cyclone Idai in Chimanimani, Chipinge and Buhera districts in Zimbabwe. Final project report. SAICH Platform, Chinhoyi
Muchenje B, Pwiti G, Mhizha A, Nyaruwata S (2023) Understanding the African intangible cultural heritage as a way of life and a form of tourism: a case of Korekore Cultural Village, Western Zimbabwe. Int J Innov Sci Res Technol 8:2255–2266
Munjeri D (1995) Spirit of the people. Nerve of heritage. In: Munjeri D (ed) African cultural heritage and the world heritage convention. UNESCO and NMMZ, Harare, pp 52–58
Munjeri D (2004) Tangible and intangible heritage: from difference to convergence. Mus Int 56:12–20
Murimbika M (2006) Sacred powers and rituals of transformation: an ethnoarchaeological study of rainmaking rituals and agricultural productivity during the evolution of the Mapungubwe state, AD 1000 to AD 1300. Unpublished PhD thesis. University of the Witwatersrand, Johannesburg
Ndoro W (2005) The preservation of great Zimbabwe: your monuments our shrine. ICCROM, Rome
Ndoro W, Wijesuriya G (2015) Heritage management and conservation from colonization to globalization. In: Meskell (ed) Global heritage: a reader. Wiley, Singapore, pp 131–149
Ndorom W, Chirikure S, Deacon J (eds) (2018) Managing heritage in Africa: who cares? Routledge, London and New York
Nhambura C (2024) Supporting and sustaining the indigenous intangible cultural heritage (IICH) of Zimbabwe. In: Olumide B et al (eds) Evaluating indigenous African tradition for cultural reconstruction and mind decolonization. IGI Global, Pennyslavia, pp 1–9
Nhimbe Trust (2022) Report: intangible cultural heritage. Nhimbe Trust, Harare
Ntoi L (2006) Contesting sacred space: a pilgrimage study of the Mwali cult of southern Africa. Africa World Press, Eritrea
Nyathi P, Ndiweni B (2005) A living religious shrine under siege. The Njelele Shrine/King Mzlikazi's grave conflicting demands on the Matopo Hills area of Zimbabwe. In: Stovel H, Stanley-Price N, Killick R (eds) Conservation of living religious heritage. ICCROM, Rome, pp 58–66
Ortiz LS, Jiménez de Madariaga C (2021) The UNESCO convention for the safeguarding of the intangible cultural heritage: a critical analysis. Int J Cult Policy 28:327–341
Pwiti G, Mvenge G (1996) Archaeologists, tourists, and rainmakers: problems in the management of rock art sites in Zimbabwe, a case study of Domboshava national monument. In: Pwiti G, Soper R (eds) Aspects of African archaeology: papers from the 10th congress of the Pan-African Association for Prehistory and Related Studies. University of Zimbabwe Publications, Harare, pp 817–824
Pyykkönen M (2015) UNESCO and cultural diversity: democratisation, commodification or governmentalisation of culture? Routledge, London
Schoffeleers JM. (Ed.). (1979) Guardians of the land: essays on Central African territorial cults. Mambo Press: Gweru
Shoko T (2009) Komba: girls' initiation rite and inculturation among the VaRemba of Zimbabwe. Stud Hist Eccles XXXV 1:31–45
Sinamai A (2020) 'We are still here': African heritage, diversity and the global heritage knowledge templates. Archaeologies 16:57–71
Smith L (2006) Uses of heritage, Routledge: New York
Smith L, Akagawa N (2009) Intangible heritage. Routledge, London
Smith L, Campbell G (2017) The tautology of 'intangible values' and the misrecognition of intangible cultural heritage. Herit Soc 10:26–44
The Southern African Intangible Cultural Heritage Cooperation (SAICH) Platform (2019) SAICH news 2019: on the tracks of living heritage in southern Africa. SAICH Platform, Chinhoyi
Tracey A (1963) Three tunes for 'Mbira dza Vadzimu. Afr Music J Int Libr Afr Music 3:23–26
Tracey A (1970) The Matepe mbira music of Rhodesia. Afr Music J Int Libr Afr Music 4:37–61
Tracey A (1972) The original African mbira? Afr Music J Int Libr Afr Music 5:85–104

Tracey A (2021) The mbira of the Ndau. Afr Music J Int Libr Afr Music 11:1–32
Uchiyama M (2021) The mbira: an African musical tradition. North Atlantic Books, Berkeley
UNESCO (2003) Convention for the safeguarding of the intangible cultural heritage. UNESCO, Paris
UNESCO (2008a) The intangible cultural heritage intergovernmental committee for the safeguarding of intangible cultural heritage. Third session: incorporation of items proclaimed masterpieces in the representative list. ITH/08/3.COM/CONF.203/1 UNESCO, Paris
UNESCO (2008b) Nomination file no. 00169- Mbende Jerusarema dance, Zimbabwe. UNESCO, Paris
UNESCO (2014) Report on the implementation of the convention and on the status of elements inscribed on the representative list of the intangible cultural heritage of humanity, periodic report no. 00820/Zimbabwe. UNESCO, Paris
UNESCO (2015) Decision of the Intergovernmental Committee: 10.COM 15.A. Tenth session. UNESCO, Paris
UNESCO (2020) Nomination file no. 01541 for inscription in 2020 on the representative list of the intangible cultural heritage of humanity. UNESCO, Malawi and Zimbabwe. Paris
UNESCO (n.d.) Priority Africa. https://ich.unesco.org/en/priority-africa. Accessed 11 Jan 2025
Zulu J, Hermione N, Boko K (2020) The intangible in world heritage in Africa: recognising the invisible: case studies of the Mosi-oa-Tunya/Victoria Falls World Heritage Zambia, Pendjari National Park, Benin, and Matobo Hill World Heritage Zimbabwe. In: Abungu GO, Ndoro W (eds) Cultural heritage management in Africa. Routledge, London, pp 189–203

Jesmael Mataga is an associate professor and the inaugural Head of Humanities at Sol Plaatje University. He has experience in teaching, research, training and community engagement in museum and heritage management on the African continent. His current research, situated in the emerging focus on critical and decolonial heritage, explores the role and place of communities in museums and heritage.

Rethinking Craftsmanship, Restoration and Reconstruction

The Relevance of Building Crafts for Cultural Heritage Conservation and the Quality of Life: Case Studies from Egypt

Ingy Waked, Koenraad van Balen, and Christian Ost

1 Introduction

This chapter explores traditional craftsmanship in architecture as a vulnerable yet vital form of living heritage that significantly contributes to cultural heritage conservation, unique identities, and the achievement of quality and sustainability in buildings and places. Based on research conducted at KU Leuven on traditional building crafts, it examines the intangible values associated with craftsmanship in sectors such as stone-, marble-, brick-, plaster-, stucco-, wood-, metal-, and glasswork in contemporary societies. Understanding traditional craftsmanship as the most tangible manifestation of intangible heritage (UNESCO 2003), this chapter highlights its role as a living tradition deeply rooted in cultural, ethnic, and geographical contexts.

With reference to a recent survey on craftsmanship applications, the chapter analyses case studies from conservation and architectural practices in Egypt and international sites. It reflects on factors affecting the viability of building crafts in historical places facing significant challenges, particularly in Egypt. Work experiences in Historic Cairo have provided valuable insights into both the challenges and opportunities of preserving tangible and intangible heritage, inspiring contemporary research into building crafts applications. Through a methodological and scientific approach, this research contributes new knowledge to the field. Ultimately,

I. Waked (✉) · K. van Balen
KU Leuven, Leuven, Belgium
e-mail: ingywaked@gw-de.com

K. van Balen
e-mail: koenraad.vanbalen@kuleuven.be

C. Ost
ICHEC Brussels Management School, Brussels, Belgium
e-mail: christian.ost@ichec.be

B. Zwegers and R. Vulto (eds.), *The Spillover Effect of Intangible Cultural Heritage*,
Studies in Art, Heritage, Law and the Market 13,
https://doi.org/10.1007/978-3-032-25352-1_4

this chapter underscores the relevance of skills and knowledge affiliated with craftsmanship in architecture for maintaining quality of life and ensuring the sustainability of cultural heritage.

1.1 Craftsmanship in a Globalized World

Skills and know-how of traditional and indigenous communities helped to maintain resources and the quality of life on our planet for thousands of years (ICOMOS 2019). Yet, threats on the ecosystem have increased, because of the negative effects of modernisation, the growing population and urbanization, and the exploitation of resources. Besides, cultural heritage values are endangered due to accelerated globalisation, as well as socio-economic, environmental, and political factors. To fulfil human needs without neglecting those of future generations, sustainability concepts became important. While these are primarily affiliated with the environmental, social and economic pillars, the role of culture as a driver for sustainable development is acknowledged, and many people believe that culture should be recognized as the fourth sustainability pillar.

Cultural heritage includes tangible heritage, such as buildings, sites, and artifacts (UNESCO 1972), as well as intangible heritage, which comprises oral traditions and expressions, performing arts, social practices, knowledge, and traditional craftsmanship (UNESCO 2003) (Fig. 1). Tangible and intangible cultural heritage are inherited assets that make people across the globe unique, thus, that need to be passed down to future generations. They are resources that link between the past and the future and that promote the sustainability concept. Nevertheless, in the contemporary world, threats to cultural heritage, such as deterioration, extraction of resources, tourism, management deficiencies and cultural changes need to be addressed to safeguard cultural heritage values and unique identities (ICOMOS 2000, 2005).

The heritage community increasingly understood connections between tangible and intangible cultural heritage (Bouchenaki 2003), and their potentials for achieving well-being and resilience (Jigyasu et al. 2013), which led to a search for a holistic understanding of cultural heritage as a resource. Contributions of urban heritage as socioeconomic and cultural resources of a city were recognized (UNESCO 2011), and the importance of culture as a driver for sustainable development was reaffirmed (UNESCO 2013). In recent years, the heritage community furthermore provided improved insights into threats and opportunities of cultural heritage and sought to activate living heritage as a tool to address challenges such as climate change (McDermott et al. 2023). Consequently, studies and guiding principles exist that aim to support professionals and communities in preserving tangible and intangible heritage values (De la Torre, 2002), not only to preserve uniqueness, but also to maintain a sustainable future.

Regarding intangible cultural heritage, different forms of living traditions, including traditional craftsmanship, can be found worldwide; especially among communities that are not overwhelmed by globalization and who maintained special

Fig. 1 Carved wooden panels of the *minbar* of Altinbughā al-Mārīdanī Mosque in Historic Cairo, Egypt (© Egyptian Heritage Rescue Foundation)

relations with their environment. These communities provide lessons learnt regarding subjects affecting our present-day societies, such as environment protection, social cohesion, creative economies, and environmentally friendly buildings. From this perspective, building crafts are seen as a unique form of cultural heritage that bears tangible and intangible heritage values (Fig. 2) represented in building traditions and human-centric architecture. UNESCO even defined traditional craftsmanship as the most tangible manifestation of intangible heritage (UNESCO n.d.). Craftsmanship in architecture corresponds to traditional building materials, skills, and techniques handed down over generations in specific cultural and geographical contexts. It correlates with know-how associated with building crafts sectors, such as traditional stone-, marble-, brick-, plaster-, stucco-, wood-, metal-, and glasswork. Building crafts are living traditions that transform intangible values of people into tangible heritage, i.e., architecture that expresses uniqueness and that depicts shared heritage values in specific territories. In agreement with Mason (2002), building crafts applications are furthermore seen as sociocultural activities rather than merely technical interventions (Fig. 3).

In this context, the present chapter sheds light on intangible qualities affiliated with craftsmanship in built heritage conservation and in contemporary architecture. With reference to a field study that examined traditional building materials, skills, and techniques through a small number of case studies representing conservation- and architectural practices which were mostly in Egypt, the chapter discusses how building crafts applications contribute to preserving heritage values and unique identities, along with promoting the community well-being and sustaining our planet for future generations.

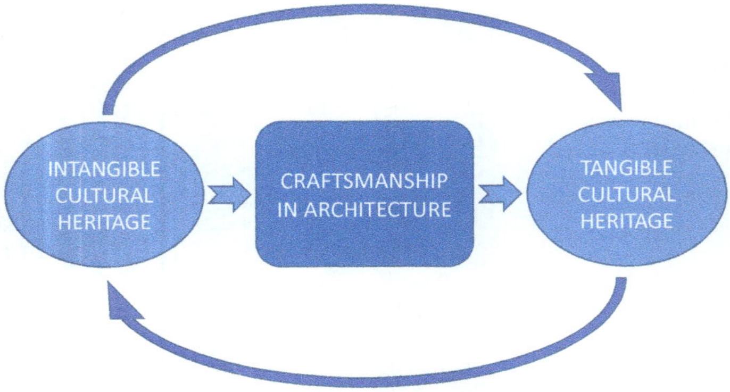

Fig. 2 Craftsmanship in architecture as a cultural heritage that bears tangible and intangible values (© authors, 2024)

Fig. 3 Craftsman reassembling decorative wooden panels, al-Imam al-Shafi'i Dome project (© ATHAR LINA)

2 Theoretical Framework

'Cultural heritage' was defined in the World Heritage Convention, as monuments, groups of buildings, and sites of outstanding universal values (UNESCO 1972). The convention points out the importance of preserving cultural heritage for future generation that is threatened due to natural and socioeconomic causes. In the last decades, the concept of cultural heritage evolved and broadened to include the cultural significance of a place in the Burra Charter (Australia ICOMOS 2013), the 'authenticity' concept in the Nara Document (UNESCO, ICCROM and ICOMOS 1994), and built vernacular heritage (ICOMOS 1999). The importance of protecting living heritage, such as oral traditions, performing arts, social practices, know-how of people, and craftsmanship was recognized in the Convention for the Safeguarding of Intangible Cultural Heritage (UNESCO 2003).

Besides, the Historical Urban Landscape approach (UNESCO 2011) moved beyond preserving the physical environment to an understanding of urban heritage as socioeconomic and cultural resources of a city (Fig. 4). Apart from the institutional approach to cultural heritage, especially in traditional communities, people feel attached to places of meaning (National Trust 2017) and are devoted to objects and practices that represent cultural heritage in their environments (Brumann 2015). Yet, our present-day societies, which have different cultural backgrounds and ideologies, face accelerating challenges that affect their values and identities. An inclusive approach to heritage conservation, which is founded on understanding cultural heritage as a resource and a cultural capital, became crucial. This idea is based on studies, such as the ones of Throsby (1999) and Klamer (2012), who defined the term 'cultural capital' and its significance beyond the economic sphere.

Correspondingly, understanding the notion of traditional craftsmanship is based on a holistic approach. In addition to being the most tangible manifestation of intangible heritage (UNESCO 2003), craftsmanship is affiliated with cultural and creative industries that provide economic development potentials (RICHES 2016). In general, craftsmanship is defined as skilful production by hand and is linked with the quality of creating functional objects (Donkin 2001). Sennett (2008, pp. 15–52) introduced craftsmanship as part of the human nature that seeks perfection while

Fig. 4 View of al-Muizz Street in Historic Cairo, Egypt (© Aischa Mahmoud)

carrying out a job for its own sake. With reference to craftsmanship in architecture, the idea that traditional construction materials, as well as skills and knowledge possessed by craftsmen are crucial for built heritage conservation is accepted at the international level. The Venice Charter (ICOMOS 1964) and the Charter on Principles for the Analysis, Conservation and Structural Restoration of Architectural Heritage (ICOMOS, ISCARSAH 2003) highlight the importance of traditional skills and techniques for architectural restoration. Reports of heritage institutions, such as Historic Environment Scotland, helped to categorize traditional skills and materials, and conservation principles required for built heritage conservation. Similar to the resources identified by Historic Environment Scotland (2017) to preserve built heritage, the study adapted the idea that building crafts depend on traditional materials, skills, and techniques.

3 Historical Cairo as an Inspiration for the Study

The idea of the study on traditional building crafts was derived from experiences in Historic Cairo, where living traditions and built heritage are evidence of outstanding universal values. Moreover, where craftsmen who have inherited traditional know-how can be found, as well as traditional activity patterns that represent part of the daily lives of the people. Nevertheless, the heritage values of the historical site are threatened due to globalisation and socioeconomic pressures, and insufficient conservation policies (UNESCO 2024). Many buildings of high heritage value are in a bad state of conservation, and historical buildings are being replaced by poor structures or new roads. Regarding the status of building crafts, the demand on craftsmanship applications in the conservation and architectural fields, and the knowledge transfer channels are not sufficient to safeguard know-how associated with traditional building crafts in Egypt. Initiatives that aim to preserve cultural heritage and living traditions exist; however, they are not enough to overcome the accelerating threats.

Limited literature was found on building crafts in Historic Cairo. While references describe the city's evolution, architecture, and decorative arts, few Arabic and international studies were found that refer to the competences of craftsmen mastering traditional techniques in Egypt. It should be noted that Ancient Egyptian wall paintings reveal that traditional construction techniques using local materials and specific tools are rooted in the Egyptian history. An important documentation goes back to a nineteenth century publication of the French Expedition *Description de l'Égypte* in a section on artisans in medieval Cairo entitled *Art et MÉtiers*. This provides information on building crafts that served constructing and furnishing houses, in addition to a description of materials, tools, and drawings of craftsmen at work (Commission des sciences et arts d'Egypte 1809–1822). In a further examination of building crafts in Historic Cairo, Dobrowolska (2005) briefly presented materials, skills and techniques related to building crafts as endangered living traditions and referred to guilds between the fifteenth and the nineteenth centuries who played a vital role in the lives of craftsmen. Moreover, some scholars examined the social and economic conditions of artisans and craftsmen from a historical perspective, such as Hanna (2011) who studied the role of artisan entrepreneurs in Egypt's economy between 1600 and 1800 AD.

4 Study of Building Crafts Applications in Conservation and Architectural Practices

A field study on building crafts applications in conservation- and architectural practices was conducted in the framework of a doctoral research carried out at KU Leuven. It was founded on the idea that safeguarding building crafts is relevant, not only because they represent living traditions, but due to their importance for preserving heritage values and for maintaining a sustainable built environment in Egypt and worldwide. The qualitative study aimed to find ways for recognizing tangible and intangible qualities affiliated with building crafts in different contexts, and to validate their relevance through assessing the impact of craftsmanship applications on buildings and places.

Even though the study was inspired by Historic Cairo, which is a World Heritage site that faces challenges in Egypt, the scope broadened to include examinations in few other Egyptian, Arab/Middle Eastern and Belgian sites to recognize the status and the demand on building crafts, and their contributions in specific cultural and geographical contexts. The case studies were classified according to three building types: monuments, unlisted or partially listed buildings of heritage values, and contemporary architecture. Despite the relatively small number of the case studies (11) which were surveyed in Egypt (7),[1] Algeria (1), Palestine (1) and Belgium (2), these revealed the diversity and uniqueness of building crafts, their relevance in contemporary societies, as well as dynamics affecting their livelihood in specific places.

The case studies enabled the elaboration of a methodology that helps to recognize tangible and intangible attributes related to building crafts applications; this used a comprehensive survey form and stakeholders' questionnaires. The survey form examined technical, operational, financial, and intangible aspects associated with building crafts in each project that was analysed. It is composed of four parts investigating building crafts applications from a macro-level to a micro-level through queries about the project, the building, and the execution works, while focusing on interventions that required craftsmanship know-how. A detailed analysis of technical, operational, and financial outcomes is out of the scope of this chapter that discusses intangible values affiliated with craftsmanship in architecture.

[1] Four were surveyed in Historic Cairo, and one in each Downtown Cairo, Sheikh Zayed City, and Upper Egypt.

On the other hand, the stakeholders' questionnaires were developed as a complementary tool to test theoretical concepts and to understand intangible attributes associated with building crafts in the projects' sites. The questionnaires explored perceptions towards the notion and characteristics of craftsmanship, the appreciation and preservation levels of building crafts, the availability and demand on building crafts sectors, in addition to knowledge transfer systems and challenges facing craftsmanship in the contemporary context. They furthermore examined the background, the integration process, and the responsibilities of craftsmen in the surveyed projects. Despite the small sample size of the questionnaires, which were predominantly conducted with stakeholders of the Egyptian case studies,[2] these enabled gaining insights into aspects influencing craftsmanship applications in conservation- and architectural practices, factors affecting the liveability of building crafts in historical places, and challenges causing a shortage in traditional building skills in Egypt (Fig. 5).

For the analysis of data acquired from the survey and the questionnaires, different spreadsheets were created, in addition to an assessment model that evaluates the impact of craftsmanship applications on buildings and places. The tools developed for the field study on building crafts applications generated the following results: (1) comprehensive report for each project, (2) analysis of intangible values affecting building crafts in specific contexts, (3) comparative analysis between craftsmanship applications in the surveyed projects, and (4) impact assessment of building crafts applications, which was tested on the 11 case study projects that are briefly presented in the following part in chronological order, i.e., according to the construction date of each case study building (Figs. 6 and 7).

5 Case Studies as Examples of Projects Incorporating Craftsmanship that Contributed to Maintaining the Quality of Life

5.1 Al-Imām al-Shafi'ī Dome Project

This project dealt with the conservation of a thirteenth century mausoleum-dome of a prominent scholar[3] in the monumental cemeteries of Historic Cairo. It contributed to preserving the mausoleum that has unique values and that is a place of visitation for Muslims worldwide. It also promoted the revitalization of the monumental cemeteries

[2] Thirty-six questionnaires were conducted with project stakeholders including 18 with craftsmen.

[3] Al-Imām al-Shāfi'ī (767 AD–819 AD) was a leading scholar and the founder of the Shāfi'ī school of *fiqh*. The mausoleum was built by the Ayyubid Sultan Al-Kamil in 1211 AD.

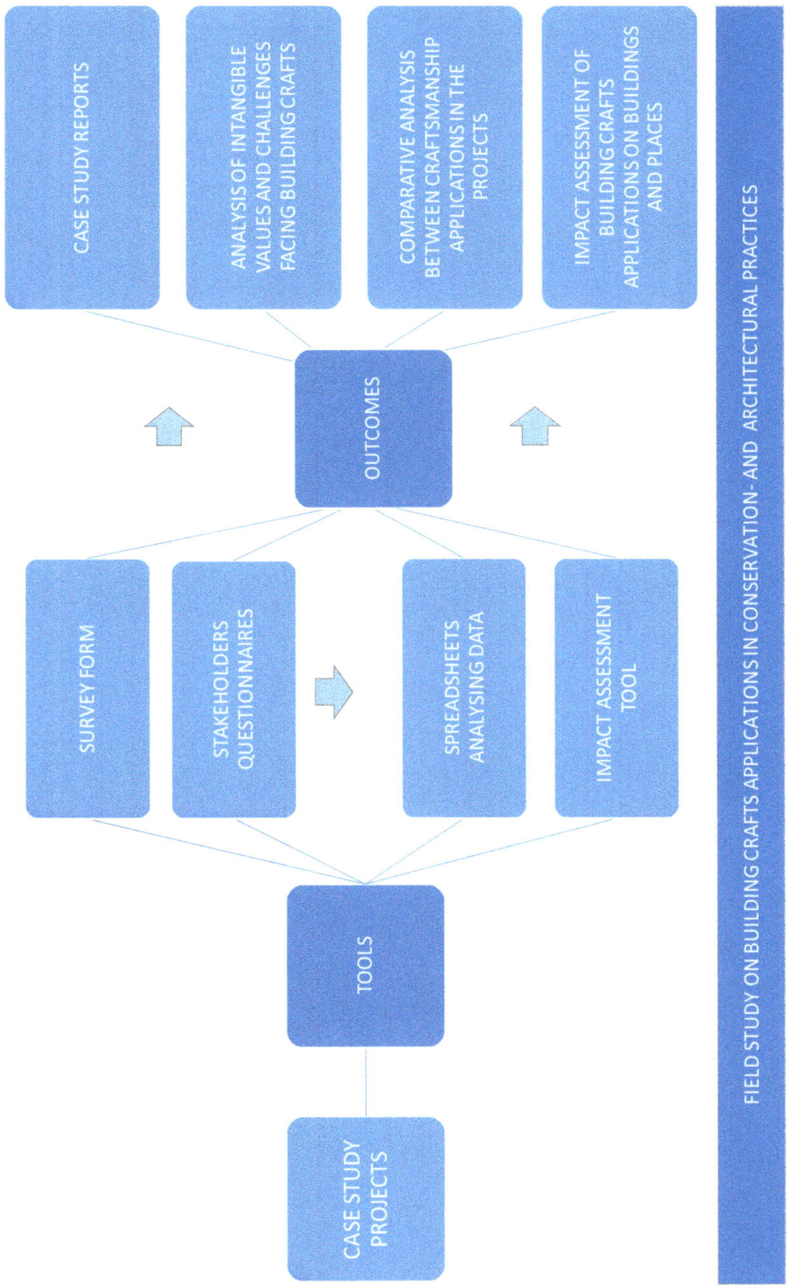

Fig. 5 Methodology developed to assess building crafts applications in conservation practices and in contemporary architecture

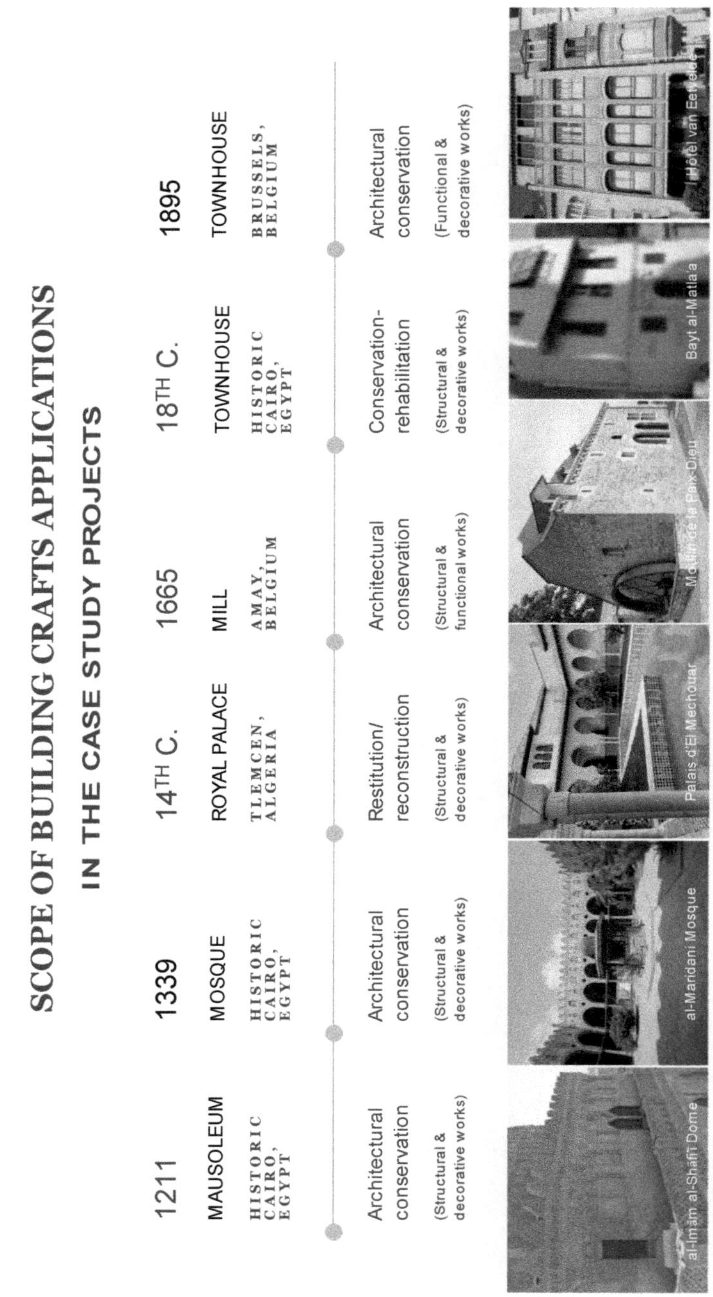

Fig. 6 Case studies projects that integrate craftsmanship applications—Part 1 (© authors, 2024)

Fig. 7 Case studies project that integrated craftsmanship applications—Part 2 (© authors, 2024)

that are threatened by urbanization challenges.[4] The project was initiated by a participatory initiative[5] concerned with the regeneration of Historic Cairo; this manages to create partnerships and receive funding for preserving the unique architectural heritage of the historical site along with sustaining living traditions and stimulating socio-economic development. A visitors' centre was created in the building complex, which promotes awareness about the heritage values of the mausoleum.

5.2 Al-Māridāni Mosque Project

This project dealt with the conservation of the Bahri Mamluk mosque of Alitunbugha al-Māridāni (1339–1340 AD) in Historic Cairo, that has high heritage values for scholars and for the local people. It is one of several monuments' conservation projects carried out by an international organization[6] experienced in the revitalization of al-Darb al-Ahmar area in Historic Cairo: their work is based on a holistic approach that considers the needs and socio-economic conditions of the community, while preserving cultural built heritage and craftsmanship as living traditions. The project contributed to revitalizing the historical area that faces socio-economic challenges; it helped to preserve its cultural heritage values along with promoting socio-economic development potentials for the community.

5.3 Palais royal d'El Mechouar Project

This project dealt with the restitution of a fourteenth century royal palace in Tlemcen City[7] as a landmark of cultural heritage in Algeria. It is an example of an institutional initiative[8] that promoted resilience and inclusion in a historical place that suffered for decades from occupation and unrest. The project depended on traditional skills and knowledge of Algerian and Moroccan craftsmen and contributed to regenerating El Mechouar Citadel that kept local people out for hundreds of years.[9] It helped to reintegrate the citadel into its urban context, and to create viable local economies in the place. Palais El Mechouar is today a Centre for Traditional Algerian Costumes

[4] New highways causing the destruction of Cairo's monumental cemeteries.

[5] Athar Lina is an Egyptian participatory initiative specialized in cultural heritage conservation.

[6] The project was carried out by Aga Khan Cultural Service—Egypt (AKCS-E)/Aga Khan Historic Cities Programme (AKHCP) which are affiliated to Aga Khan Development Network (AKDN).

[7] A historical city in Western Algeria known as the city of art and history.

[8] The initiative of the Algerian government to preserve cultural identities through the restitution/reconstruction of a medieval palace that represents an important historical era of the Zayyanid dynasty in Central Maghreb.

[9] An imperial city that was transformed later into a military site.

that hosts cultural activities addressed to the community and visitors from around the world.

5.4 *Moulin de la Paix Dieux Project*

This project dealt with the conservation-rehabilitation of a mill that dates to the seventeenth century in the Walloon region, Belgium. The mill's project[10] was part of a larger project addressing the conservation-rehabilitation of the historical abbey of l'Abbaye de la Paix-Dieu, in which the mill is located. The historical mill was transformed into a tourists' office that attracts visitors to the abbey. The project provided decent jobs and promoted the liveability of the place. Today, the abbey hosts a heritage skills centre[11] established to sustain know-how associated with traditional building crafts, and further activities addressing a wide scope of people. It became a hub for craftsmen, professionals, and the community, which promotes cultural heritage awareness, and fosters quality education in the Walloon region.

5.5 *Bayt al-Matla'a Project*

This project dealt with the conservation-rehabilitation of a privately-owned eighteenth century townhouse overlooking the famous Ibn Tulun Mosque in Historic Cairo. Like many unlisted buildings of heritage values in the site, the traditional townhouse was in a ruined state and caused environmental- and visual pollution. The small-scale conservation project is an example of projects that are based on private initiatives of professionals[12] concerned with the preservation of Historic Cairo. It contributed to revitalising the historical site and to sustaining its heritage values, while promoting socio-economic potentials and eliminating environmental risks. Today, Bayt al-Matla'a is reused as an architectural office visited by people from outside the area. It is well-accepted by the local people due to its integrative approach that respected the historical neighbourhood.

[10] This incorporated traditional techniques for conservation of the structure, and modern techniques in the interior.

[11] Centre des Métiers du Patrimonies - la Paix-Dieu is affiliated to l'Agence wallonne du Patrimoine (l'AWaP).

[12] The project was the initiative of Dr. Mona Zakaria, a conservation architect and the owner of the townhouse.

5.6 *Hôtel van Eeetvelde Project*

This project dealt with a recent conservation phase of an art-nouveau townhouse of the late nineteenth century designed by Victor Horta in Brussels.[13] Until recently, it was used as the headquarter of a Belgian company[14] and opened its doors for visitor in specific days of the year. The project[15] was designed by a conservation architect experienced in restoring Victor Horta's architecture,[16] and a specialized contracting firm was assigned for coordinating the execution works. The project represents one of several conservation and adaptive-reuse projects of historical buildings in Brussels that integrate craftsmanship. It is an example of projects that promote cultural heritage tourism, while sustaining heritage values and promoting socio-economic development in the historic urban core of Brussels.

5.7 *La Viennoise Project*

This project dealt with the conservation and adaptive reuse of a nineteenth century European style apartment building in Downtown Cairo.[17] It is one of several conservation-rehabilitation projects carried out by a real estate development company[18] that invests in Downtown Cairo to reclaim its glory; thus, that contributes to the revitalization of the historical place. La Viennoise building was transformed into a mixed-used building that offers modern office spaces, as well as cultural, commercial, and artistic activities addressed to a wide scope of users. La Viennoise project, which integrated social development concepts, focused on achieving economic growth along with preserving cultural heritage and stimulating arts and culture in Downtown Cairo. Nevertheless, there are debates about the contribution of similar projects to the gentrification process of Cairo's Downtown area.

[13] Together with three buildings of Victor Horta, the townhouse is part of UNESCO World Heritage since 2000.

[14] Hôtel van Eetvelde is owned by Synergrid, the Federation of electricity and gas network operators since 1950.

[15] In addition to conservation works, the project incorporated modern interventions that helped to increase the energy efficiency of the historical townhouse.

[16] Architect Barbara Van der Wee, who is specialized in the restoration of art nouveau architecture in Belgium.

[17] Downtown Cairo, also known as Khedivial Cairo, is the prestigious city centre that was designed by French architects in the nineteenth century. In the past decades, the liveable historical area suffered from neglect.

[18] Al-Ismaelia for Real Estate Investment Co.

5.8 *Hosh al-Huqqiyya Project*

This project in Qalandiya Village, Palestine, was part of a larger project initiated by local professionals[19] that aimed to revitalize villages and historical centres in rural Palestine to sustain their heritage values and identities. The project dealt with the conservation-rehabilitation of a historical mansion of the nineteenth century,[20] using traditional materials, skills, and techniques. It is an example of conservation projects that promote resilience and sustainable development, i.e., cultural heritage preservation along with socio-economic development in historical rural areas in Palestine. Today, Hosh al-Huqqiyya is used as a cultural and community centre, and a place for micro-entrepreneurs that generates incomes for further conservation and development projects in the urban surroundings.

5.9 *El Foustat Ceramics Centre Project (2001/2005)*

This project dealt with the construction of a cultural-education centre in Historic Cairo, which is affiliated to the Egyptian Ministry of Culture. It was built close to an archaeological site in a place famous for ceramics manufacturing since centuries. The project incorporated design concepts[21] that respected the environment and the skyline of al-Foustat historical area. Today, El Foustat Centre is a hub for artisans and craftsman, which fosters traditional knowledge transfer related to ceramics manufacturing and other traditional crafts sectors. It contributes to sustaining crafts communities, while promoting creativity and socio-economic development. Besides, it helps to provides decent jobs and to realize resilience and inclusion, while preserving cultural heritage values of the site.

5.10 *Eco-Nubia Ecolodge Project (2018)*

This project was part of Bigeh Island Revitalization project. The project dealt with building few new structures on a historical island in Aswan, Upper Egypt, using environmental-friendly building materials and traditional techniques. The project was initiated by the Nubian community and carried out by local professionals; it contributed to the revival of the abandoned island and the heritage values of the Nubian community. Eco-Nubia project promoted local economies that depend on

[19] The project was initiated by Riwaq Centre for Architectural Conservation, which was founded by Suad Amiry, a prominent architect and writer. Today, the Centre is managed by Palestinian professionals.

[20] The historical mansion includes three peasant houses that date to the Ottoman period.

[21] El Foustat Centre was designed by Architect Gamal Amer, a disciple of the late Architect Hassan Fathy.

Fig. 8 Egyptian craftsman constructing a traditional brick vault (© Architect Gamal Amer)

new models of sustainable tourism and responsible producers and consumers. It is an example of small-scale projects that contribute to protecting cultural and natural heritage in historical places; at the same time, which enhance resilience, environmental protection, socio-economic development, as well as safeguarding the identity of indigenous people.

5.11 The Architects' House Project (2019)

This project dealt with the construction of a residence for an architects' couple in a desert area in Sheikh Zayed City, Greater Cairo. It is one of few examples of contemporary residential architecture in Egypt constructed using craftsmanship techniques; it integrates design concepts that adapt to the climatic conditions in hot and arid zones. The residence of the architects' couple,[22] was built in the middle of an olive grove in harmony with the environment. It contributed to the liveability and increasing the land value in the desert area. It is a model that attracts people to live in environmental-friendly architecture and in residential communities in the outskirts of Cairo, which respect the natural environment and promote socio-economic prosperity (Figs. 8 and 9).

[22] Both architects, Rami El Dahan and Soheir Farid, were disciples of the late Egyptian Architect Hassan Fathy, who reintroduced vernacular traditional architecture in Egypt and in the Arab region.

Fig. 9 Traditional domes built by craftsmen (© Architect Gamal Amer)

6 Findings from the Case Studies about Intangible Qualities of Traditional Building Crafts

Understanding factor affecting the liveability of traditional craftsmanship was based on the field study and the analysis of the questionnaires, which were mostly carried out with Egyptian professionals and craftsmen in the framework of the study on building crafts applications. The interviewees had common views regarding the notion and characteristics of traditional craftsmanship. They agreed that craftsmanship in architecture corresponds to know-how about building traditions, the ability to use traditional materials and techniques, and to create architectural elements of aesthetic/ artistic and historical values. They had common opinions about the relevance of building crafts for the conservation of listed and unlisted historical buildings, for the rehabilitation of historical sites, and for safeguarding living traditions.

The interviewees pointed out that in Egypt, craftsmen mastering building crafts, such as traditional stone-, marble-, brick-, and woodwork can be found; however, many thought that they are only partially appreciated, and that the preservation level of these building crafts is rather low. Regarding the market demand, it was agreed that there is a partial demand on specific building crafts sectors in the conservation and the construction markets. Professionals moreover stated that owners and users of unlisted historical buildings are often not willing to pay for conservation works that integrate traditional skills and techniques, due to insufficient awareness about the values of these buildings as cultural assets, the lack of financial means, and the lack of support provided by local authorities. According to the interviewees' opinions, investors and funding agencies are to some extent willing to pay for monuments' conservation projects that incorporate craftsmanship. As for the knowledge transfer systems, the respondents agreed that the current channels are not sufficient to protect skills and knowledge associated with craftsmanship in architecture. It was also agreed that factors that could attract young people to learn building crafts techniques that require time and patience include attractive salaries, good knowledge transfer channels, and awareness about the values of craftsmanship.

Based on the interviewees' responses, an analysis of reasons causing a shortage in traditional building skills in Egypt was conducted. The outcomes were represented in a Pareto Chart[23] (Fig. 10) which helped to identify few factors that are seen as major causes for the shortage in traditional knowledge and skills; thus, that need to be addressed as a priority. The results represent the opinions of a small group based on their experiences and interests. Although the outcomes cannot be generalized at this stage, they enabled getting insights into obstacles threatening building crafts in Egypt. According to the interviewees, the lack of interest and insufficient awareness about the values of craftsmanship, especially among younger people, the old age of craftsmen mastering traditional techniques, and the difficulty to sustain family businesses are major causes threatening building crafts in the Egyptian context. Besides, the difficulty to compete with cheaper skills, the low salaries, the gap in traditional knowledge transfer systems, and social obstacles were further reasons agreed upon as major causes. Although some people believed that low return of investment, high labour costs, environmental obstacles, difficulty to supply materials, as well as legislations are obstacles affecting the livelihood of craftsmanship, according to this analysis, these were not seen as major challenges.

Based on the survey data analysis and the questionnaires outcomes, the following factors were identified as key aspects that can positively or negatively influence the liveability of traditional building crafts in present-day societies:

- Globalization and urbanization
- Policies, conservation strategies, and investments[24]
- Socio-economic conditions
- Cultural heritage awareness (tangible and intangible)
- Quality of academic education and vocational training

The study conducted on building crafts applications in Egyptian- and international sites, helped to shed light on contradictions between the contributions of building crafts in facing global challenges and their vulnerable status in specific places. Special reference was given to the Egyptian context were most of the case studies were surveyed.[25] In Egypt, deficiencies related to the above-mentioned factors led to the

[23] Also known as the 80–20 rule, assumes that 80% of the outcomes are the result of 20% of the inputs.

[24] Investments in cultural heritage conservation and in sustainable architecture integrating building crafts.

[25] Seven case study projects and the majority of the stakeholders' questionnaires were conducted in Egypt.

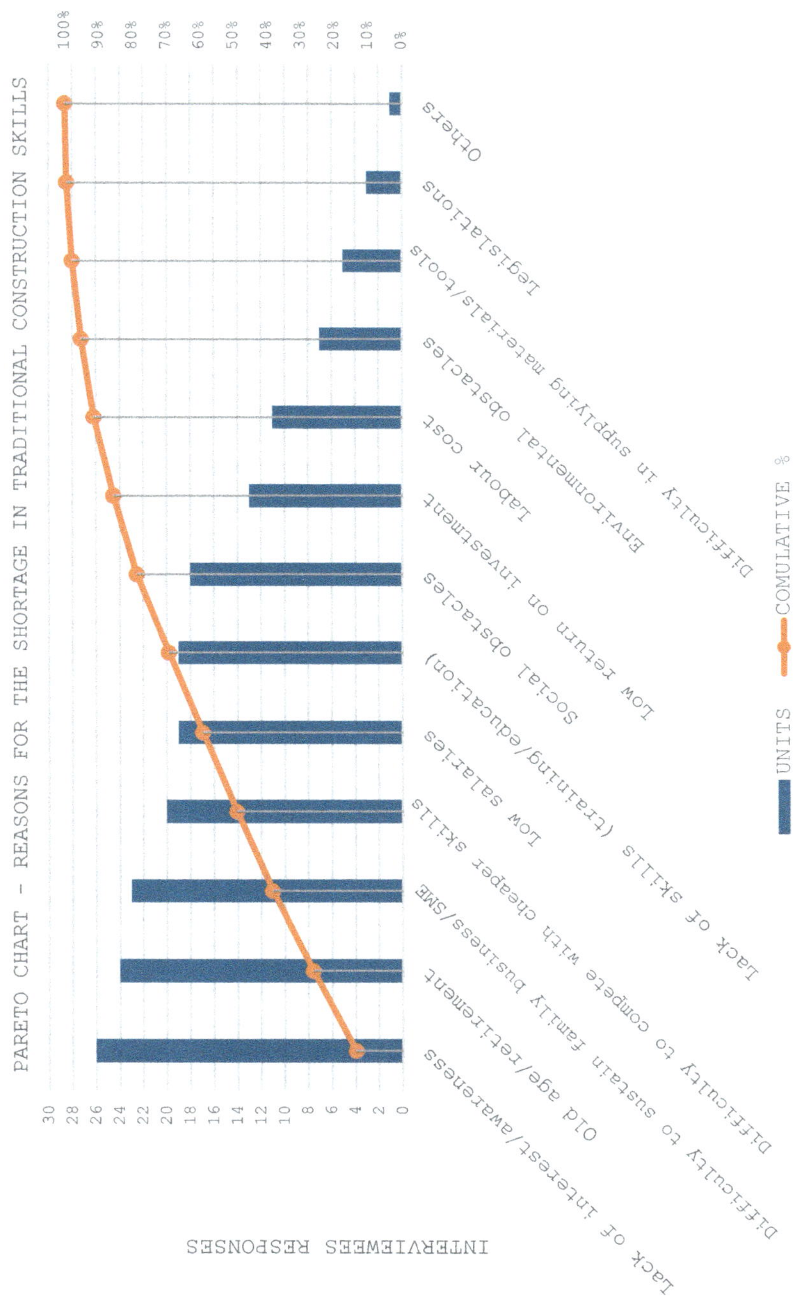

Fig. 10 Pareto Chart showing reasons for the shortage in traditional skills in Egypt (© authors, 2024)

vulnerability of building crafts that represent unique living traditions, and to existential threats that risk traditional skills and knowledge affiliated with craftsmanship in the conservation and architectural fields. On the other hand, the case study projects, which were selected to demonstrate good examples of conservation- and architectural projects integrating craftsmanship applications, revealed that despite the challenges that endanger building crafts, there are strengths and opportunities associated with building crafts in the surveyed sites. These need to be addressed and strengthened to safeguard traditional know-how in built heritage conservation and in contemporary architecture, and to reinforce the contributions of craftsmanship in preserving heritage values and cultural identities, and in facing global challenges, not only in the Egyptian context but worldwide.

Case studies in Arab/Middle Eastern- and Belgian sites revealed the contributions of a holistic approach towards improved conservation practices beyond the Egyptian context. For example, the analysis of high-quality conservation projects in Belgium confirmed the in-valuable contributions of craftmanship in preserving heritage values of the surveyed places, despite the relatively high cost of labour in Belgium compared to Egypt. The study furthermore gave insights into traditional building skills in diverse cultural and geographical contexts: For instance, crafts communities and families specialized in building crafts were found in Egypt whereas these were difficult to find in Belgium where craftsmanship is primarily seen as a profession. This can be partially explained by differences in socioeconomic standards, as well as regulations affecting the integration of craftsmen in conservation- and architectural practices, which helps in understanding the difficulty that the conservation sector faces to find and integrate craftspeople in Belgium.

Despite the challenges that threaten traditional building skills in the Egyptian context due to the above-mentioned factors that might be valid for other places worldwide, case studies surveyed in different contexts helped to reveal the importance of awareness and supportive mechanisms provided by professionals, communities, and institutions in safeguarding building crafts through their appropriate integration in conservation- and architectural practices. They also helped to understand their contributions for maintaining the quality of life and for solving issues that confront our societies.

7 Contributions of Craftsmanship to Maintaining the Quality of Life in Contemporary Societies

To evaluate the impact of building crafts applications on buildings and places, an assessment model was developed that evaluates their relevance and impact in the contemporary context. Taking into consideration interdisciplinary literature on the topic, the assessment was based on three vital criteria: (1) quality of interventions, (2) sustainability level, and (3) cultural heritage values. This approach is in line with UNESCO Hangzhou Declaration (2013) that places culture as a driver for sustainable development through contributions to inclusive social, economic, and cultural development, as well as environmental sustainability.

The impact assessment was applied for the post-evaluation of conservation- and architectural practices surveyed as case studies in Egyptian-, Arab/Middle Eastern-, and Belgian sites. It showcased the positive contributions of craftsmanship applications, which embody intangible values that are transformed into architectural elements, on the quality of the execution works in terms of materials, skills, and techniques integrated in the projects. Moreover, the case studies highlighted the relevance of building crafts for preserving values of historical buildings, and for creating new values in buildings and places. Assessing the impact of building crafts on cultural heritage values was based on the assessment of values typologies[26] that were identified as sub-criteria, namely, artistic/aesthetic, historical, social and economic, and scientific/technological values. The impact of craftsmanship on the artistic/aesthetic and historical values of the surveyed buildings was always high, as well as their impact on the scientific/technological values whenever this was applicable. As for their impact on the social- and economic values of buildings and places, this greatly varied and depended on the project's context. Nevertheless, the analysis showed positive relations between craftsmanship and preserving social and economic values. For example, historical buildings and new buildings integrating craftsmanship were appreciated and often used by the community, craftsmen representing traditional communities participated in the projects, and traditional crafts clusters existed in some of the projects' sites. Besides, craftsmanship applications helped to preserve traditional economic activities found in places surveyed in the context of the study.

Besides, the case studies were evidence for the contributions of building crafts to improving the sustainability level of buildings and places, based on the evaluation of their impact on social, economic, and environmental issues. The impact assessment helped to identify correlations between craftsmanship in architecture as a living tradition and achieving sustainable development goals (SDGs). For example, integrating craftsmanship in the projects promoted sustainable cities and communities (SDG 11); with special reference to Goal 11.4 on protecting the world's cultural and natural heritage, Goal 11.1 on safe and affordable housing, and Goal 11.3 on inclusive and sustainable urbanization. Building crafts applications, which often integrate circular economy principles, helped to realize further goals such as no poverty (SDG 1), quality education (SDG 4), decent jobs and economic growth (SDG 8), in addition to responsible consumption and production patterns (SDG 12) in the surveyed sites. The study indicated that craftsmanship applications also contributed to achieving goals related to environmental sustainability, such as good health and well-being (SDG 3), through design concepts and the application of traditional construction techniques that helped to achieve a healthy indoor environment in the buildings. They also supported climate action (SDG 13) with special reference to Goal 13.1 on strengthening resilience and adaptive capacity to climate-related hazards, because

[26] In the context of the study, heritage values are derived from the Nara Document on Authenticity (1994), the Burra Charter (1998). the 'Nara Grid' developed at KU Leuven, and Getty Conservation Institute report on 'Assessing the Values of Cultural Heritage (2002)'.

building crafts usually depend on low-carbon manufacturing processes and respect the climatic and geographic conditions of the sites.

8 Conclusions

Know-how and skills associated with traditional craftsmanship are seen as the most tangible manifestation of intangible cultural heritage. Based on this perspective, and considering the ability of building crafts to transform heritage values of communities of different cultural backgrounds into tangible and unique architecture; the present chapter discussed intangible values of traditional building crafts, based on the outcomes of research on building crafts applications carried out at KU Leuven. Special reference was given to research findings showcasing the importance of traditional building crafts for safeguarding cultural heritage values and for facing global challenges; also, findings about factors affecting the livelihood of building crafts in historical places, especially in the Egyptian context where most of the case studies were surveyed.

Through a methodology developed to analyse data acquired from the survey on building crafts applications; it was possible to recognize tangible and intangible values of traditional building crafts as discussed in the present chapter. Moreover, it was possible to highlight their contributions to preserving cultural heritage, along with achieving quality and sustainability in buildings and places. The case studies surveyed in the context of the study were presented as examples of conservation- and architectural practices integrating craftsmanship that contributed to maintaining the quality of life in specific sites. Consequently, the chapter threw light on discrepancies between the contributions of traditional craftsmanship in facing global challenges, and the vulnerable status of building crafts sectors in historical sites, such as Historic Cairo. Furthermore, factors affecting their liveability were discussed, as well as challenges threatening traditional building skills in Egypt.

This chapter opens the door for an improved understanding of intangible qualities affiliated with traditional building crafts, and for assessing the impact of craftsmanship applications on the values, the quality, and the sustainability of buildings and places. Using the proposed assessment methodology on a broader context, i.e., for investigations in different cultural, ethnical and geographical contexts, can support decision making regarding planning and evaluating craftsmanship applications in conservation practices and architecture; also, regarding the preservation of cultural heritage in historical places. The integrated methodology facilitates recognizing tangible and intangible attributes affiliated with craftsmanship in conservation- and architectural practices. It is founded on in-depth examinations of building crafts applications supported by the analysis of factors affecting the involvement of craftspeople in the projects, as well as aspects affecting their liveability in the surveyed places based on perspectives provided by craftspeople and professionals. This holistic approach allows a fine-grained evaluation of the impact of craftsmanship interventions on built heritage conservation, living traditions, and on the quality of the built environment. It paves the way for future studies that examine ways to transform the vulnerability of building crafts into potentials, i.e., that focus on strengths, overcome weakness, reduce threats, and exploit opportunities of building crafts not only in Egypt, but worldwide. This would contribute to safeguarding cultural heritage values, along with realizing quality and sustainability in our present-day societies.

References

Bouchenaki M (2003) The interdependency of the tangible and intangible cultural heritage. In: Proceedings of the 14th ICOMOS General Assembly and International Symposium, ICOMOS, pp 1–5. https://openarchive.icomos.org/id/eprint/468

Brumann C (2015) Cultural heritage. In: Smelser NJ, Baltes PB (eds) International encyclopedia of the social and behavioral sciences. Elsevier, Amsterdam, pp 414–419. https://doi.org/10.1016/B978-0-08-097086-8.12185-3

Commission des sciences et arts d'Égypte (1809–1822) Description de l'Égypte, état moderne, vol 2. French Government, Paris. https://digitalcollections.nypl.org/collections/description-de-lgypte-ou-recueil-des-observations-et-des-recherches-qui-ont-t#/?tab=navigationandroots=1:cfdaa7b0-c632-012f-8cef-58d385a7bc34/1:17852570-0cb6-0139-3063-0242ac110003

De la Torre M (ed) (2002) Assessing the values of cultural heritage: research report. Getty Conservation Institute, Los Angeles. http://hdl.handle.net/10020/gci_pubs/values_cultural_heritage

Dobrowolska A (2005) The building crafts of Cairo – a living tradition. AUC Press, Cairo

Donkin L (2001) Crafts and conservation: synthesis report for ICCROM. International Centre for the Study of the Preservation and Restoration of Cultural Property, Paris

Hanna N (2011) Artisan entrepreneurs in Cairo: aAn early modern capitalism 1600–1800. AUC Press, Cairo

Historic Environment Scotland (2017) Scotland's traditional building materials: a consideration of current provision, challenges and opportunities. Historic Environment Scotland, Edinburgh. https://www.historicenvironment.scot/archives-and-research/publications/publication/?publicationid=d528a605-e25a-4824-933d-a77700968f1f

ICOMOS (1964) International charter for the conservation and restoration of monuments and sites. ICOMOS, Venice. https://www.icomos.org/images/DOCUMENTS/Charters/venice_e.pdf

ICOMOS (1994) The Nara document on authenticity. ICOMOS, Nara. https://www.icomos.org/en/charters-and-texts/179-articles-en-francais/ressources/charters-and-standards/386-the-nara-document-on-authenticity-1994

ICOMOS (1999) Charter on the built vernacular heritage. ICOMOS, Mexico City. https://www.icomos.org/images/DOCUMENTS/Charters/vernacular_e.pdf

ICOMOS (2000) Heritage at risk: trends, threats and risks – world report 2000 on monuments and sites in danger. ICOMOS, Paris. https://www.icomos.org/public/risk/world_report/2000/trends_eng.htm

ICOMOS (2019) The future of our pasts: engaging cultural heritage in climate action. Outline of climate change and cultural heritage. Technical report, ICOMOS, Paris

ICOMOS (2005) Threats to world heritage sites 1994–2004: an analysis. ICOMOS, Paris. https://openarchive.icomos.org/id/eprint/2981/

ICOMOS (2013) The Burra charter: the Australia ICOMOS charter for places of cultural significance 2013. ICOMOS, Burra. https://australia.icomos.org/wp-content/uploads/The-Burra-Charter-2013-Adopted-31.10.2013.pdf

ICOMOS, ISCARSAH (2003) Recommendations for the analysis, conservation and structural restoration of architectural heritage. ICOMOS, Paris

Jigyasu R, Murthy M, Boccardi G, Marrion CE, Douglas D, King J, O'Brien G, Dolcemascolo G, Kim Y, Albrito P, Osihn M (2013) Heritage and resilience: issues and opportunities for reducing disaster risks. Global Platform for Disaster Risk Reduction, Paris. https://openarchive.icomos.org/id/eprint/3359/
Klamer A (2012) Crafting culture: the importance of craftsmanship for the world of the arts and the economy at large. Erasmus University Rotterdam, Rotterdam. http://www.klamer.nl/wp-content/uploads/2017/08/crafting.pdf
Mason R (2002) Assessing values in conservation planning: methodological issues and choices. In: De la Torre M (ed) Assessing the values of cultural heritage: research report. The Getty Conservation Institute, Los Angeles, pp 5–31
McDermott D, Mathisen B, Sarıkaya Levent Y, Wallace P, Truscott M (eds) (2023) Living heritage and climate change. ICOMOS, Paris. https://openarchive.icomos.org/id/eprint/2908
National Trust (2017) Places that make us: research report. National Trust, Swindon. https://nt.global.ssl.fastly.net/binaries/content/assets/website/national/pdf/places-that-make-us.pdf
RICHES (2016) Towards a craft revival: recalibrating social, cultural, economic and technological dynamics. European Commission, Brussels. https://resources.riches-project.eu/wp-content/uploads/2016/04/EUROPEAN-POLICY-BRIEF_Craft_final.pdf
Sennett R (2008) The craftsman. Penguin Books, London
Throsby D (1999) Cultural capital. J Cult Econ 23:3–12. https://doi.org/10.1023/A:1007543313370
UNESCO (1972) Convention concerning the protection of the world cultural and natural heritage. https://whc.unesco.org/archive/convention-en.pdf
UNESCO (2003) Convention for the safeguarding of the intangible cultural heritage. Paris, France.
UNESCO (2011) Recommendation on the historic urban landscape. UNESCO World Heritage Centre. https://whc.unesco.org/uploads/activities/documents/activity-638-98.pdf
UNESCO (2013) The Hangzhou declaration: placing culture at the heart of sustainable development policies. https://www.icomos.org/images/DOCUMENTS/Working_Groups/SDG/UNESCO_2013_Hangzhou_Declaration-_Culture_and_Sustainable_Development.pdf
UNESCO (2024) Historic Cairo. State of conservation report 2024. https://whc.unesco.org/en/soc/4604
UNESCO (n.d.) Traditional craftsmanship. https://ich.unesco.org/en/traditional-craftsmanship-00057

Ingy Waked completed her PhD research in 2025 at Raymond Lemaire International Centre for Conservation, Faculty of Engineering Science, KU Leuven, Belgium on 'contributions to understanding building crafts applications in built heritage conservation and in contemporary architecture'. The empirical-based research delivers new knowledge on traditional craftsmanship in architecture through a holistic approach that considers tangible and intangible heritage values. She is an Egyptian architect and urban planner with years of experience in cultural heritage preservation, especially in Historic Cairo World Heritage site, Egypt. Since 2017, she lives in Germany, and she is a member of ICOMOS Germany.

Koenraad van Balen is an emeritus professor at the Civil Engineering department, KU Leuven. Van Balen carries out research and teaches on binders, masonry and sustainable construction methods. He has been the holder of the UNESCO Chair on preventive conservation, monitoring and maintenance of monuments and sites since 2008. He is a member of ICOMOS and was the first secretary-general of the International Scientific Committee of ISCARSAH.

Christian Ost is economist with extensive experience in heritage economics, business cycle theory, and education institution management. He graduated from UC Louvain (Ph.D.), Georgetown University, Washington D.C. (M.A.), and Institut International d'Etudes Européennes (Geneva). He is honorary rector (dean) from ICHEC Brussels Management School, President of the Raymond Lemaire International Centre for Conservation (KU Leuven) and guest lecturer at UC Louvain, and Burgundy School of Business in Dijon.

From CNC Machine to Chisel: Balancing (3D) Technology and Craftsmanship in the Restoration of Notre Dame, Dom Tower, and Grote Kerk

Liselore Tissen and Hendrik-Jan Tolboom

1 Introduction

Over the past few decades, the cultural heritage sector has undergone significant transformations due to technological advancements. These innovations are now swiftly revolutionizing our practices in previously inconceivable ways. Current advanced three-dimensional (3D) scanning methods, including photogrammetry, Light Detection And Ranging (LiDAR), and laser scanning, digitalize cultural heritage objects for documentation, preservation, and analysis (Acke et al. 2021, pp. 272–288; Aure Calvet 2019; Basu et al. 2023, pp. 2–30; Fico et al. 2023, pp. 2–13; Tissen et al. 2020; Tissen 2024, pp. 58–78).[1] The seamless integration of digital data with additive manufacturing methods, including 3D printing, makes it possible to translate digital data and enables the limitless production of high-quality physical reproductions of heritage objects in various materials and complexities. This process is achieved by building the object layer by layer using a liquid (photosensitive) material that hardens upon exposure to an energy source or in the air or by carving material from a solid block, like stone (e.g., Computer Numerical Control (CNC)

[1] For an overview of all technologies used in cultural heritage conservation, see: Tissen, L.N.M. "Indistinguishable Likeness - The Impact Of The Original Artwork And Its 3D-Printed Twin On The Discipline Of Art History, Conservation, And Museum Practice." Doctoral Dissertation, Leiden University and Delft University of Technology 2024 and Verykokou, S., and C. Ioannidis. "An Overview on Image-Based and Scanner-Based 3D Modeling Technologies." *Sensors* 23, no. 2 (2023).

L. Tissen (✉)
Leiden University, Leiden, The Netherlands
e-mail: l.n.m.tissen@hum.leidenuniv.nl

H.-J. Tolboom
Dutch Cultural Heritage Agency (RCE), Amersfoort, The Netherlands
e-mail: h.tolboom@cultureelerfgoed.nl

B. Zwegers and R. Vulto (eds.), *The Spillover Effect of Intangible Cultural Heritage*, Studies in Art, Heritage, Law and the Market 13,
https://doi.org/10.1007/978-3-032-25352-1_5

milling (Tissen 2024, pp. 79–85). As a result, numerous studies demonstrate how these methods facilitate the visualization of different conservation options, stages of the object's materials, and the reconstruction of entirely or partially lost artworks (Acke et al. 2021, pp. 272–288; Acke 2024; Basu et al. 2023; Tissen et al. 2022; Tissen 2024, pp. 50–78). For instance, 3D laser scanning empowers conservators to create detailed digital models of structures, which can then be faithfully reproduced with CNC machining, ensuring millimeter-level accuracy (Bayram 2021, pp. 173–193; Fico et al. 2023, pp. 2–15; Gamal et al. 2024, pp. 121–140). One significant advantage of these methods for large-scale projects, including conserving buildings, architecture, and substantial stone structures, is their ability to lessen the amount of manual labor and physically strenuous tasks. The concurrent restoration of Notre Dame in Paris (2019–2024), the Grote Kerk in Breda (from 2014 onwards), and the Dom Tower (2016–2024) have demonstrated that replacing stone masonry and sculptures benefits significantly from modern tools (Bold et al. 2017, pp. 315–320; Gallet 2024, pp. 46–48; Pereira et al. 2019). Conventional stone shape techniques involve laborious and complex procedures such as hand tooling and molds. Automated machines can now supersede these methods, considerably improving repair speed and accuracy and simultaneously addressing labor shortages and the economic constraints of such manual tasks (Acke et al. 2021, pp. 272–288; Dillmann 2024; Göktas 2024; Gros et al. 2023; Repinskiy et al. 2021; Tolboom and Dubelaar 2009; Vanhellemont et al. 2016, pp. 141–150).

While modern technologies like CNC milling may speed up the restoration process and improve precision, there is a danger that the human touch and the conservator's knowledge will vanish completely. Numerous scholars express concern regarding the latter since their expertise, experience, and humanity are essential to conserving the object's intangible and more conceptual qualities, such as its cultural value, societal meaning, and, in these cases, its religious role (Acke 2024; Ashley-Smith 2016; Brückle 2019; Caple and Williams 2023; Muñoz Viñas 2022, pp. 173–180; Ng et al. 2017a, b; Otero 2024; Schlegel and Kraus 2021). Moreover, without the conservator's knowledge, even the material components of an object cannot be restored, as their judgment is always necessary for authentic conservation (Castriota 2024, pp. 59–86; Macedo 2024, pp. 147–162; Muñoz Viñas 2022, pp. 173–182).

The restoration efforts for Notre Dame, Grote Kerk, and Dom Tower highlight the necessity of balancing machine use and conservators' roles, ensuring the preservation of both tangible and intangible elements. Although all aim to uphold historical accuracy, material authenticity, and aesthetic similarity, their philosophical approaches to conserving both material and immaterial heritage—encompassing conservators' expertise and traditional methods—differ notably in their degree of mechanization. These cases present a unique opportunity to explore how the three restorations balance technology and craftsmanship and their effects on preserving the historical integrity of the monument's tangible and intangible cultural values and the conservator's expertise.

This chapter compares the restoration methods used to recreate the stonemasonry and ornaments of Notre Dame, the Grote Kerk, and the Dom Tower, emphasizing the implications of combining modern technologies with traditional craftsmanship. The analysis relies on data from academic literature, firsthand restoration project reports, and expert interviews to provide a thorough and reliable assessment. This mixed-method approach highlights the challenges and successes of integrating technological innovations with traditional techniques throughout large-scale restoration projects. Emphasizing historical accuracy and quality in these endeavours, the analysis will explore how philosophical views on restoration influence the connection between conventional craftsmanship and modern methods. We will pay specific attention to the roles of artisans in making restoration choices and the degree of mechanization used in the process. By examining these three case studies, the chapter aims to deepen our understanding of how modern restoration practices can incorporate technological advancements while respecting the intangible cultural heritage of traditional stone-masonry and sculpture. While this study primary focuses on stone restoration, this discussion will also contribute to broader conversations regarding the sustainable preservation of material heritage and the intangible qualities of both the object and the conservator amidst evolving technological trends.

2 Authenticity and Craftsmanship in Heritage Conservation

The idea of authenticity in conservation has led to significant debates over time, owing to its intricate and varied nature, which includes many stakeholders who often hold differing opinions (Muñoz Viñas 2023, pp. 130–157). The still-influential example that illustrates these conflicting views is the opposing philosophies of French architect Eugène Viollet-le-Duc (1814–1879) and British art critic John Ruskin (1819–1900) (Tissen 2024, pp. 252–270). Viollet-le-Duc, a pivotal figure in nineteenth-century restoration and known for designing the spire on the Notre Dame Cathedral that collapsed in 2019 during the fire, advocated for restoring monuments to an idealized state—one that reflected what the building "should have been" rather than its historical reality (Viollet-le-Duc 1858). His approach often involved significant interventions, including introducing elements that were never part of the original structure to preserve the monument's visual and symbolic integrity (Viollet-le-Duc 1875, pp. 3–6). Maintaining a building's aesthetic cohesion, using traditional methods, and allowing artistic freedom were considered more important than strict historical accuracy (Giombini 2024, pp. 82–92; Marchesi 2017, pp. 30–31; Muñoz Viñas 2020, pp. 9–14; Van de Vall and van Saaze 2024, pp. 1–6).

In contrast, Ruskin advocated a "hands-off approach" in which buildings were allowed to age naturally (Ruskin 1849, pp. 17–20). To him, any form of unnecessary intervention would alter the historical, aesthetical, and material integrity of a building; hence, it would diminish its material authenticity (Ruskin 1849, pp. 8.242–8.244). For Ruskin, restoration was akin to destruction, as it erased the traces of time that conveyed the building's history. He believed that the decay and deterioration of materials were essential to a structure's identity, emphasizing preserving original materials as central to maintaining its authenticity (Ruskin 1849, pp. 17–20; Ryynanen and Kaverina 2024, pp. 1–8). His philosophy directly opposes Viollet-le-Duc's interventionist approach, focusing instead on conserving the material history of the building (Tissen 2024, pp. 252–270).

The relevance of these foundational debates remains central to contemporary conservation practices. However, with the high-profile and high-tech restoration projects of repairing the damage from the Notre Dame fire, the Dom Tower, and the ongoing restoration of the Grote Kerk, this discussion has resurfaced more prominently than ever. With the rise of modern techniques, a common question is whether prioritizing the preservation of art materials through high-resolution digital reproduction methods compromises or enhances the authenticity of the building (Tissen 2024, pp. 13–31, pp. 256–270). Moreover, the increasing role of science in heritage conservation, alongside the museumification of cultural objects—where monuments are often treated primarily as artifacts for display—has further entrenched the focus on material conservation (Castriota 2024, pp. 59–86; Muñoz Viñas 2015). Museums, prioritizing the physical stability of objects, usually emphasize the preservation of material aspects over other considerations (Dudley 2013; Macedo 2024; Tissen 2021, 2024, pp. 13–31, pp. 256–270). Following Ruskin, this predominantly Eurocentric idea about authenticity, reproduction methods cannot be 'authentic.'

At the same time, an increasing number of studies show a shift in the perception of authenticity (Castriota 2024, pp. 58–86; Di Giuseppantonio Di Franco et al. 2018; Schwarz and Williams 2021; Tissen 2024, pp. 180–191; Tissen and van Veldhuizen 2022, pp. 2–7; Tom 2024). In a world that is becoming increasingly connected through digitalization and the rapid development of technology, authenticity should not be considered solely static, fixed, and based on materials alone (Latour and Lowe 2011; Tissen 2024, pp. 180–190). After the fire at the Notre-Dame, for instance, significant debates emerged over whether the cathedral should be reconstructed using only original materials or whether modern methods and materials should be incorporated to enhance the building's resilience against future vulnerabilities (Tissen 2019; Voisenat 2024, pp. 177–179). This shows that authenticity is becoming increasingly more complex as the value of art also relies on intangible qualities, such as one's emotional connection to an artwork or its significance in a cultural context. The proliferation of digital tools in heritage conservation, including high-resolution scanners, 3D printers, and VR/AR systems, has added a layer of complexity to this debate. These tools allow for precise measurements, the creation of accurate replicas, and even virtual tours of historical sites, fundamentally altering the methodologies employed in restoration (Cimino et al. 2018; Giombini 2024; Innocente et al. 2023; Lehtola et al. 2021; Neumüller et al. 2014; Scopigno et al. 2017; Tissen 2024, pp. 30–90). However, many scholars express concerns that over-reliance on these tools could erode manual skills and experiential knowledge—essential to traditional restoration work (Ashley-Smith 2016, pp. 119–132; Brückle 2019, pp. 287–310; Lawson et al. 2024; Macedo 2024; Muñoz Viñas 2022, pp. 173–198; Reich et al. 2024; Reich and Drummer 2024; Valle Noronha 2024; Wei 2024). Although scientific methods such as spectroscopy, microscopy, and environmental monitoring allow for precise interventions to stabilize materials and minimize degradation, this approach tends to overlook the intangible values of heritage. These include the cultural, emotional, and historical significance that give monuments lasting meaning (Castriota 2024, pp. 59–86; Muñoz Viñas 2020, pp. 2–7).

3 Balancing Craft and Industry in Stone Conservation

Digital tools excel at replicating form and structure. However, they may miss the unique flaws and subtle differences vital to handcrafted works. The philosophy of idealized restoration proposed by Viollet-le-Duc remains relevant today, reflecting the precision found in digital restorations. In such cases, we often neglect the crucial role reproduction plays in reconstructing the aesthetic values of our heritage that we admire, as well as in the conservation process itself. During the nineteenth century, professional stonemasons and sculptors typically did not design their works; instead, they meticulously reproduced designs created by other artists. Consequently, these arts evolved into industrialized processes, differing significantly from how craftsmen operate according to Thomas Crombez's definition in his essay, *De steenhouwer en de robot: Reflecties over handwerk en ambacht* (The Stone Mason and the Robot: Reflections on Arts and Crafts). He argues that a craftsman is involved in every step, from design to execution, and is consistently engaged and learning; consequently, alterations and improvements in the final product are allowed to an extent (Crombez 2019). In his renowned book, *The Craftsman*, Richard Sennett asserts that a craftsman hones his skills throughout the process, making choices regarding the tools, techniques, and materials employed (Sennett 2016, pp. 150–155). This implies that machinery can play a role in craftsmanship, provided design and execution remain intertwined, unlike the separation seen in the nineteenth century and typical industrial practices.

To clarify the differences between industrial and artisanal processes, Belgian sculptor Geo Verbanck outlines the distinction between a sculpture initially created in plaster by an artist and later transformed into stone by a skilled craftsman. The latter, described as "thought in stone," undergoes modifications during creation, ensuring the final piece is well-suited to its material. This method infuses a personal touch and optimizes the stone's inherent qualities (Tolboom and Van der Star 2020; Verbanck 1949).

Ruskin explored similar themes, particularly the distinction between design and execution, in *The Stones of Venice*:

> "Understand this clearly: you can teach a man to draw a straight line, and to carve it; and to copy and carve any number of given lines or forms, with admirable speed and perfect precision; and you find his work perfect of its kind: but if you ask him to think about any of those forms, to consider if he cannot find any better in his own head, he stops; his execution becomes hesitating; he thinks, and ten to one he thinks wrong; ten to one he makes a mistake in the first touch he gives to his work as a thinking being. But you have made a man of him for all that. He was only a machine before, an animated tool" (Ruskin 1892, 1899, p. 168).

Ruskin critiques a craftsman who works with 'perfect precision,' viewing the results as mechanical and lacking a human touch. Even when stonemasonry relied on hand tools, skilled artisans produced work that Ruskin deemed unnaturally uniform. Sharing this sentiment, Arend Odé, a Dutch sculptor and architecture scholar, criticizes pre-1920 restorations for their lack of beauty and authenticity compared to earlier stonework (Odé 1919; Caple and Williams 2023, pp. 45–60; Lawson et al. 2024, pp. 315–339). Odé championed a methodology that has become standard in the Netherlands, Belgium, and Germany (Tolboom 2023): rather than strictly adhering to measured drawings or molds, stonemasons should consider the interplay of light and shadow to create nuanced surfaces that appear 'vivid.' These surfaces should not result from strictly adhering to the shape of the original mold but from granting the craftsman creative freedom, moving away from the strict precision typical of the period before 1918. Thus, he emphasizes the importance of creative decision-making over simple mechanical execution in craftsmanship, arguing that the expressiveness and irregularities of original craftsmanship reveal that restoration involves much more than accurate mechanical imitations.

Ruskin and Odé's examples illustrate a common belief in stonemasonry that machines, regardless of their precision, cannot achieve results as vivid as those produced by traditional hand-carving techniques. This is attributed to their lack of human intervention, which should be preserved and recognized as equally valuable to aesthetic authenticity. Nevertheless, this has drastically changed over the past few years with the advent of sawing and CNC machines in stonemasonry workshops replacing traditional hand tools. (Bayram 2021, pp. 179–193; Bold et al. 2017; Castañeda et al. 2015; Gamal et al. 2024; Žujović et al. 2022) The potential loss of these methods and their implicit knowledge reignites the discussions initiated by Ruskin and Odé, prompting questions about the value of human artistry in today's mechanized landscape precision.

As technology evolves, preserving traditional craftsmanship's expressive qualities while integrating modern efficiencies remains challenging. The survival of these time-honored techniques depends on a commitment to valuing and transmitting the knowledge that has defined stonemasonry for centuries. Various scholars have highlighted the significance of tacit knowledge in heritage conservation, noting that it includes technical proficiency and the discernment of when and how to intervene to maintain a monument's authenticity (Ashley-Smith 2009, 2018; Castriota 2024; Macedo 2024; Muñoz Viñas 2022; Otero 2024; Tom 2024). This expertise comes only through experience and physical interaction with materials and is often not transferable to machines (Ashley-Smith 2016, pp. 119–132; Brückle 2019, pp. 287–310; Otero 2024, pp. 2–10; Polanyi 2009, pp. 10–35; Tolboom and Dubelaar 2009). For example, in stone conservation, the feedback from chiseling or carving stones provides invaluable insights into the material's integrity. Knowing when to stop or how to adjust one's technique based on this feedback is a skill that machines cannot replicate (Cook 2020; Kuipers and De Jonge 2017, pp. 33–63; Roeck 2024, pp. 101–125; Tolboom and Dubelaar 2009). This knowledge is vital for maintaining a monument's historical integrity and the potential erosion of such skills through the increased use of technology raises critical concerns about the future of conservation practices (Hagendijk et al. 2021, pp. 119–224; Stols-Witlox 2021, p. 166; Van Veldhuizen 2022, pp. 19–22).

Investing in high-tech equipment, such as high-resolution scanners, 3D printers, and specialized software, requires significant initial costs and ongoing maintenance, updates, and training. For smaller institutions with limited financial means, the gap between well-funded and under-resourced organizations may continue to widen, potentially undermining the equity of conservation efforts (Acke et al. 2021; Acke 2024; Brückle 2019, pp. 278–310; Caple and Williams 2023, pp. 45–60; Lawson et al. 2024, pp. 315–339; Schlegel and Kraus 2021). Economic constraints may lead smaller institutions to depend on more traditional methods, which, while potentially slower and less accurate, preserve essential craftsmanship skills. However, this disparity might create a two-tiered preservation system, where some heritage sites benefit from the latest technologies while others struggle to maintain authenticity using outdated or underfunded methods (Repinskiy et al. 2021, p. 12170). Hence, the debates surrounding authenticity in heritage conservation focus on balancing historical integrity with modern restoration techniques. While technology offers the potential for precision and efficiency, it raises significant ethical and financial concerns. Combining modern tools with traditional methods requires caution to preserve the material and immaterial values that define heritage (Ashley-Smith 2016).

This section will examine the restorations and techniques used to restore Notre Dame in Paris, the Dom Tower in Utrecht, and the Grote Kerk in Breda. It will explore how the integration of technology has influenced these efforts and what this signifies for the future of conserving both the material and immaterial aspects of cultural heritage.

4 Restoration Methodologies in Practice

4.1 Notre Dame

The construction of the Notre Dame de Paris cathedral started in the twelfth century, becoming a symbol of national pride, historical events, and religious pilgrimage. The 2019 fire caused severe damage to the cathedral, particularly its iconic spire and roof, initiating a significant restoration project (Friends of Notre Dame de Paris 2019; Lassus 2020, pp. 15–34; Tissen 2019). The National Commission for Heritage and Architecture (CNPA) and Emmanuel Macron, the president of France since 2017, jointly agreed to reconstruct the cathedral to its "original state", relying on traditional methods and materials to preserve its authenticity (Isnart et al. 2024, pp. 205–211; Monferran et al. 2024, pp. 184–188). For example, French limestone from quarries near the original stone's site north of Paris, along with the recreation of Viollet-le-Duc's original spire to its pre-fire condition, ensured the cathedral's material and aesthetic authenticity (Gallet 2024, pp. 46–48). Yet, establishing the cathedral's 'original state' and its 'authenticity' remains a contentious and intricate issue due to its phased construction, evolving look over the centuries, and the shifts in its purpose (Giombini 2024, pp. 40–46; Ryynanen and Kaverina 2024, pp. 82–92; Tissen 2024, pp. 250–256). Consequently, there was an ongoing debate about whether the cathedral should be reconstructed in Viollet-le-Duc's nineteenth-century style, with the spire replaced by a more modern version, such as one made of glass (Theodossopoulos 2024, pp. 79–92; Tissen 2024, pp. 252–257). Nevertheless, its status as a global icon and the involvement of many stakeholders, investors, and public opinion strongly influenced the decision, with citizens and heritage professionals advocating for a swift reconstruction to restore the cathedral to its familiar form (Isnart et al. 2024, pp. 205–211; Monferran et al. 2024, pp. 181–188; Sagnes 2024, pp. 190–197; Voisenat 2024, pp. 177–179).

Since great emphasis is placed on tradition and historical materials, this would signify that modern methods would not be allowed, let alone reproducing elements. Despite this emphasis on tradition, American professor and specialist in the cathedral's history, Andrew Tallon (2015), finished a 20-year project to record and 3D digitize the entire building, its structure, and its contents, which is only one of the numerous novel technologies vital in the restoration of the cathedral's visual and symbolic function before it was destroyed (Art Graphique et Patrimoine 2019; Cook 2020; Dillmann 2024; Mouaddib et al. 2024). Tallon's 3D scan produced detailed maps of the cathedral's structure, enabling the conservation team to create digital models that facilitated the swift restoration work needed for replacing damaged components (Gros et al. 2023). At the Monument Vandekerckhove firm in Zottegem, CNC machinery was essential for ensuring precision in the stonemasonry performed on the French limestone sourced from the original quarries of Saint-Maximin (see Fig. 2). In this case, CNC milling was necessary to replicate and repair crucial architectural and structural features such as stone vaulting and tracery, guaranteeing that every element was meticulously crafted (Tolboom 2023). CNC milling has been similarly crucial in ensuring the rebuilding adheres to the original design while incorporating modern reinforcements essential for maintaining the cathedral's long-term stability (Cook 2020; Gallet 2024, pp. 47–49; BRGM n.d.; Tiegelaar 2024; Tolboom 2023).

Although traditional stonemasons continued to play a role in applying the finishing touches, their influence was limited to superficial finishing with a pneumatic hammer and a tooth chisel (Pereira et al. 2019, pp. 11–18; Tolboom 2023). Additionally, the stonemasons in Zottegem utilized a CNC-controlled milling machine to carve stone blocks, yet they intentionally left the carved ornaments—like the crockets on pinnacles and cornices—untouched. This decision allowed sculptors in Paris to further refine the remaining mass of stone into elegant ornaments using traditional manual techniques (see Fig. 1) (Tolboom 2023). In this case, the restorers primarily focused on enhancing the shapes that the milling machine could not access, relying on conventional manual methods to erase traces left by the machine on the prepared surfaces (see Fig. 2). The stonemasons' work on the surface textures contributed to a final result that exhibited a distinctly handcrafted quality, albeit in a minimal manner. Art historian Bruno Phalip publicly criticized how the stonemason's knowledge and

Fig. 1 Paris. Sculpture workshop near Notre Dame de Paris (© Monument Vandekerckhove, 2023)

expertise were used to verify the CNC milling machine's work (Phalip 2006). Phalip suggests that the significance of a stonemason's experience is often overlooked. He argues that introducing "La taille numerique" (CNC milling) during this restoration process contributes to the erosion of tacit knowledge.

Fig. 2 Zottegem. Stonemasonry Monument Vandekerckhove. Stacks of reconstructed parts of the Notre Dame de Paris. These parts were made with limestone from the quarry of Saint-Maximin(© Monument Vandekerckhove, 2023)

4.2 Dom Tower: Balancing Authenticity and Modern Practicality

Conversely, the restoration of the Dom Tower in Utrecht embraced a more traditional approach, emphasizing artisanal skills alongside modern technology. Dating to the fourteenth century, it is the tallest church tower in the Netherlands and stands as an emblem of national heritage with profound cultural significance (Göktas 2024; Domtoren n.d.; Restauratie Domtoren | Gemeente Utrecht n.d.). Like many historic buildings, it needed regular restoration to address weathering and aging. However, worries about the tower's structural integrity prompted a large-scale restoration project in the early twenty-first century (Tolboom and De Wild 2024; den Hartog 2015). Similarly to the Notre Dame, the project involved aesthetic repairs and significant engineering interventions to ensure its long-term preservation (Beukers and Koot 2014, pp. 5–40; Göktas 2024; Tolboom and De Wild 2024). The restoration of the Dom Tower adopted a pragmatic approach, merging modern techniques with traditional craftsmanship. This allowed machinery to manage some of the work while maintaining the structure's authenticity through artistic skill (Quist 2016, pp. 3–35; Tolboom 2019; Tolboom and De Wild 2024). While upholding the historical accuracy of the tower, the restoration team needed to tackle urgent structural problems and practical challenges arising from time and environmental wear.

Modern technology was used in restoring the Dom tower, especially in the initial phases (Tolboom and De Wild 2024). Laser scanning technology was utilized to create accurate digital models of the tower's intricate stonework; however, the results were unsatisfactory. The inaccuracies were not due to the scanning technology but to mistakes in interpreting the acquired data. As a result, drawings and molds for the replacement blocks were crafted using measuring tools and perpendicular lines. CNC machines were then employed to shape these stone blocks, particularly for the areas of the tower's exterior that were decayed or damaged (Van Doesburg 2017). CNC machining effectively tackled one of the significant challenges in restoring the Dom Tower: the large volume of stonemasonry needed (Fig. 3). Without these modern tools, relying solely on traditional techniques would have severely delayed the project's completion.

Still, a significant amount of stonemasonry was completed with hand tools. While the machines shaped the rough outlines of the blocks, stonemasons focused on refining the intricate profiles and details. The final step for the stonemasons involved surface finishing with the same tools used to finish the replacement blocks, mainly wooden mallets and flat chisels (Fig. 6). However, the Slotboom stonemasons from Winterswijk, responsible for the restoration of the Dom Tower, did not use machines for milling sculptures; this intricate work was left entirely to sculptors (Quist 2016, pp. 5–25; Tolboom and De Wild 2024). Occasionally, sculptors used a basic sawing machine to trim excess stone that could quickly be finished by hand with pneumatic hammers and chisels—flat, rounded, and tooth chisels. This process converted the square stone block from the stonemasons into an ornament that accentuated its essential features, such as the various crockets, while removing any excess stone (see Fig. 4

Fig. 3 Winterswijk. Slotboom Steenhouwers. Milling of an element at the base of a pinnacle for the Dom Tower in Portland whitbed (© H.J. Tolboom 2024)

and 5) (Tolboom and De Wild 2024; Quist 2016, pp. 5–35; Tolboom 2019, Tolboom and Van der Star 2020).

Relying on these traditional methods is necessary because making ornaments involves manually cutting and shaping partially decayed parts with modelling clay, a relatively common technique that sculptors have relied on for centuries. This technique allows the sculptor to analyse the ornament's features in detail, improving their ability to reproduce it accurately in stone. In this context, manual methods are significantly more efficient since relying on automated techniques alone would not have been possible. This approach also removes the need for expensive equipment typically associated with digital reconstruction.

Fig. 4 Achterveld. Workshop sculptor Koen van Velzen. Replacing element for the Dom tower. Work in progress at the workshop of the sculptor (© H.J. Tolboom, 2024)

4.3 *Grote Kerk Breda: Leaving Space for Handcrafting*

The restoration of the Grote Kerk's choir and chapels in Breda commenced in 2016. It required the replacement of specific stone masonry and decorative elements that predominantly date back to a previous restoration between 1900 and 1940. The detailed features, such as pinnacles, canopies, and balustrades made of different types of French limestone, showed significant signs of weathering (Fig. 7). For replacements, Portland stone (whitbed) and a small amount of French Massangis limestone were utilized (Tolboom 2023).

A digital scan of the original stonemasonry and ornaments provided the foundation for reconstruction by the drafting technicians at Monument VandeKerckhove in Zottegem, who had previously worked on the Notre Dame restoration. Weathered

Fig. 5 Achterveld. Workshop sculptor Koen van Velzen. According to the model in the background, a fleuron is made of Portland stone for the Dom Tower in Utrecht (© H.J. Tolboom, 2024)

ornaments from the church were taken to the workshop, where sculptors rebuilt the missing sections using plasticine alongside the existing artifacts (see Fig. 7) (Tolboom 2023). After the architect's approval, the models were digitized and included in the digital drawings, allowing CNC machines to mill the new stone masonry and decorative elements (see Fig. 8). Once milled, stonemasons and sculptors finalize the pieces, refining edges and surfaces to eliminate visible milling marks (see Fig. 9). This process ensured that the new stonework replicated the characteristics of the original early twentieth-century pieces, known for their 'perfect precision'. In 2021, additional restoration efforts focused on components from post-1920, revealing that their masonry and ornaments lacked this precision and exhibited a more 'vivid' quality, diverging from strict moulds. Reproducing this historical craftsmanship with CNC milling proved challenging, leading to innovative solutions. Ultimately, a 3 mm layer

Fig. 6 Winterswijk. Stonemasonry Slotboom Steenhouwers. A stonemason detailing and finishing stonemasonry with hand-tools, that a CNC-machine partly preprocessed (© H. J. Tolboom 2024)

of stone was added to the surface of the reconstructed elements, allowing traditional chiselling with wooden mallets to create the necessary irregularities and tools historically used in this craft (see Fig. 9). This approach effectively transferred much of the original vividness and irregularity to the newly crafted stonework.

Fig. 7 Zottegem. Stonemasonry Monument Vandekerckhove. Reconstructing a weathered ornament from the Grote Kerk of Breda with plasticine (clay) (c H.J. Tolboom 2021)

5 Comparative Analysis: Impact of Technology on Restoration at Notre Dame Cathedral, the Dom Tower in Utrecht, and the Grote Kerk in Breda

The restorations of Notre Dame in Paris, the Dom Tower in Utrecht, and the Grote Kerk in Breda highlight contrasting approaches to heritage conservation (see Table 1). While all three projects integrate modern technology, their use of traditional craftsmanship varies significantly, raising questions about the balance between material authenticity and technological efficiency. Notre Dame's restoration highlights the tension between technological precision and traditional craftsmanship. CNC milling machines and 3D scanning technologies were extensively utilized to shape stones

Fig. 8 Zottegem. Monument Vandekerckhove NV. Ornament after milling, Portland stone (whitbed) (© H.J. Tolboom 2021)

and replicate architectural details with accuracy and efficiency. Although these tools offer practical advantages, their overuse risks marginalizing human artisanship, a fundamental aspect of the tacit knowledge that historically endowed Notre Dame with its cultural significance.

Additionally, Notre Dame's status as a national symbol and global icon increased pressure for rapid restoration, prioritizing visual continuity over strict adherence to traditional techniques. While 3D scanning and CNC milling enhanced efficiency, their overuse risked sidelining artisans, reducing their role to finishing tasks rather than core construction. This shift threatens the transmission of tacit knowledge, potentially turning Notre Dame into a static artifact rather than a living cultural site.

Unlike Notre Dame, the Dom Tower restoration demonstrates a more balanced integration of craftsmanship and technology. Rather than prioritizing efficiency, this

Fig. 9 Zottegem. Monument Vandekerckhove NV. The same type of ornament, after cutting away with hand tools the stone left during the milling (© H.J. Tolboom 2021)

Table 1 Overview of the techniques used in the restoration of Notre Dame, Dom Tower, and Grote Kerk

	Stonemasonry (a)			Sculpture + ornament (b)		
	Rough shape	Details	Finish	Rough shape	Details	Finish
Notre Dame	Sawing machines + CNC-machines	CNC-machines	Handcrafted (air tools)	Handcrafted	Handcrafted	Handcrafted
Dom Tower	Sawing machines + CNC machines + handcrafted (air tools)	CNC machines + handcrafted (air tools)	Handcrafted (traditional tools)	Handcrafted (Air tools)	Handcrafted (air tools)	Handcrafted (air tools and traditional tools)
Grote Kerk (c)	Sawing machines + CNC-machines	CNC machines + handcrafted (air tools + traditional tools)	Handcrafted (Traditional tools)	Sawing machines + CNC-machines	Handcrafted (traditional tools)	Handcrafted (Traditional tools)

(a, b) the difference between stonemasonry and sculpture is defined by the fact that the first can be precisely measured, using 2-dimensional molds and drawings, while the latter can only be measured using a 3D-model and is executed on sight mostly. (c) replacing stonework originating from the restoration works 1920–1940

project emphasized the role of artisans at every stage of the restoration process. While modern technologies like CNC milling and laser scanning were employed to enhance precision, they were used as supplements rather than replacements. The final and most critical stages of the restoration, including intricate stone carving, were carried out by artisans, underscoring the importance of manual labour. This approach preserved not only the material authenticity of the structure but also the immaterial values—skills and traditions—that define its historical character.

The Dom Tower restoration achieved this balance partly because it did not face the same public or time pressures as Notre Dame, allowing the restoration team greater freedom to focus on craftsmanship and authenticity. The decision to engage human artisans in every stage of the restoration ensured the continuation of traditional stone working techniques, aligning with a more conservative model of heritage conservation. Authenticity extended beyond visual replication to encompass the cultural practices that shaped the tower's original construction. This decision preserved the historical narrative of the building—conveyed through the imperfections and textures of handcrafted stonework—in a way that machine precision could not.

The Grote Kerk in Breda presents yet another approach, emphasizing the importance of digital tools and manual craftsmanship. While CNC milling and digital scans were used to produce initial forms for stone elements, artisans significantly refined these pieces. Unlike Notre Dame, where machinery dominated, the Grote Kerk project ensured that finishing details were completed manually to maintain the aesthetic continuity of the original work. Additionally, the restoration team experimented with techniques to replicate the irregularities of early twentieth-century masonry, ensuring that the new stone elements harmonized with the older structure. This balance between modern efficiency and traditional handcrafting allowed for technical accuracy and material authenticity.

While Notre Dame's restoration focused on symbolic replication, the Dom Tower and Grote Kerk restorations ensured historical authenticity in appearance and technique. Engaging artisans throughout the process preserved the tangible structure and the intangible skills associated with traditional stone working. The restorations of the Dom Tower and Grote Kerk in Breda offer sustainable models in which technology supports, rather than replaces, traditional craftsmanship. They demonstrate that the survival of cultural heritage depends not only on material integrity but also on the transmission of artisanal skills. Future restorations must strike this balance to ensure heritage sites remain historically authentic and culturally meaningful.

6 Lessons for the Future

The comparative analysis of the restorations of Notre Dame in Paris, the Dom Tower in Utrecht, and the Grote Kerk in Breda offers valuable insights into future heritage conservation. Although each project utilized modern digital tools, it followed distinct approaches to balancing efficiency, authenticity, and craftsmanship. These restorations prompt essential questions about preserving tangible and intangible heritage while maintaining historical continuity and embracing innovation.

6.1 The Role of Technology: Efficiency vs. Authenticity

The application of CNC milling, 3D scanning, and digital modelling has significantly changed how historic monuments are restored, but these technologies need strategic implementation. At Notre Dame, digital tools were extensively utilized to speed up the rebuilding efforts. Precise 3D scans before the 2019 fire allowed restorers to recreate missing parts accurately, while CNC-milled stone blocks provided structural consistency. However, this method reduced the involvement of human artisans, limiting stonemasons to only minor surface touch-ups. In contrast, the sculpture that needed to be replaced was executed in a very traditional way.

Conversely, the restoration of the Dom Tower combined CNC milling for structural components with a focus on hand-carved stonework for details and finishing. Instead of replacing craftsmanship, digital tools were used to prepare rough stone shapes, which stonemasons refined manually. This method ensured that the final product maintained a human touch, upholding the historical integrity of traditional stonemasonry techniques. The execution of the ornaments and sculpture was done in the same way as for the Notre Dame.

The restoration of the Grote Kerk in Breda found a balanced approach, utilizing CNC milling for efficiency and to facilitate traditional chiselling methods. By leaving extra material on the CNC-milled blocks, stonemasons and sculptors could employ historical tools and hand-finishing techniques to replicate the textured, uneven details and finish typical of the church's original early twentieth-century designs. This innovative approach illustrated how technology can enhance craftsmanship, allowing human artisans to perfect and refine machine-cut stone elements. On the other hand, the sculpture and ornaments in this case were, like the stonemasonry, partly milled by a machine and not completely cut out of a rectangular piece of stone, like at the Dom Tower and Notre Dame, appealing less on the craft of the sculptor.

6.2 Preserving Tacit Knowledge and the Role of Artisans

A key takeaway from these restorations is the importance of safeguarding artisans' expertise to prevent the loss of traditional skills in the face of technological progress. At Notre Dame, stonemasons mainly focused on verification and surface finishing, sparking worries that "La taille numérique" (CNC milling) undermines the passing down of tacit knowledge. French heritage scholars have criticized this method, stating it reduces the roles of conservators and stonemasons to mere technicians operating machines instead of skilled artisans.

Conversely, the Dom Tower restoration preserved a more significant role for artisans, especially in the final shaping of decorative stonework. Stonemasons and sculptors participated throughout the entire process, rather than just applying finishing touches, which helped ensure the transmission of skills to younger generations and kept traditional techniques vital to conservation efforts. The Grote Kerk restoration presents an innovative approach by intentionally designing digital interventions that support traditional techniques. By programming CNC machines to leave an additional 3 mm layer of stone on each piece, the restoration team allowed artisans to finish the final details by hand. This approach balanced efficiency with artistic interpretation, allowing craftsmanship to remain an essential part of the restoration process. For sculptors, however, this method enables them less to develop their ability to give the stone a which is primarily derived from a model, since a machine partially milled this shape.

6.3 Balancing Public Expectations with Historical Integrity

The urgency and visibility of a restoration project significantly impact the decision-making process. Notre Dame's worldwide importance pressured restorers to expedite the reconstruction. Consequently, the cathedral was rebuilt with modern tools while maintaining its nineteenth-century look. This choice ensured aesthetic fidelity but raised questions about whether the intangible elements of its historical construction methods were adequately preserved.

In contrast, the Dom Tower restoration enjoyed a longer timeline and fewer external pressures, enabling a more systematic approach emphasizing historical accuracy over speed. Opting for partly handcrafted stonemasonry and completely hand-carved sculptures instead of digital milling exemplified a dedication to authentic craftsmanship rather than mere efficiency.

The Grote Kerk restoration illustrates how smaller projects can effectively manage these pressures by adopting a flexible strategy. The restoration team intentionally preserved early twentieth-century craftsmanship aesthetics, ensuring the masonry's visual and tactile authenticity remained intact. By blending CNC precision with skilled craftsmanship, they developed a nuanced approach that satisfies public expectations and respects conservation ethics.

6.4 The Future of Hybrid Conservation Models

The Grote Kerk's approach to restoring stonemasonry highlights an emerging model in which digital tools prepare materials, but craftsmanship remains central to the final result. In contrast to Notre Dame, where technology prevailed, and the Dom Tower, known for its handcrafting, the Grote Kerk's team effectively employed digital tools to foster human involvement. The structural uniformity achieved through CNC milling was balanced with hand-finishing processes that enabled artistic enhancement.

This hybrid method offers a promising framework for future conservation projects, where technology is not merely a tool for replication but a mechanism to support the work of artisans. By integrating digital fabrication to encourage hands-on craftsmanship, restorers can ensure that traditional techniques remain relevant in the twenty-first century.

6.5 Educational and Ethical Strategies for Future Conservation

The analysis emphasizes the significance of educational programs that merge technological training with traditional hands-on techniques. Future conservators need a skill set to navigate the complexities of using modern tools while preserving craftsmanship. Mentorship programs, workshops, and apprenticeships are essential for ensuring that tacit knowledge is passed down to the next generation of artisans, protecting the intangible heritage of traditional methods. In addressing this issue, various initiatives and studies, including ICOM-CC, present a solution by discussing the benefits of developing community-led initiatives that effectively educate fellow conservation experts, thereby preserving the conservator's knowledge and the intangible qualities of art (Acke 2024; Acke et al. 2024; Seymour 2024).

Furthermore, ethical frameworks are vital for integrating technology into conservation. Clear guidelines from international bodies and professional organizations can assist practitioners in addressing the moral dilemmas that arise when balancing technological intervention with authenticity (Ashley-Smith 2018). Sustainability is also a key consideration, as environmentally responsible solutions, such as energy-efficient tools and e-waste management, should be integral to any technological strategy in heritage conservation since it has been proven that digital data has a detrimental environmental effect due to the large amounts of energy it requires to keep these digital models operable (Jaheer et al. 2024, pp. 369–420). Therefore, assessing what is being preserved and carefully considering whether using digital tools to conserve a single material object justifies the potential environmental damage that could lead to the future loss of heritage artifacts.

6.6 Data-driven Research and Continuous Improvement

Another key lesson is the need for ongoing research that evaluates the effectiveness of technological methods compared to traditional practices. By gathering data-driven insights, conservators can identify the best conservation technology applications, ensuring that efficiency does not come at the cost of authenticity. Learning from past projects, like Notre Dame and the Dom Tower, is crucial in preparing for continuous improvement in the field. Adapting restoration techniques to strike the right balance between technological advancements and preserving immaterial heritage is a key part of this process.

6.7 *Importance of Collaboration and Resource Sharing*

The analysis also underscores the need for collaboration between institutions to democratize access to technological tools and expertise. Partnerships between well-funded institutions and smaller organizations can help bridge the gap in resources and skills, ensuring that all heritage sites benefit from the latest advancements in conservation. Promoting open-source technologies and affordable solutions can level the playing field and ensure that even smaller heritage sites can implement modern tools without sacrificing authenticity.

7 Conclusion: Crafting a Sustainable Future for Heritage Conservation

The restorations of Notre Dame, the Dom Tower, and the Grote Kerk provide valuable lessons for the future of heritage conservation. Notre Dame serves as a cautionary tale, illustrating the risks of over-reliance on technology at the expense of craftsmanship and historical techniques. At the same time, the Dom Tower offers a more holistic model where technology supports rather than replaces traditional methods. Both cases highlight the importance of preserving tangible and intangible heritage that define historical monuments. Moving forward, the field of heritage conservation must adopt a balanced approach that integrates modern tools while safeguarding the legacy of craftsmanship. Implementing ethical frameworks, educational programs, and sustainability practices will ensure that future conservation efforts maintain the authenticity and integrity of the world's cultural heritage. Without these efforts, we risk losing the essence of our historical monuments, reducing them to mere replicas of their former selves. By learning from the successes and shortcomings of projects like Notre Dame, the Dom Tower, and the Grote Kerk, conservators can ensure that heritage sites are preserved for future generations in material form and the traditions, skills, and stories that make them culturally significant. Without this legacy of craftsmanship, our material heritage, too, will eventually perish.

References

Acke L (2024) 3D digital conservation and restoration skills for the 21st century. University of Antwerp, Antwerp

Acke L, Corradi D, Verlinden J (2024) Comprehensive educational framework on the application of 3D technologies for the restoration of cultural heritage objects. J Cult Herit 66:613–627

Acke L, de Vis K, Verwulgen S, Verlinden J (2021) Survey and literature study to provide insights on the application of 3D technologies in objects conservation and restoration. J Cult Herit 49:272–288

Art Graphique et Patrimoine (2019) The 3D scan come to the rescue of Notre-Dame. Art Graphique et Patrimoine, Saint Denis. https://www.artgp.fr/agp-digitized-notre-dame-in-3d.html?lang=fr

Ashley-Smith J (2009) The adolescence of the profession. In: Conservation: principles, dilemmas, and uncomfortable truths [Conference presentation]. The Royal Academy of Arts, London
Ashley-Smith J (2016) Losing the edge: the risk of a decline in practical conservation skills. J Inst Conserv 39:119–132. https://doi.org/10.1080/19455224.2016.1210015
Ashley-Smith J (2018) The ethics of doing nothing. J Inst Conserv 41:6–15
Aure Calvet X (2019) The application of 2.5D and 3D technologies for the conservation and presentation of surface texture in paintings. University of West England, Bristol
Basu A, Paul S, Ghosh S, Das S, Chanda B, Bhagvati C, Snasel V (2023) Digital restoration of cultural heritage with data-driven computing: a survey. IEEE Access 1:53939–53977. https://doi.org/10.1109/ACCESS.2023.3280639
Bayram AKŞ (2021) Digital fabrication shift in architecture. Archit Sci Technol 42:173–193
Beukers M, Koot R (2014) Jaarboek Oud Utrecht 2014. Vereniging Oud Utrecht, Utrecht. https://books.google.nl/books?id=gOv4rQEACAAJ
Bold J, Larkham P, Pickard R (2017) Authentic reconstruction: authenticity, architecture and the built heritage. Bloomsbury Publishing, Bedford
BRGM (n.d.) Restoration of Notre-Dame Cathedral: methodological guide to the selection of stones. https://www.brgm.fr/en/reference-completed-project/restoration-dame-cathedral-methodological-guide-selection-stones. Accessed 26 Sep 2024
Brückle I (2019) The development of skill knowledge in conservation. J Restor Int J Preserv Libr Arch Mate 40:287–310. https://doi.org/10.1515/res-2019-0016
Caple C, Williams E (2023) Conservation skills for the 21st century: judgement, method, and decision-making. Taylor and Francis, Milton Park
Castañeda E, Lauret B, Lirola J, Ovando G (2015) Free-form architectural envelopes: digital processes opportunities of industrial production at a reasonable price. J Facade Design Eng 3:1–13
Castriota B (2024) The enfolding object of conservation: artwork identity, authenticity, and documentation. In: van de Vall R, van Saaze V (eds) Conservation of contemporary art: bridging the gap between theory and practice. Springer, Cham, pp 59–86. https://doi.org/10.1007/978-3-031-42357-4_4
Cimino D, Rollo G, Zanetti M, Bracco P (2018) 3D printing technologies: are their materials safe for conservation treatments? IOP Conf Ser Mater Sci Eng 364:1–7
Cook L (2020) Technology to freeze time at Lassus and Viollet-le-Duc's Notre-Dame of Paris: learning from the past for the cathedral of the future. Future Anterior J Hist Preserv Hist Theory Crit 17:47–59
Crombez T (2019) De steenhouwer en de robot: Reflecties over handwerk en ambacht. Uitgeverij Vrijdag, Antwerp
den Hartog E (2015) De bouwsculptuur van de Utrechtse Dom: Een andere kijk op de bouwgeschiedenis. Rijksdienst voor het Cultureel Erfgoed, Amersfoort
Di Giuseppantonio Di Franco P, Galeazzi F, Vassallo V (2018) Authenticity and cultural heritage in the age of 3D digital reproductions. Cambridge University Press, Cambridge
Dillmann P (2024, May) Notre-Dame de Paris: the contribution of (materials) science to the rebirth of a cathedral. E-MRS Spring Meeting. https://hal.science/hal-04594684
Domtoren (n.d.) Lees alles over de restauratie van de Domtoren. https://www.domtoren.nl/het-verhaal/restauratie/. Accessed 26 Sep 2024
Dudley SH (ed) (2013) Museum materialities: objects, engagements, interpretations. Taylor and Francis, Milton Park
Fico D, Rizzo D, Montagna F, Esposito Corcione C (2023) Fused filament fabrication and computer numerical control milling in cultural heritage conservation. Materials 16:1–15. https://doi.org/10.3390/ma16083038
Friends of Notre Dame de Paris (2019) Reconstruction process report. Friends of Notre Dame de Paris, Paris. https://www.friendsofnotredamedeparis.org/reconstruction-progress/#elementor-toc__heading-anchor-6

Gallet Y (2024) Of stone and mortar: studying Notre-Dame cathedral's core materials. J Cult Herit 65:46–48. https://doi.org/10.1016/j.culher.2023.09.014
Gamal A, Nashaat B, Shahda MM, Nosier SR (2024) Ten questions concerning the integration of digital fabrication techniques into the architectural design process. Archit Eng Des Manag 20:120–149. https://doi.org/10.1080/17452007.2023.2269559
Giombini L (2024) Integrity in cultural heritage preservation: unveiling the challenges. In: Somhegyi Z, Giombini L (eds) The Routledge companion to the philosophy of architectural reconstruction. Routledge, London, pp 1–18
Göktas M (2024, April 11) Restauratie natuursteen Domtoren te Utrecht in goede handen bij VRS-lid Slotboom Steenhouwers. Vereniging Restauratie Steenhouwers (VRS). https://restauratiesteenhouwers.nl/restauratie-natuursteen-domtoren-te-utrecht-in-goede-handen-bij-vrs-lid-slotboom-steenhouwers/
Gros A, Guillem A, De Luca L, Baillieul É, Duvocelle B, Malavergne O, Leroux L, Zimmer T (2023) Faceting the post-disaster built heritage reconstruction process within the digital twin framework for Notre-Dame de Paris. Sci Rep 13:5981. https://doi.org/10.1038/s41598-023-32504-9
Hagendijk T, Dupré S, Vilarigues M (2021) Re-working recipes and experiments in the classroom. In: Stols-Witlox MJN, Harris A, Dupré S, Kursell J, Lulof P (eds) Reconstruction, replication and re-enactment in the humanities and social sciences. Amsterdam University Press, Amsterdam, pp 199–224
Hartigan R (2019, April 16) Historian uses lasers to unlock mysteries of Notre Dame Cathedral | National Geographic. https://www.nationalgeographic.com/adventure/article/150622-andrew-tallon-notre-dame-cathedral-laser-scan-art-history-medieval-gothic
Innocente C, Ulrich L, Moos S, Vezzetti E (2023) A framework study on the use of immersive XR technologies in the cultural heritage domain. J Cult Herit 62:268–283
Isnart C, Raulin A, Menezes R, Pereira E, de Pinto DS, Pinheiro TM, Loir-Mongazon E, Girard G, Goacolou E, Fonseca VL (2024) Mourning, reconstruction, and the future after heritage catastrophes: a comparative social science perspective agenda. J Cult Herit 65:199–205. https://doi.org/10.1016/j.culher.2023.09.010
Jaheer MKP, Vishal J, Bing T, Sang W, Chia W (2024) Digital innovations for renewable energy and conservation. IGI Global, Hershey
Kuipers M, de Jonge W (2017) Designing from heritage. Strategies for conservation and conversion. TU Delft, Delft
Lassus JP (2020) Projet de restauration de Notre-Dame de Paris, vol 1. Library of Alexandria, Alexandria
Latour B, Lowe A (2011) The migration of the aura, or how to explore the original through its facsimiles. In: Bartscherer T, Coover R (eds) Switching codes: thinking through digital technology in the humanities and the arts. University of Chicago Press, Chicago, pp 1–18
Lawson L, Harvey D, Ribeiro A, Marçal H (2024) The living process of conserving performance: theory and practice in the conservation of performance-based artworks at Tate. In: van de Vall R, van Saaze V (eds) Conservation of contemporary art: bridging the gap between theory and practice. Springer, Cham, pp 315–339. https://doi.org/10.1007/978-3-031-42357-4_16
Lehtola VV, Nikoohemat S, Nüchter A (2021) Indoor 3D: overview on scanning and reconstruction methods. In: Chiang YY, Werner M (eds) Handbook of big geospatial data. Springer, Cham, pp 55–97
Macedo R (2024) Visible issues: insights into the professional identity of the conservator. In: van de Vall R, van Saaze V (eds) Conservation of contemporary art: bridging the gap between theory and practice. Springer, Cham, pp 147–162. https://doi.org/10.1007/978-3-031-42357-4_8
Marchesi M (2017) Forever young: the reproduction of photographic artworks as a conservation strategy. Leiden University, Leiden
Monferran JC, Salatko G, Voisenat C (2024) Crafting exceptionality: Notre-Dame de Paris between materiality and sacrality. J Cult Herit 65:180–188. https://doi.org/10.1016/j.culher.2023.02.002

Mouaddib EM, Pamart A, Pierrot-Deseilligny M, Girardeau-Montaut D (2024) 2D/3D data fusion for the comparative analysis of the vaults of Notre-Dame de Paris before and after the fire. J Cult Herit 65:221–231. https://doi.org/10.1016/j.culher.2023.06.012

Muñoz Viñas S (2015) Who is afraid of Cesare Brandi? Personal reflections on the Teoria del restauro. CeROArt, HS, 2015

Muñoz Viñas S (2020) On the ethics of cultural heritage conservation. Archetype, London

Muñoz Viñas S (2022) Conservation science, conservation practice and the conservator's knowledge: a naïve exploration. J Inst Conserv 45:173–189

Muñoz Viñas S (2023) A theory of cultural heritage: beyond the intangible. Taylor and Francis, Milton Park

Neumüller M, Reichinger A, Rist F, Kern C (2014) 3D printing for cultural heritage: preservation, accessibility, research and education. In: Ioannides M, Quak E (eds) 3D research challenges in cultural heritage: a roadmap in digital heritage preservation. Springer, Cham, pp 119–134

Ng WX, Chan HK, Teo WK, Chen IM (2017a) Capturing the tacit knowledge of the skilled operator to program tool paths and tool orientations for robot belt grinding. Int J Adv Manuf Technol 91:113–124. https://doi.org/10.1007/s00170-016-9813-8

Ng WX, Chan HK, Teo WK, Chen IM (2017b) Programming a robot for conformance grinding of complex shapes by capturing the tacit knowledge of a skilled operator. IEEE Trans Autom Sci Eng 14:912–922

Odé AWM (1919) No. 1903. Nota van Professor A.W.M. Odé betreffende de behandeling van steenhouwwerk en beeldhouwwerk bij restauraties. In: Notulen van de vergaderingen van afdeeling B gehouden in het jaar 1919

Otero J (2024) Beyond skills: reflections on the tacit knowledge-brain-cognition nexus on heritage conservators. Herit Sci 12:223. https://doi.org/10.1186/s40494-024-01341-y

Pereira T, Kennedy JV, Potgieter J (2019) A comparison of traditional manufacturing vs additive manufacturing, the best method for the job. Procedia Manuf 30:11–18. https://doi.org/10.1016/j.promfg.2019.02.003

Phalip B (2006) Techniques et technologies: Nouvelles approches de recherche. Université Blaise-Pascal, Clermont-Ferrand

Polanyi M (2009) The tacit dimension. University of Chicago Press, Chicago. https://press.uchicago.edu/ucp/books/book/chicago/T/bo6035368.html

Quist W (2016) Het besluitvormingsproces met betrekking tot natuursteenrestauratie. Delft University of Technology, Delft. http://resolver.tudelft.nl/uuid:3403bd5f-cd37-4299-b005-aeffc6c209f0

Reich J, Drummer C (2024) Digital archaeology between hype and reality: the results of a survey on the use of 3D technologies in archaeology. In: Hostettler M (ed) The 3 dimensions of digitalised archaeology. Springer, Cham, pp 181–203

Reich J, Drummer C, Hostettler M (2024) 3D archaeology and cultural heritage: where are we today? In: Hostettler M (ed) The 3 dimensions of digitalised archaeology. Springer, Cham, pp 3–8

Repinskiy OD, Romaneskul NB, Studenkova NA (2021) Using of additive manufacturing (AM) in construction economics–shortcomings, advantages, prospects. IOP Conf Ser Mater Sci Eng 751:12170

Restauratie Domtoren | Gemeente Utrecht (n.d.). https://www.utrecht.nl/wonen-en-leven/bouwprojecten-en-stedelijke-ontwikkeling/bouwprojecten/restauratie-domtoren. Accessed 26 Sep 2024

Roeck C (2024) Languages of conservation: a comparison between internet-based art and built heritage. In: van de Vall R, van Saaze V (eds) Conservation of contemporary art: bridging the gap between theory and practice. Springer, Cham, pp 101–125. https://doi.org/10.1007/978-3-031-42357-4_6

Ruskin J (1849) The seven lamps of architecture. Wiley, Hoboken

Ruskin J (1892) The nature of gothic: a chapter of the stones of Venice. Kelmscott Press, London

Ruskin J (1899) The stones of Venice. George Allen, London

Ryynanen M, Kaverina K (2024) Questioning heritage. In: Somhegyi Z, Giombini L (eds) The Routledge companion to the philosophy of architectural reconstruction. Routledge, London, pp 82–95

Sagnes S (2024) Mediators, users and narratives: the cathedral experience. J Cult Herit 65:189–198. https://doi.org/10.1016/j.culher.2023.06.011

Schlegel D, Kraus P (2021) Skills and competencies for digital transformation—a critical analysis in the context of robotic process automation. Int J Organ Anal 31:804–822. https://doi.org/10.1108/IJOA-04-2021-2707

Schwarz KC, Williams JP (2021) Introduction to the social construction of identity and authenticity. In: Schwarz KC, Williams JP (eds) Studies on the social construction of identity and authenticity. Routledge, London, pp 1–24

Scopigno R, Cignoni P, Pietroni N, Callieri M, Dellepiane M (2017) Digital fabrication techniques for cultural heritage: a survey. Comput Graph Forum 36:6–21

Sennett R (2016) De ambachtsman: De mens als maker. Meulenhoff Boekerij B.V., Amsterdam

Seymour K (2024) Solidarity project: community-led training. ICOM-CC On Board 2:19–23

Stols-Witlox MJN (2021) Imperfect copies. In: Stols-Witlox MJN, Kursell J, Dupré S, Harris A, Lulof P (eds) Reconstructions in conservation research and practice. Amsterdam University Press, Amsterdam, pp 169–198

Theodossopoulos D (2024) A reversal from hi-tech to authenticity: the case of fire safety for cathedral roofs in France. Mater Strutt Probl Di Conserv 25:79–92

Tiegelaar M (2024, April 29) VRS-lid Monument Vandekerckhove is bijna klaar met haar opdracht aan de Notre-Dame in Parijs. Vereniging Restauratie Steenhouwers (VRS). https://restauratiessteenhouwers.nl/vrs-lid-monument-vandekerckhove-is-bijna-klaar-met-haar-opdracht-aan-de-notre-dame-in-parijs/

Tissen LNM (2019, April 25) The threat after the fire: the restoration of the Notre-Dame. Leiden Arts In Society Blog. https://www.leidenartsinsocietyblog.nl/articles/the-threat-after-the-fire-the-restoration-of-the-notre-dame

Tissen LNM (2021) Authenticity and meaningful futures for museums: the role of 3D printing. In: Tissen LNM, Tomberge T, de Roest A, Raia A, van den Berg C, Powell-Warren C, Caers B (eds) Reinventing boundaries of crisis. Leiden University Libraries, Leiden, pp 94–122

Tissen LNM (2024) Indistinguishable likeness—the impact of the original artwork and its 3D-printed twin on the discipline of art history, conservation, and museum practice. Leiden University and Delft University of Technology, Leiden and Delft

Tissen LNM, Frequin S, Wiersma RT (2022) The case of the golden background, a virtual restoration and a physical reconstruction of the medieval crucifixion of the Lindau Master (c. 1425). Digit Humanit Q 16:1–8

Tissen LNM, Seymour K, Dubbeldam S, Jerdonekova I, Molenaar C, Schilder J, Elkhuizen WS (2020) Using 3D scanning to support conservation treatments for paintings. Mater Sci Eng 949:1–8

Tissen LNM, van Veldhuizen MJE (2022) Picture-perfect – the perception and applicability of facsimiles in museums. Art Percept 11:1–53. https://doi.org/10.1163/22134913-bja10043

Tolboom HJ (2019) Het veranderde aanzicht van de Utrechtse Domkerk. Over de omgang met natuursteen in de Nederlandse restauratiepraktijk. In: La pierre comme porteur de messages du chantier de construction et de la vie du bâtiment. Actes du XXIe Colloque international de Glyptographie. Academia Biology, Bruxelles, pp 389–402

Tolboom HJ (2023) Veranderingen in de uitvoering van steen- en beeldhouwwerk in de restauratiepraktijk. In: van 't Hof J, De Ceukelaire M (eds) Complexe binnenstedelijke projecten. 8e Vlaams-Nederlandse natuursteendagen. Rijksdienst voor het Cultureel Erfgoed, Amsterdam, pp 53–63

Tolboom HJ, de Wild KLM (2024) De uitvoering. Steen- en beeldhouwwerk. In: Tolboom HJ (ed) Icoon in de steigers: Restauratie van de Domtoren 2016–2024. WBOOKS, Zwolle, pp 168–179

Tolboom HJ, Dubelaar CW (2009) Avendersteen in Nederland. Bull KNOB 108:173–182. https://doi.org/10.7480/knob.108.2009.5-6.164

Tolboom HJ, van der Star C (2020) Ontwerp en uitvoering. Over het vervangen van beeldhouwwerk in natuursteen bij restauraties. Prof Papers Geol Surv Belg 318:105–117
Tom C (2024) When old was new: rethinking traditional and contemporary art and their paradigms of care. In: van de Vall R, van Saaze V (eds) Conservation of contemporary art: bridging the gap between theory and practice. Springer, Cham, pp 87–100
Valle Noronha M (2024) No longer artwork. In: van de Vall R, van Saaze V (eds) Conservation of contemporary art: bridging the gap between theory and practice. Springer, Cham, pp 127–143
Van de Vall E, van Saaze V (2024) Conservation of contemporary art: bridging the gap between theory and practice. Springer, Cham. https://doi.org/10.1007/978-3-031-42357-4
van Doesburg P (2017) Steenhouwersmerken opnieuw beschouwd: Steenhouwers en fabrieksrekeningen van de Dom in Utrecht. Bulletin KNOB 116:161–183
Vanhellemont Y, de Bouw M, Dekeyser L, Dubois S, Vermeir S, van Damme P, van der Have JA (2016) Application of digital technologies in the restoration of historic buildings and heritage objects: a selection of practical examples. In: Ioannides M, Fink E, Moropoulou A, Hagedorn-Saupe M, Fresa A, Liestøl G, Rajcic V, Grussenmeyer P (eds) Digital heritage: Progress in cultural heritage, documentation, preservation and protection. Springer, Berlin, pp 141–150
van Veldhuizen M (2022) A pearl is forever. Comparing facsimile methods on their characteristics, limits and potential for technical art history, conservation and the museum. University of Amsterdam, Amsterdam
Verbanck G (1949) De techniek in de beeldhouwkunst. Mededelingen van de Koninklijke Vlaamse Academie voor Wetenschappen, Letteren en Schone Kunsten in België. Klasse der Schone Kunsten 11:5–9
Viollet-le-Duc EE (1858) Dictionnaire raisonné de l'architecture française du XIe au XVIe siècle. B. Bance, Nashville. http://archive.org/details/dictionnairerais02viol
Viollet-le-Duc EE (1875) On restoration. Sampson Low, Marston, Searle and Rivington, London
Voisenat C (2024) Notre Dame de Paris: emotions and mobilisations. J Cult Herit 65:177–179. https://doi.org/10.1016/j.culher.2023.09.013
Wei W (2024) Innovative technology in art conservation: original appearance, viewer perception. Routledge, London
Žujović M, Obradović R, Rakonjac I, Milošević J (2022) 3D printing technologies in architectural design and construction: a systematic literature review. Buildings 12:1319. https://doi.org/10.3390/buildings12091319

Liselore Tissen is a postdoctoral researcher at Leiden University and Delft University of Technology, and the coordinator of communication, education, research, and ethics at the Royal Netherlands Academy of Arts and Sciences (KNAW) and the Social Sciences and Humanities Open Cloud (SHHOC-NL). Her research focuses on the intersection of the humanities, social sciences, natural sciences, the arts, and technology. By integrating philosophical and ethical evaluations with field research and museum visitor studies, she explores the moral and practical implications of emerging technologies for the art field, contemporary artists, technical art historical research, conservation, and museum presentation.

Hendrik-Jan Tolboom is working for the Dutch Cultural Heritage Agency as a specialist on stonemasonry and sculpture since 1999. In this position he was involved as an advisor in many conservation projects in the Netherlands. He was trained as a stonemason and sculptor, studied art history at Utrecht University and is a PhD candidate at the University of Amsterdam. During the last decades he published regularly about conserving stonemasonry and sculpture.

The Reconstruction of Kāṣthaṃaṇḍap: As Seen through its Intangible Ritual Practices

Binita Magaiya

1 Introduction

Kāṣthaṃaṇḍap is derived from two Sanskrit words: 'kāṣtha' (meaning 'wood' or 'made of wood') and 'maṇḍap' (referring to an enclosed space, either physical or spiritual, in Hinduism). Accordingly, 'Kāṣṭhamanḍap' translates to 'the pavilion made of wood'. The capital city of Nepal, Kathmandu, takes its name from this very structure. Locally known as *Maru Satah*, it is situated within the UNESCO monument zone under the Kathmandu Valley World Heritage Site. Measuring approximately seventy by seventy feet, with three tiers of tiled roofs and open spatial planning on every level, the Kāṣthaṃaṇḍap served primarily as a public building and was a culturally and historically significant landmark in the Kathmandu Valley (Joshi, Tamrakar and Magaiya 2021; Joshi et al. 2022; Magaiya and Shrestha 2023).

Archaeological excavations carried out between 2015 and 2018 by Nepal's Department of Archaeology, in collaboration with a Durham University research team, dated the structure's construction to the seventh century, with its central wooden bracket traced as far back as the fifth century (Coningham et al. 2017). During the 2015 Gorkha earthquake, the Kāṣthaṃaṇḍap collapsed, tragically killing ten individuals who had gathered on the ground floor for a blood donation. Following this catastrophe, deliberations on how to appropriately reconstruct this historic shrine commenced. The Department of Archaeology proposed a reconstruction plan, which was met with sharp criticism from conservators, scholars, architects, and engineers who objected to the proposed use of modern materials, including cement and reinforced concrete. They advocated for adherence to traditional construction techniques and materials (Joshi et al. 2022).

The Department's proposal alarmed the local community, raising concerns that the traditional craftsmanship might be lost in a hurried reconstruction process.

B. Magaiya (✉)
Baakhan Nyane Waa, Kathmandu, Nepal

B. Zwegers and R. Vulto (eds.), *The Spillover Effect of Intangible Cultural Heritage*,
Studies in Art, Heritage, Law and the Market 13,
https://doi.org/10.1007/978-3-032-25352-1_6

In response, an activist initiative emerged to educate the public about the technical and cultural intricacies involved in restoring historical structures like the Kāṣthaṃaṇḍap. This grassroots movement was spearheaded by the Campaign to Rebuild Kāṣthaṃaṇḍap (CRK), a volunteer-based organization welcoming individuals from both technical and non-technical backgrounds. CRK activists championed the use of traditional materials and construction technologies in the rebuilding of heritage structures.

Simultaneously, the intangible aspects of the monument—its ritual practices, oral traditions, and cultural significance—were largely overlooked in the post-disaster context. This oversight created a considerable knowledge gap regarding the culturally appropriate restoration of such a nationally significant religious monument. Nevertheless, a broad coalition of experts expressed solidarity with CRK's movement, rallying under the theme "Let us rebuild our heritage ourselves" (Bhattarai 2018). The public critique targeted architectural plans that deviated from traditional methods, including directives to replace mud mortar construction with lime mortar. CRK volunteers undertook research and documentation of salvaged timber, prepared inventories, and organized thematic workshops that emphasized both the tangible and intangible values embedded in the Kāṣthaṃaṇḍap. In April 2017, CRK formalized itself as a non-governmental organization (NGO).

Following the earthquake, the government established the National Reconstruction Authority (NRA) in December 2015, to oversee post-disaster rebuilding efforts (NRA 2015). Tasked with coordinating reconstruction projects, including heritage sites, the NRA aimed to rebuild ancient settlements and monuments using disaster-resilient techniques while preserving their original form and fostering community resilience (Rastriya Punarnirman Pradhikaran 2015). Although earlier restoration initiatives by the Department of Archaeology received little public scrutiny, the 2015 earthquake dramatically shifted public sentiment, making heritage preservation a highly sensitive issue. Amid concerns over project quality—especially with tenders awarded to the lowest bidders—the new government-led reconstruction proposal lacked consideration of the Kāṣthaṃaṇḍap's intangible heritage dimensions.

Debates ensued between two opposing perspectives: one supporting the government-led 'build back better' campaign, proposing to using modern materials like reinforced concrete, and the other, led by CRK, advocating for a return to traditional materials and construction techniques. On May 12, 2017, a formal memorandum of understanding was signed between the National Reconstruction Authority, the Department of Archaeology, the Kathmandu Metropolitan City (KMC), and CRK, granting CRK initial responsibility for the reconstruction of Kāṣthaṃaṇḍap. However, this authority was short-lived. The reconstruction project was later transferred to a newly formed Kāṣthaṃaṇḍap Reconstruction Committee (KRC), comprising over 60 members and led by the mayor of Kathmandu. KRC continued CRK's vision but operated under municipal oversight, successfully completing the reconstruction within three and a half years.

Unlike previous reconstruction projects where stakeholder identification was largely absent and the Department of Archaeology unilaterally managed efforts,

CRK's grassroots movement actively engaged local communities traditionally associated with the Kāṣthaṃaṇḍap. This community involvement ultimately restored local ownership of the reconstruction process. In Nepal, a system of indigenous self-functioning patron groups exists, known as *Guthis* (Maharjan and Barata 2020), which have historically maintained such cultural sites. CRK identified eight *Guthis*, including the *Mahabali Guthi*, whose practitioners guided the reconstruction according to *Vajrayāna*—a Buddhist tradition that emphasizes esoteric practices and rituals aimed at spiritual awakening. Bennett (2013) observes that "culture is constantly being re-created by people acting out their experience of the cultural institutions they were born into". Traditions rooted in ancestral practices have long been intertwined with systems of power dynamics, shaped by the custodianship of influential patrons. In contemporary times, modern institutions with standardized policies often fail to grasp the soul of legacies sustained through trade, rituals, and intergenerational knowledge-sharing. In Nepal, particularly within the Kathmandu Valley, the Guthis historically endowed with land by wealthy patrons, were established to support various activities—from monument maintenance and cultural festivals to death rituals, financial management, scholarly pursuits, and music. As Maharjan (2018) notes, Guthis can serve multiple purposes. Traditionally hierarchical and governed by oral directives passed down by elders, Guthis have been tightly knit, often limited to members of the same extended family. They play a crucial role in bridging generational divides and facilitating the transmission of intangible heritage, particularly in the context of conservation (Toffin 2005).

This chapter offers both a case study and a reflective report on the intangible dimensions of the Kāṣthaṃaṇḍap, specifically as practiced through ritual performances during its reconstruction phase. While various religious groups participated at different times, *Vajrayāna* rituals remained the most consistently observed. The reconstruction process involved strict adherence to ritual prescriptions, determining elements such as timber selection, the shape, size, and layering of bricks, and the sequencing of construction stages, all governed by *Vajrayāna* rites. The chapter aims to document these ritual practices, which defined the pavilion's structure and spatial form, illuminating how its intangible cultural values were retained and revitalized through the rebuilding process.

2 Integrating Ritual Practices into Heritage Conservation

According to the 2003 Convention for the Safeguarding of Intangible Cultural Heritage, intangible heritage encompasses "cultural expressions that have been passed from one generation to another, have evolved in response to their environments and contribute to giving us a sense of identity and continuity" (UNESCO 2003). The defining characteristics of intangible cultural heritage rest on continuity and intergenerational transmission, both of which were actively manifest during the reconstruction of the Kāṣthaṃaṇḍap. Through CRK's activist-led initiatives, communities asserted their custodianship, sharing knowledge such as oral histories, traditions, and performing arts—including *caryāgīti* (sacred songs) and *caryānṛtya* (ritual dances) rooted in the *Vajrayāna* Buddhist tradition. These ritual performances, traditionally conducted by tantric priests or ritual practitioners, served as public religious expressions. As seen in most government-led conservation projects in Nepal, local communities have often been marginalized as primary knowledge holders. However, CRK's activism facilitated the resurgence of these knowledge forms, integrating them into the reconstruction process. This is in line with the Burra Charter (ICOMOS 2013), which defines conservation as a set of actions intended to enable people to understand and appreciate the values, meanings, and messages latent within heritage spaces. Conservation thus inherently encompasses both tangible forms and intangible practices that attest to the significance of heritage sites. When examining the spillover effects of intangible cultural heritage upon its tangible counterparts, multiple interconnected layers emerge, warranting careful exploration to reveal their mutual relationships.

There is not much research on *caryāgīti* and *caryānṛtya* in the context of Nepal's Vajrayāna Buddhist practices. Vajrayāna is a form of Mahāyāna Buddhism that developed into what is known as Mantra-yāna—a path that uses secret mantras and rituals to support spiritual growth (Upadhyaya 1988). In this tradition, key elements include *mantras* (sacred syllables given by a teacher after initiation), *mudras* (symbolic hand gestures), and *maṇḍalas* (spiritual diagrams used in meditation). Because these practices are considered sacred and are traditionally kept secret, they are rarely written down. Instead, they are passed on orally from teacher to student. As a result, truly understanding these rituals and their deeper meanings usually requires personal instruction from someone trained in the tradition.

In *Vajrayāna* Buddhism, Kāṣthaṃaṇḍap is seen as a physical representation of the *Cakrasaṃvara Maṇḍala*, a sacred cosmic diagram. In Nepal Bhasa, the local language of the Kathmandu Valley, a *maṇḍala* represents the deep connections between spiritual forces, the natural world, and human existence, especially within rituals. When Kāṣthaṃaṇḍap was rebuilt, the transformation from spiritual concept to physical structure was guided by ritual practices, including sacred songs (*caryāgīti*) and devotional dances (*caryānṛtya*). These performances involved specific gestures and footwork (*padcālan*), which conveyed meaning to the audience. At the core of these songs is the *Bijākṣara*, or "seed mantra"—a single sacred syllable that expresses the essence of the performance. The hymns are written in *Sandhyābhāṣā*, or 'twilight language', a symbolic and poetic form of speech that can only be fully understood with the help of a spiritual teacher.

In his books *Nepālkā Prācīn Vajrācārya: Līlāvajra Kāṣthaṃaṇḍap Nirmātā* (2010) and *Kāṣthaṃaṇḍapko Nālībelī* (2020), Yagaman Pati Bajracharya identifies Kāṣthaṃaṇḍap as a traditional learning pavilion built by his ancestors. He highlights the importance of the *Bijākṣara* system—a set of sacred syllables—that guided the construction process. These syllables, expressed through mantras and ritual performances like *caryāgīti* and *caryānṛtya*, were central to the spiritual and architectural design of the structure. As a representative of the *Mahabali Guthi*, Bajracharya led the reconstruction rituals of Kāṣthaṃaṇḍap and traced its spiritual and architectural lineage back to Nepal's Licchavi period (300–879 CE). His research revealed that specific mantras were directly linked to structural components, meaning the pavilion itself was a physical manifestation of intangible spiritual codes.

This blending of tangible elements with intangible heritage offers a valuable model for cultural preservation. Yet integrating these esoteric philosophies into modern conservation practices remains difficult, as they are often viewed as incompatible with scientific or technical approaches. Nevertheless, the reconstruction of Kāṣthamaṇḍap showed that these ancient traditions still hold relevance. The rebuilding process became a living expression of heritage, where material construction and spiritual meaning came together through the collaboration of diverse stakeholders.

3 Oral Traditions and Guthi Custodianship

This chapter draws on firsthand fieldwork conducted between 2015—immediately after the Gorkha Earthquake—and 2023, which marked the completion of Kāṣthamaṇḍap's reconstruction. The research combined extensive documentation, community engagement, oral history collection, and the recovery and cataloguing of salvaged wooden architectural elements. These methods helped bridge oral traditions with physical design details such as measurements, materials, and construction techniques (Magaiya and Shrestha 2023).

According to longstanding belief, Kāṣthamaṇḍap was originally built using wood from a single tree. One of its most enduring legends describes the structure as a perfect cube, each side measuring 36 *hāth*—a traditional Nepali unit of length (Pant and Funo 2007). This ancient system of measurement is still followed by the Guthis responsible for the maintenance of the pavilion and associated structures. Practitioners from the *Ta Caṭah Guthi* and *Sā Guthi* explain that these measurements are encoded within ritual and performative practices.

One particularly significant ritual text, the *Anilā Caryāgīti*, captures the symbolic design principles of Kāṣthamaṇḍap, reinforcing the sacred significance of the number 36 in its architectural form. Performed in secret and inaccessible to outsiders, this ritual links the structure's proportions to spiritual cosmology. During reconstruction, archaeological investigations confirmed these proportions, uncovering foundation lines that likely date back to between the seventh and ninth centuries (Simpson et al. 2019).

Additional symbolic features were also observed during the rebuilding process. The first floor includes ten central joists, symbolizing the *Daśa Pāramitā* ("Ten Perfections") –key virtues in Buddhism. Surrounding them are 64 columns, also reflecting a number of ritual significance in Vajrayāna Buddhism. On the uppermost floor, ten beams correspond to the *Daśa Śīla* ("Ten Ethical Precepts"), another core aspect of Vajrayāna teachings (Majumdar 1968). Other ritual texts, such as the *Vajrasattva Hundred-Syllable Mantra*, specify that 100 pillars and rafters should support the ground floor, further reinforcing the pavilion's design as a sacred architectural expression of spiritual philosophy (Figs. 1 and 2).

Fig. 1 The ritual performed before commencing the works for the pavilion's first floor. © Binita Magaiya

During the rituals and reconstruction phase, many heritage and cultural experts widely criticized the dominance of *Vajrayāna* rituals, arguing that the rituals overshadowed the heritage values and practices of other communities historically associated with the Kāṣthamaṇḍap. Experts repeatedly voiced concerns over the need for ritual practices by other associated groups, traditionally managed by their respective *Guthis*, to be equally represented. Although, when these other *Guthis* were invited to participate, their rituals were neither as elaborate nor as specific as the *Vajrayāna* ones. This process underscored the significance of symbols, oral histories, ritual practices, traditions, engineering techniques, and other elements as defining features of a heritage building, regardless of its monumental status. The technical team of the CRK expressed deep gratitude to the ritual practitioners who willingly shared their knowledge and expertise within their respective scopes.

Today, only two *Guthis*—the aforementioned *Ta Cataḥ Guthi* and *Sā Guthi*—actively continue their cultural practices, maintaining their annual traditions even in the absence of Kasthamandap's physical structure. Notably, during *Ta Cataḥ Guthi*'s annual ritual, almsgiving is conducted within a wooden *maṇḍala* formation. According to Guthi member Hira Tamrakar, this *maṇḍala* represents the true Kāṣthamaṇḍap, simlpy a maṇḍala made up of wood. (Fig. 3).

4 Ritual, Community, and Conservation: Lessons from Kāṣthamaṇḍap

According to the 2013 Burra Charter, "[c]onservation means all the processes of looking after a place so as to retain its cultural significance" (ICOMOS 2013). In Nepalese society, conservation has historically extended beyond physical upkeep to encompass the ritualistic and communal practices ensuring a site's spiritual and

Fig. 2 The placement of ten beams as *Daśa Pāramitā* in between the central columns. © Binita Magaiya

cultural integrity. Cultural heritage in Nepal is thus regarded as a continuum of practices passed through generations, which may not always be tied to tangible materials but are nonetheless integral to societal identity.

The country's institutional framework for heritage conservation involves three tiers of government, alongside key organizations such as the Department of Archaeology, the *Guthi Sansthan* (Guthi Corporation), and provincial and municipal cultural heritage departments. Despite formal structures and standards, coordination among these agencies has often been inconsistent and insufficiently inclusive of community stakeholders. Notably, the presence and engagement of international bodies like UNESCO and ICOMOS during the reconstruction of the Kāṣthamaṇḍap were minimal.

Fig. 3 Receiving alms for the annual *Pancadān* ritual by Ta Chatan Guthi. © Binita Magaiya

As explained in the earlier texts, conservation practices in Nepal have historically been guided by community-based rituals carried out by communal *Guthis*, fostering intergenerational knowledge transfer and preserving the specialized skills needed for heritage maintenance. While ownership of monuments may rest with state agencies such as the Department of Archaeology or municipal authorities, the intangible knowledge vested within these *Guthis* remains largely outside formal institutional reach. International heritage laws and policies, when applied to grassroots, self-sustaining communities like the *Guthis*, often clash with traditional practices, limiting their autonomy and operational flexibility.

The *Kāṣthamaṇḍap* reconstruction project proved a rare exception where ritual practitioners and community members were integral to the process. As a participant immersed in both the physical and spiritual rebuilding of the Kāṣthamaṇḍap, the author gained firsthand insight into the 'sacred secret-keeping' roles preserved through these ancient systems and ritual initiations for the upcoming professionals in conservation of religious and secular heritage structures. The reconstruction, therefore, embodied not just the restoration of a monument, but the continuation of an intricate network of beliefs, practices, and symbolic knowledge, affirming the resilience and relevance of intangible heritage within contemporary heritage conservation (Fig. 4).

When shaping a framework for heritage conservation that reflects local norms and values, it is crucial to address the question of cultural continuity over time. The paradox inherent in the relationship between culture and property must also be considered. Culture, by nature, is dynamic and constantly evolving, while property implies ownership, control, and fixity. As Harding argues, "cultural property does not really belong to anyone […] all of us have a duty towards cultural property because of its relative scarcity and profound significance" (Harding 1997, p. 760). This recognition positions cultural property as a collective inheritance, to be respectfully preserved and responsibly transmitted.

The conservation of the Kāṣthamaṇḍap illuminates these tensions vividly. The reconstruction process revealed how ownership, heritage management, community participation, and the safeguarding of intangible cultural practices are complex, often contested issues. It highlighted the necessity of integrating both local community

Fig. 4 The final pinnacle ritual with *Caryā giti* and *Caryā nritya*. © Binita Magaiya

perspectives and technical expertise into heritage conservation practices. Such integration ensures not only the continuity of the physical structure but also the cultural practices, beliefs, and values embedded within it. A careful examination of the initial reconstruction proposals showed that traditional knowledge systems and conservation practices were largely overlooked, with limited recognition of the community as a vital stakeholder. Without incorporating traditional conservation wisdom attuned to local geography, such projects risk undermining both cultural authenticity and public trust. Policies frequently neglected the inclusion of ritual practitioners, favouring cost-effective, modern methodologies reliant on the lowest bidding processes—a tendency that jeopardized the long-term integrity and resilience of heritage sites.

The 'Kāṣthamaṇḍap Reconstuction project' demonstrated the importance of revaluing these neglected knowledge systems. It emphasized that to achieve holistic conservation, modern institutions must be willing to accommodate pluralistic methodologies, including those rooted in oral traditions, esoteric philosophies, and ritual-based practices. This approach ensures that both tangible structures and their intangible cultural dimensions are preserved for future generations. Moreover, the experience highlighted how heritage conservation cannot be separated from issues of access, control, and power. In a multicultural society with diverse custodial claims over cultural heritage, negotiations over authenticity, repatriation, and ownership are inevitable. The reconstruction of the Kāṣthamaṇḍap revealed these dynamics, as different community groups and institutional bodies navigated claims of authority, knowledge, and custodianship.

Ultimately, the project underscored that the essence of cultural heritage lies not only in its material form but in its living, evolving traditions. The act of rebuilding the Kāṣthamaṇḍap became more than a technical challenge; it was a platform for reaffirming community identities, ritual practices, and intergenerational bonds. This case study thus serves as a valuable model for inclusive, culturally sensitive, and contextually grounded approaches to heritage conservation in Nepal and beyond (Fig. 5).

5 Conclusion

Following the successful reconstruction of the Kāṣthamaṇḍap, the foremost challenge remains ensuring the long-term conservation of the structure and the intergenerational transfer of the intangible knowledge and practices surrounding it. The reconstruction initiative demonstrated the importance of sustained traditional practices within ancestral contexts and illuminated the gaps that exist between these time-honoured customs and modern conservation methodologies. It revealed how integrating local communities and traditional custodians as primary stakeholders can enrich heritage conservation practices and ensure both the material integrity and cultural authenticity of heritage monuments. The project also illustrated the necessity of documenting and systematizing indigenous knowledge systems that, while

Fig. 5 *Kāṣthamaṇḍap* after the reconstruction, before the final unveiling. © Binita Magaiya

historically transmitted orally, risk being marginalized within contemporary, institutionalized frameworks. By identifying and involving stakeholders with ancestral knowledge of construction techniques, rituals, and oral histories, the reconstruction of the Kāṣthamaṇḍap reaffirmed the relevance of community-led heritage practices.

Understanding how traditional systems of conservation, rooted in ancestral practices, were established—along with the techniques they developed—can offer deeper insight into the relationship between Nepali heritage, its monuments, and the caretakers, communities, and stakeholders involved. Even today, these practices largely rely on systems of patronage rather than institutionalized state bodies and modern conservation frameworks. However, the adoption of Western Conservation Theories and preservation policies at the state level has introduced confusion and tension among traditional groups, whose knowledge and skills have been passed down through generations within familial and community lineages.

As Nepal increasingly adopts global conservation frameworks, it must navigate the tensions between universally applied preservation policies and localized, culturally embedded practices. The Kāṣthamaṇḍap experience highlights that the universal value of cultural heritage must be balanced with the rights, roles, and claims of local communities, whose practices have historically shaped and sustained these sites. The idea of cultural heritage as a universally valuable asset invites the involvement of multiple stakeholders, whose primary concerns may not always align with its historical significance. This raises complex questions about access, use, and control. The claims, rights, and restrictions asserted by particular cultural groups can create power struggles and revive colonial dynamics, ultimately shaping who has authority and autonomy over culturally significant sites. Within this context, cultural communities also grapple with events such as disputes over authenticity, repatriation, appropriation, and preservation. The field of research finds itself caught in a dilemma: negotiating between the conservation of cultural heritage, which often challenges notions of ownership of the past, and determining what cultural legacy the current generation will leave for the future.

References

Bajracharya YP (2010) Nepālkā Pŕācīn Vajŕācāŕya- Līlāvajŕa (Kāṣthaṃaṇdap Niŕmātā). Virinchi Moti Smriti Guhyatara Kosh, Kathmandu

Bajracharya YP (2020) Kāṣthaṃaṇdapko Nālībelī. Lilavajra Prajna Pratishthan, Kathmandu

Bennett MJ (2013) Constructivism, intercultural. https://www.idrinstitute.org/resources/constructivism. Accessed 16 June 2025

Bhattarai A (2018) Storeyed past: the movement to rebuild an iconic monument in earthquake-hit Nepal. https://caravanmagazine.in/reportage/storeyed-past. Accessed 16 June 2025

Coningham RA, Acharya KP, Davis CE, Kunwar RB, Simpson IA, Schmidt A, Tremblay JC (2017) Preliminary results of post-disaster archaeological investigations at the Kasthamandap and within Hanuman Dhoka, Kathmandu Valley UNESCO World Heritage Property (Nepal). Ancient Nepal 1997:28–51

Harding S (1997) Justifying repatriation of native American cultural property. Indiana Law J 72:723–774

ICOMOS (2013) The Burra charter: the Australia ICOMOS charter for places of cultural significance. ICOMOS, Burra

Joshi A, Magaiya B, Shakya A, Shrestha M, Weise K (2022) Rehabilitation of the Kasthamandap: using local resources and traditional knowledge. In: Weise K, Joshi A (eds) Kasthamandap Marusatta. Kasthamandap Reconstruction Committee and Nepal Heritage Research Centre, Kathmandau, pp 209–321

Joshi R, Tamrakar A, Magaiya B (2021) Community-based participatory approach in cultural heritage reconstruction: a case study of Kasthamandap. Prog Disaster Sci 10:1–9

Magaiya B, Shrestha M (2023) From past to future: learning from reconstruction of Kasthamandap. In: Hilal S, Bedir M, Thomsen MR, Tamke M (eds) Design for partnerships for change. Springer, Copenhagen, pp 249–259

Maharjan M (2018) Indigenous practices of heritage conservation: the Guthi system of Kathmandu valley. ICH Courier 36:26–27

Maharjan M, Barata FT (2020) The Kathmandu valley's indigenous practices of safeguarding heritage: an assessment of present-day challenges. J Cult Hert Manag Sustain Dev 11:214–225

Majumdar RC (1968) Ancient India. Motilal Banarsidass, Delhi

NRA (2015) Nepal Government- National Reconstruciton Authority-2015 Earthquake reconstruction. https://portal.nra.gov.np/nra-timeline#yr2015. Accessed 16 June 2025

Pant M, Funo S (2007) Stupa and swastika: historical urban planning principles in Nepal's Kathmandu Valley. National Library Board Singapore Cataloguing in Publication Data, Kyoto

Rastriya Punarnirman Pradhikaran (2015) 2015 Earthquake reconstruction. https://portal.nra.gov.np/. Accessed 16 June 2025

Simpson IA, Kelly L, Kinnaird T, Graham C, Conningham R, Davis C, Mirnig N (2019) Geo-archaeological assessment of post-earthquake Kasthamandap. https://dspace.stir.ac.uk/handle/1893/29860. Accessed 16 June 2025

Toffin G (2005) From kin to caste- the role of Guthis in Newar society and culture. Social Science Baha, Lalitpur

UNESCO (2003) Convention for the safeguarding of the intangible cultural heritage. UNESCO, Paris

Upadhyaya J (1988) Vajrayana: system, perceptivity and practice. Tibet J 13:3–12

Binita Magaiya is an architect specializing in the conservation of monuments and heritage structures. She completed her master's at Katholieke Universiteit Leuven in Belgium with a degree in Conservation of Monuments and Sites. A former heritage activist, she is now engaged in the preservation of intangible heritage via her work as a storybook writer for children. She is also a co-founder of Baakhan Nyane Waa (Come, Listen to Stories!), a non-profit organization that documents and converts oral histories and stories into illustrated children's books.

New and Future Uses of Intangible Cultural Heritage

Reframing Museum Practice: The ICHC's Impact on Museums

Alix Ferrer-Yulfo

1 Introduction

Since the adoption of UNESCO's 2003 *Convention for the Safeguarding of Intangible Cultural Heritage* (ICHC) museums have increasingly been called on to take part, facilitate and forward the heritage protection framework it proposes. From the 2004 Seoul Declaration to the 2015 Recommendation, museums have been considered capable of playing important roles in the safeguarding of intangible cultural heritage (ICH) given their long-standing relationship with heritage. Indeed, museums have worked with "ICH" long before the adoption of the ICHC as evidenced, for example, by the development of the New Museology during the 1970s when alternative museum formats more attuned to their contexts and the community they served began to develop. However, calls for museums' involvement in ICH safeguarding were received with some hesitation. Many academics and heritage experts questioned museums' capabilities for safeguarding ICH considering the prevalence of the traditional museological model—i.e. museum practices that focus on collections and the conservation and documentation of material heritage for research and exhibition. While this limitation supported the belief that museums would not be adequate for safeguarding ICH, museums around the world began to answer UNESCO's call with varying results.

This chapter examines the impact of the ICHC on museums and their practices by critically examining the 'unconventional' relationship (Alivizatou 2006) between ICH and museums, their responses to the UNESCO-ICH paradigm and the intersection between museum practice and heritage safeguarding. It demonstrates that to support the ICHC and work towards ICH safeguarding, museums require a transformation. Most criticisms against museums' role in safeguarding ICH are based on

---

A. Ferrer-Yulfo (✉)
School of Design, Syracuse University, Syracuse, NY, USA
e-mail: anferrer@syr.edu

B. Zwegers and R. Vulto (eds.), *The Spillover Effect of Intangible Cultural Heritage*, Studies in Art, Heritage, Law and the Market 13,
https://doi.org/10.1007/978-3-032-25352-1_7

predominantly Western conventional museological theory and practice and the overarching complexity of definitions within the international heritage discourse. Therefore, museums must reframe their practices to fit within the established parameters of the ICHC and accommodate the UNESCO-ICH paradigm.

The chapter starts by tracing the relationship between museums and ICH to the work of ethnographic museums and the New Museology while examining their role in managing and developing safeguarding strategies for ICH, as well as some of their limitations. This discussion leads to an overview of the paradigm shift in heritage protection and the debates surrounding museums' involvement in the implementation of the ICHC. The impact of the UNESCO-ICH paradigm on museums and their practices at the international level is also explored, along with some of the museological responses on the ground. The challenges and opportunities brought on by the ICHC are discussed throughout the chapter, concluding that the UNESCO-ICH paradigm caused a reframing of museum practices as an ongoing process that still requires further exploration whilst the ICHC continues to be implemented worldwide.

2 Ethnographic Museums and ICH

In her keynote speech for the International Society for Ethnology and Folklore, Barbara Kirshenblatt-Gimblett (2004b) stated that "[m]useums, while repositories of tangible heritage in the form of artifact collections, have always had to address intangible aspects of culture – indigenous knowledge, belief systems, techniques of the body, performance" (p. 74). This statement echoed museologists' beliefs of the origins of the relationship between museums and ICH: the longstanding work of ethnographic museums,[1] or museums with ethnographic collections.[2] It is widely believed that ethnographic museums' interest in researching, documenting and interpreting the meanings and values of their collections strongly connects them to UNESCO's notion of ICH (Kirshenblatt-Gimblett 2004b; Ferreira da Costa 2009b; Mingote Calderón 2013b; Fromm 2016).[3]

While Fromm (2016) recognises that earlier ethnographic museums followed a similar model to that of their ancestor, the cabinets of curiosity—which were object-focused and based on the curator's knowledge (the basic tenets of traditional museology)—she links the relationship between ethnographic museums and ICH to "salvage ethnography", transformed through the mid-twentieth century (p. 90). According to her, ethnographic museums collected "both the tangible and the intangible remnants of the ways of life of the past" to preserve the traditional knowledge

[1] See for instance Vieregg and Davis (2000) and Vieregg et al. (2004).

[2] Alivizatou's (2012) research demonstrated how the "ethnographic museum label" is being increasingly contested and completely dismissed by some museums considered to be "embedded in the colonial project", such as the Musée Quai Branly, which prefers to be referred to as a "museum with an ethnographic collection" (p. 23).

[3] See Ferreira da Costa (2009a) and Mingote Calderón (2013a) for additional information on these views from a South European perspective.

endangered by "the prevalent forces of assimilation, dislocation, and removals of [I]ndigenous people and rural dwellers worldwide" (p. 91). Indeed, Kreps (2009) suggests that the "rescuing" mission behind some of UNESCO's initiatives for ICH safeguarding parallels the intentions of "salvage ethnography" (p. 203). Similarly, but more critically considering the relationship between ethnology as a discipline and heritage in general, Kirshenblatt-Gimblett (2004b) argues that ethnographic museums have aided in producing and reproducing what UNESCO has defined as ICH. However, both agree that the relationship between ethnographic museums and ICH has endured changes in anthropological approaches to cultural heritage and is now being reconsidered due to the UNESCO-ICH paradigm.

Reflecting on the relationship between museums and ICH, most museologists have considered ICH the essence of material cultural heritage, giving meaning and value to cultural objects and spaces, rather than a category within cultural expressions (Maranda 2000). ICH has been gathered and recorded to contextualise material cultural evidence collected by ethnographic museums. Furthermore, ICH in the form of knowledge and performance has been archived as photographs, films, and sound recordings throughout the twentieth century, serving as supporting data for museums' interpretations of their collections (ibid. p. 92). From this perspective, ICH is seen as "a broader framework within which tangible heritage takes on its shape and significance" (Bouchenaki 2004b, p. 8). Thus, by collecting, studying, preserving and presenting objects of specific cultural groups, museums must also recognise and deal with the intangible cultural aspects from where these objects originate.

Recording intangible knowledge and values allows museums to remain relevant for research purposes and to stakeholder communities to some extent. However, it has been recognised that the narratives presented in ethnographic museums were—and in many cases still are—generally those of the curator/anthropologist (Smith 2006; Alivizatou 2012; Fromm 2016). Indeed, if we consider the colonial context where many of these museums developed, the relationship between the museum and the community has been uneven in many ways. This challenges UNESCO's ICH safeguarding framework which requires the active participation and engagement of the cultural bearers in all safeguarding processes.[4]

Nevertheless, scholars have noticed a shift in this tradition, especially after the UNESCO-ICH paradigm. Ethnographic museums have been attempting to become more inclusive in their efforts to present and safeguard the knowledge, values and practices their collections represent by adopting participatory approaches to heritage interpretation and management and recognising the importance of the ICH community in these processes (Blake 2015, 2018; Kreps 2009; Alivizatou 2012, 2022). While a difficult task, ethnographic museums in certain countries are changing their engagement dynamics by giving voice to communities (e.g. involving them

[4] As per Article 15 of the ICHC—Participation of communities, groups and individuals—"each State Party shall endeavour to ensure the widest possible participation of communities, groups and, where appropriate, individuals that create, maintain and transmit such heritage, and to involve them actively in its management" (UNESCO 2003).

in museum work), recognising and valuing cultural diversity, and striving to reconcile their colonial past (Yoshida 2004; Van Huy 2006; Ferreira da Costa 2009a: Alivizatou 2012, 2022).

For example, the Vietnam Museum of Ethnology promotes the participation of local communities in the research, collection, and preservation of ethnographic artefacts that reflect the culture and life of Vietnam's 54 ethnic groups (Van Huy 2006). In Spain, the Museo do Pobo Galego in Galicia and the Museo del Pueblo de Asturias in Asturias also involve the local population in collecting oral history through recordings. In these cases, ICH is represented by the oral history and memories of the local population, which is "musealised" through documentation techniques and dissemination strategies. Both museums include a documentation centre that promotes the documentation, study and dissemination of their respective regional ICH and provide training for those helping with research (Fernández Cerviño 2008; López Álvarez and Suárez López 2009). These examples consider the importance of the human element in their work. Since "living" ICH bearers cannot be preserved themselves, the best way to safeguard their memories and values is through documentation (Fernández Cerviño 2008). This view contradicts experts' concerns about the limitations of documenting ICH and the creation of "proxies" for ICH bearers (Kirshenblatt-Gimblett 2004a, p. 61; Kurin 2004b), thus illustrating the different understandings regarding the safeguarding of ICH in the museum.

However, these museums still face many limitations and have yet to engage fully with the UNESCO-ICH paradigm. Notwithstanding the application of participatory methods for documenting and interpreting collections by engaging with the stakeholder communities, museum strategies for ICH safeguarding are still limited to documentation, recording, exhibition, and research (Blake 2018). This limitation is a combination of the persistence of the traditional museology focused on objects and their interpretation by an expert curator, and the ambivalent character of UNESCO's safeguarding guidelines. Furthermore, knowledge sharing might prove difficult for ethnographic museums that still determine how community participation develops, and what the purpose of such participation will be, often in response to an underlying agenda. Indeed, Alivizatou (2012) suggests caution in co-curatorial projects since "exhibitions curated by the community are often considered to lack scientific authority, often deemed as political propaganda" (p. 192).

Museums could also limit stakeholder participation through restrictions imposed on their collections, thus denying access and hindering ICH transmission. Blake (2015) observes this trend and questions why museums do not instead focus on enhancing and promoting ICH as part of the local community's everyday life (p. 32). This strategy might be possible in the case of ethnographic museums' whose collections belong to neighbouring communities, but perhaps not in the case of collections with a colonial history. This leads to another limitation when considering the relationship between ethnographic museums and ICH: the importance of "place" in ICH practices.

The role of place when referring to ICH is often overlooked in ethnographic museums. Some heritage scholars argue that place is an important aspect of ICH creation, as it is part of the everyday life of bearers and carries a set of shared values and practices (Smith 2006; Corsane et al. 2008; Davis 2011). Place, conceived as a dynamic and permeable "web of understanding between people and the environment, between people and their neighbours, between people and their history" (Davis 2011, p. 44) is key in the formation of community identities and the continuation of ICH. Corsane et al. (2008) suggest that the traditional museum would not be able to capture the elusive qualities of place nor the complexity of its role in the development and experience of ICH. This is another reason why ethnographic museums were initially dismissed by scholars when examining their potential in ICH safeguarding, being critiqued for perpetuating the top-down, unidirectional approach to heritage safeguarding that has characterised the traditional museology and, in certain aspects, UNESCO's heritage framework (Kurin 2007; Stefano 2012). The traditional museological principles followed by ethnographic museums do not consider the spatial context and cultural ecosystem in which ICH is conceived and operates. In this regard, while ethnographic museums' relationship with ICH has been and will remain complex, another more open, stronger relationship between them can be traced back to the 1970s with the birth of the New Museology.

3 The New Museology and ICH

The New Museology is a movement and historical phenomenon that emerged during the 1970s and 1980s. Although the term appeared in museum literature earlier (van Mensch 1992), it was not until the 1980s that it gained momentum and became a philosophy about museums' social role, developing a set of values to follow (Maure 1995). As a specific movement, it takes different forms according to the socio-cultural contexts where it is applied. Given the circumstances of its development, many scholars believe that New Museology is completely opposed to traditional museology which regards museums as static institutions, superficial and monolithic, elitist and uncommitted, too focused on methods rather than on a critical reflection and theoretical evaluation of their mission (de Varine 2006a; dos Santos 2009; Giménez-Cassina 2010). For others, it is not something separate from traditional museology, but rather an "awakening" of the museological science (Maure 1995; Primo 2013, p. 55). Nevertheless, responses to this awakening differed around the world and two different strands within the New Museology developed; a "Latin" version and an "Anglo-Saxon" or "British" version (Giménez-Cassina 2010; Davis 2011). While both strands are equally displeased with the old, traditional museology and seek to democratise museum processes, each developed different approaches to achieve their goal and relate differently to ICH.

The "original" New Museology developed during ICOM's *Round Table on the Role of Museums in Today's Latin America* held in Santiago, Chile in 1972 (Santiago Roundtable) when a group of museum experts and academics met to discuss the transformation of museums in the Latin American context and examine the ways museums could become more socially conscious and proactive (Davis 2011). As a result, the *Basic Principles of the Integral Museum* declared that the transformation in museological activities required a gradual change in the outlook of curators and administrators and on the institutional structures for which they are responsible (ICOM-UNESCO 1972). Accordingly, it established the concept of the "integral museum" as one that provided communities with a holistic view of their cultural environment. Integral or integrated museums would require the assistance of experts from different fields and would be better suited as regional museums or as museums for small- and medium-sized population centres (ibid.). While this was a turning point in museological theory and practice (de Varine 2006a), the integrated museum approach was ignored in the Anglophone world most likely due to language issues (Giménez-Cassina 2010; Davis 2011).

Following the Santiago Roundtable new non-conventional, participatory and inclusive museological practices such as "community museology" and "ecomuseums"[5] began to appear. These practices represented more "holistic" and democratic forms of museological practice as followed by the "neighbourhood museums" in the U.S.A., "open-air museums" in Scandinavia, small local and open-air museums created during the 1960s and 1970s (Corsane 2005; de Varine 2006a; Davis 2011). Their rise signalled the birth of the "New Museology", a movement that involved a departure from the traditional museum functions focused on the conservation of a collection, stored within a building and exhibited for the benefit of the public (Maure 1995).

However, the term "new museology" was not used officially in the museum world until the *first International Workshop on Ecomuseums and the New Museology* held in Quebec in 1984 since it was considered an "underground movement" and was rejected by some museum scholars (de Varine 2006a, p. 76).[6] As a result of this workshop, the 1984 Quebec Declaration established the *Basic Principles of a New Museology* which recognised the new museum formats and allowed the establishment of a new museological movement that would legitimise these forms and call for critical reflection on traditional museology (ICOM 1984). This New Museology focused on promoting and developing the socio-economic sustainability of the community and its heritage within its specific territory and natural environment as opposed to the preservation of the material artefacts of past civilizations. The community itself would be an active participant in these processes and their common heritage would serve as a resource for development. To facilitate this approach, new museological formats such as ecomuseums, community museums, and neighbourhood museums,

---

[5] A concept coined by Hughes de Varine and further elaborated by Georges Henri Rivière to describe a museum format that was oriented toward the environment and interpretation of nature. See Davis (2011) for a history of the development of ecomuseums.

[6] Indeed, this event was not organised by ICOFOM (ICOM's International Committee for Museology) but by Canadian museologists disappointed by the lack of response during ICOFOM's 1983 International Symposium in London and its failure to agree on museological concepts and terminologies (van Mensch 1992, p. 32).

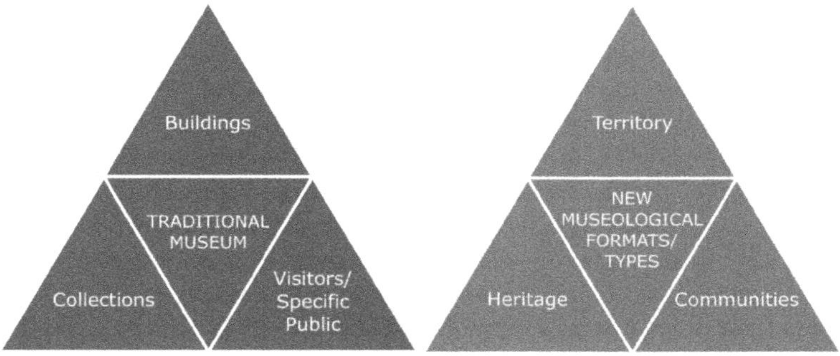

Fig. 1 The traditional museum model (left) and the "new museum" model (right) (Adapted from Maure 1995)

would develop and evolve within their specific contexts to apply the new museological principles and contrast the traditional, more conventional museum model (Fig. 1).[7]

While new museological formats could be used to better explain the approach, purpose and functions of the new museological ideals, they are only a guide and not a set of rules as each can be adapted according to the particularities of the museum context.[8] What should be highlighted about these models is the attention given to the importance of heritage (as all-encompassing) to the socio-economic sustainability of communities and the relationship between these and their heritage (e.g. territory, customs). The New Museology advocates a holistic view of heritage which can be used as a tool for social development. It is within this museological movement that a stronger, more direct relationship between ICH and museums can be traced. This frame of thought provoked transformations in museological theories and methods that allowed the creation of new and alternative forms of museum practice (de Varine 2006b). These promoted participatory approaches to heritage preservation, social wellbeing and the economic sustainability of the heritage community which would be later emphasised and promoted by the UNESCO-ICH paradigm. However, museum practices that developed under the banner of the "Latin" New Museology—i.e. ecomuseology and other integrated museum approaches—were "greatly ignored in the English-speaking museum world" (Davis 2011, p. 61), where a different interpretation of the New Museology developed.

[7] Rivard (1984 cited in Davis 2011, p. 83) provided a formula summarizing the main aspects of the ecomuseum as a new museum format to contrast the traditional museum model. However, this formula was erroneously used to call "ecomuseum" all other new museological formats, creating a terminological confusion between ecomuseums and the New Museology. The two are different as the former is one of the many ways museums can follow the basic principles of the latter (de Varine 1988, cited in Davis 2011, p. 62).

[8] De Varine (2006b) explained that "there is no accepted or compulsory standard for this kind of vernacular museology" as it is constantly expanding with new locally contextual formulas being developed and functioning in different ways all around the world (p. 83).

Introduced in 1989 by Peter Vergo's *The New Museology*, the "British" or "Anglo-Saxon" version focused on developing new techniques and theories to make museums more accessible and inclusive, calling for internal-external restructuring to cater for the needs and interests of a more diverse public (Vergo 1989; Stam 2005). As a museum philosophy, it is closely related to what Hooper-Greenhill (2000) calls the 'post-museum': a museum that will re-shape the characteristics of its parent modernist museum to open and diversify its communication and educational practices and include the broad range of visitors' experiences and emotions (p. 143). This New Museology stresses the need for an internal critical reflection of the museum's organisation and work pushing museums to become more socially conscious and serve as open and interactive platforms for communication and dialogue that consider the interests of their audiences (Stam 2005, p. 67). However, it still upholds traditional museology's emphasis on the collection, preservation, and use of objects, a defining characteristic of museums in the Anglophone world (ibid.).

Neither new museological trend (the "Latin" nor the "Britsh") provides a guide on how to put the New Museology into practice, causing confusion between the two and keeping the debate going (dos Santos 2009). Nevertheless, the "New Museologies" inspired numerous transformations in museums: from promoting the creation of alternative museum formats that are adaptable to specific contexts and needs and could potentially support ICH safeguarding; to supporting the re-framing of conventional museums towards a more self-critical and self-conscious model. Much like the UNESCO-ICH paradigm, the New Museology brought a new outlook on heritage and how it should be managed and preserved.

4 Museums and the UNESCO-ICH Paradigm

The 1990s saw a growth in museum numbers and organisations trying to apply the basic ideals of the "New Museologies". Simultaneously, the UNESCO-ICH paradigm was developing internationally with UNESCO's increasing attention to ICH. Consequently, museums faced opportunities for experimenting with new museological approaches while considering the possibilities and challenges of the UNESCO-ICH paradigm.

The 1989 *Recommendation on the Safeguarding of Traditional Culture and Folklore* was the first international normative instrument for the protection of what would later be considered ICH. While the ICHC replaced it, it nevertheless established parameters that would greatly influence the work of some museums regarding ICH such as the creation of museums or "folklore sections at existing museums" that could foster the conservation of traditional and popular culture through exhibitions and the dissemination of related knowledge (UNESCO 1989). It would serve as background for the development of more concrete museological measures focused on ICH safeguarding.

Furthermore, UNESCO's Intangible Heritage Programme and subsequent projects[9] would not only influence the development of new terminology and programmes regarding ICH safeguarding at an international scale but would also affect museological practices. These programmes were developed during the experimental phase of the "New Museologies" and, along with the emphasis on ICH, raised additional questions regarding the relationship between museums and ICH. Indeed, ICOM and UNESCO launched a series of publications to examine the developments of the new museological trends and the impact of the developing international ICH discourse on museum practice.[10]

4.1 Approaching ICH: Evidence from ICOFOM 2000

The first of these publications was the 32nd issue of the ICOFOM Study Series titled *Museology and the Intangible Heritage I* (Vieregg and Davis 2000) which gathered the views of museologists around the world on the interrelationships between museology and ICH. Themes presented ranged from the impact and challenges of the "Latin" New Museology and related movements; the roles and relationships of the museum concerning ICH; the possibilities and challenges of "musealising" ICH; to, possibly the strongest and most contested theme, the many interpretations of what constitutes ICH, especially within a museological context.

The discussion on the meaning of ICH is critical due to the implications for museological work. Defining ICH has been a long and challenging process that produced an operational concept to ease the implementation of UNESCO's safeguarding framework. In the context of ICOFOM 2000, ICH was understood as something abstract and perhaps at times unperceivable like memory, feelings and emotions or as something more visible but ephemeral such as rituals, traditions and performances.[11] Nevertheless, within a museological context, it was mainly considered as being "attached" to tangible heritage.[12] While the tangible/intangible dichotomy was called to question, conceptions of what was to be defined as ICH were still limited to values and meanings and not necessarily to practices, expressions and knowledge as defined

[9] The *1993 Living Human Treasures* system and the *1997 Proclamation of Masterpieces of the Oral and Intangible Heritage of Humanity*, precursor to the ICHC's *Representative List of Intangible Cultural Heritage of Humanity*.

[10] These publications include *ICOFOM Study Series* Volumes 33 (2000) and 34 (2004), *ICOM News* Volumes 56 (Pinna 2003) and 57 (Kurin 2004b), and the *Museum International, Special Edition on Intangible Heritage*, Volume 56 double issue (2004), which are discussed throughout the chapter. These publications were responsible for configuring the framework in which the ICHC would develop within the museum context and by which museums' approaches to ICH safeguarding would be evaluated. Additionally, the peer-reviewed *International Journal of Intangible Heritage* was launched by ICOM and the National Folk Museum of Korea in 2006 as a journal dedicated to issues related to ICH specifically.

[11] See, for example, Bedekar (2000) and Garton Smith (2000).

[12] See, for example, Bosch (2000) and Decarolis (2000).

by the ICHC. This limited view of heritage was encapsulated in ICOM's museum definition, which focused on material evidence and would not include "intangible heritage" until its 2007 revision and its most recent version.[13]

4.2 From the 2002 Shanghai Charter to 2015 UNESCO Recommendation: The Impact of the UNESCO-ICH Paradigm on Museums

The period between 2002 and 2015 represents a turning point in the international museum and ICH discourse. Discussions regarding ICH and its safeguarding in the museological context occurred simultaneously through a series of events as UNESCO developed the ICHC (Fig. 2). The first of these events was the *seventh Asia Pacific Regional Assembly of the International Council of Museums (ICOM-ASPAC) Museums, Intangible Heritage and Globalisation*, held in Shanghai in 2002, which centred on discussing heritage from a holistic perspective and considered museums' potential in ICH documentation, preservation and promotion. At the workshop, the *Charter for the Protection of Intangible Heritage* (Shanghai Charter), an important stepping stone towards the ICHC, was drafted. It recognised "museums as facilitators" of partnerships and safeguarding ICH and made several recommendations on how museums could establish holistic museum practices through "interdisciplinary and cross-sectorial approaches that bring together movable and immovable, tangible and intangible, natural and cultural heritage" (ICOM-ASPAC 2002). Of note, was the Charter's call for training and capacity building in ICH safeguarding for museum professionals and the active involvement of the bearer communities in museum work as "custodians of intangible heritage" (ibid.).

Interestingly, this set of guidelines had been proposed around 20 years earlier under the banner of the "New Museology", as previously discussed. Many museums following the principles established during the Santiago Roundtable and by the Quebec Declaration were already using integrated approaches to heritage management, proving how the "Latin" New Museology was overlooked at an international level. Nevertheless, the Shanghai Charter served to re-insert the all-encompassing notion of heritage and the optimistic view on the role of museums in safeguarding ICH in the international discourse. Furthermore, it acknowledged the development of the ICHC as the normative instrument that would bring balance to the international heritage discourse historically focused only on material cultural heritage (ICOM-ASPAC 2002).

[13] In August 2022, a new museum definition was approved after years of complex debate. This definition states the following: "a museum is a not-for-profit, permanent institution in the service of society that researches, collects, conserves, interprets and exhibits tangible and intangible heritage. Open to the public, accessible and inclusive, museums foster diversity and sustainability. They operate and communicate ethically, professionally and with the participation of communities, offering varied experiences for education, enjoyment, reflection and knowledge sharing" (ICOM 2022).

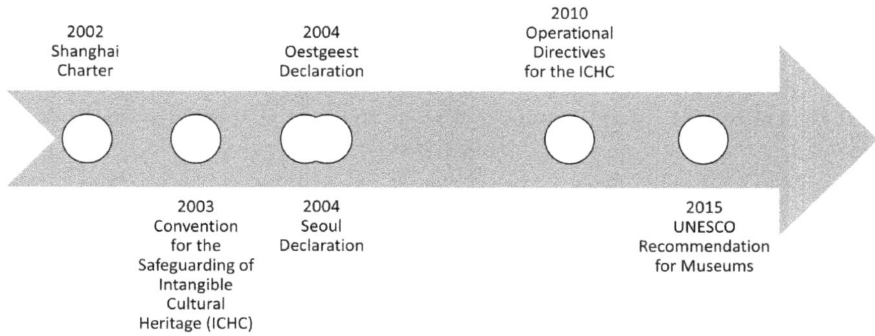

Fig. 2 Chronology of international museum-related events and documents reflecting on the potential impact of the ICHC on the museum field

After the adoption of the ICHC, a series of international discussions on the strengths and weaknesses of the UNESCO-ICH paradigm and its safeguarding framework ensued (ICOM 2009).[14] In the museological context, key events were UNESCO's *Expert Meeting on Museums and Intangible Heritage* in the Netherlands (Oestgeest Meeting), followed by ICOM's *20th General Conference and 21st General Assembly, Museums and Intangible Heritage* (ICOM Conference) in Seoul.[15] These events occurred in 2004 as countries were ratifying the ICHC,[16] highlighting the importance of museums in supporting the ICHC and encouraging countries to join in those efforts.

The issues and opportunities in safeguarding ICH highlighted by the Shanghai Charter were discussed at both events. However, attendees raised key observations regarding the limitations and challenges traditional museum processes would present, especially when participatory approaches to cultural heritage management and museum work were being advocated. As pointed out during the Oestgeest Meeting, when it came to ICH, the "experts" were "out there and not inside the museum" (Bouquet 2004, p. 13). Considering this, the Oestgeest Declaration, not only echoed recommendations stated in the Shanghai Charter but also emphasized the need for museums to re-evaluate their organisational structure and functions, reconsider their mission statements and contribute to the sustainable development of the ICH community (ibid.). Also acknowledging the shortcomings of traditional museum practices, the *Seoul Declaration of ICOM on the Intangible Heritage* (Seoul Declaration)[17] adopted during the ICOM Conference, recommended that "all training

[14] See note 10.

[15] Topics discussed during the ICOM Conference were the subject of a double issue of ICOM's peer-reviewed journal *Museum International* on the matter of Museums and ICH. Overall, the authors expressed shy optimism regarding the ICHC, and the role museums could play in helping it achieve its ambitious task questioning how museums could and should respond to UNESCO mandate (see Bouchenaki 2004a, b).

[16] The ICHC entered into force in 2006 after Romania became the 30th country to ratify it.

[17] Also known as Resolution No. 1 of ICOM's 20th General Conference.

programmes for museum professionals stress the importance of intangible heritage and include the understanding of intangible heritage as a requirement for qualification." (ICOM 2004). This task would prove challenging given the persistence of traditional museological training and the lack of integration of ICH into professional and academic museum programs. Indeed, the impact of the Seoul Declaration has been limited to museological developments in the Asia-Pacific region (Bae 2013), although this is changing.

Recognising the role museums would have in supporting the ICHC's safeguarding framework, and following the recommendations highlighted during the 2004 events, UNESCO introduced some guidelines in the 2010 version of the ICHC's Operational Directives under a new section focused on awareness-raising at the national and local levels.[18] States Parties could comply with the Operational Directives by involving research institutes, community centres, archives, libraries, documentation centres, and other similar institutions in safeguarding ICH. Particularly, museums are considered key in developing and promoting awareness-raising activities. As stated in paragraph 109, these entities are encouraged to: "involve practitioners and bearers of [ICH] when organizing exhibitions, lectures, seminars, debates and training on their heritage" and "introduce and develop participatory approaches to presenting [ICH] as living heritage in constant evolution" (UNESCO 2022). Additionally, they should "focus on the continuous recreation and transmission of knowledge and skills necessary for safeguarding [ICH], rather than on the objects that are associated with it" and "involve practitioners and bearers in their management, putting in place participatory systems for local development" (ibid.).

To further strengthen museums' commitment to the ICHC, UNESCO officially recognised museums' role as potential allies in safeguarding ICH and fostering cultural diversity with its *2015 Recommendation Concerning the Protection and Promotion of Museums and Collections, their Diversity and their Role in Society* (2015 Recommendation). This document provided principles and policy guidelines addressing different stakeholders within the museum field (UNESCO 2015). It considers museums "custodians of heritage"—"heritage" understood as tangible and intangible values and expressions and as defined by the ICHC (ibid. para. 6)—and as "spaces for cultural transmission and intercultural dialogue" (ibid. para. 2). It also emphasises museums' "important role in education (formal, informal, and lifelong learning), social cohesion and sustainable development" (ibid.). Blake (2018) considers it an "innovative document" that recognises the importance of the preservation, study and transmission of all kinds of heritage for social cohesion and sustainable development, as well as the key role museums can play in this (p. 18). However, the 2015 Recommendation does not bring anything new to the international museum and ICH discourse since it is an amalgamation of the many previous declarations and recommendations regarding museums' involvement in the safeguarding of ICH (i.e. Santiago Declaration, Quebec Declaration, Oestgeest Declaration, Seoul Declaration). This shows that museums' work with ICH during the last quarter of the

[18] The Operational Directives for the implementation of the ICHC were initially adopted in 2008 but were updated to include additional guidelines in 2010 and are revised accordingly every 2 years.

twentieth century was disregarded by the international community in general. With the events of 2004, the entering into force of the ICHC in 2006 and the subsequent establishment of guidelines for museums in the Operational Directives in 2010, those cases would be revisited by museum scholars.

Research on the ICHC's impact on museological processes in the twenty-first century would involve reconsidering and reevaluating the multiple approaches to ICH management already in place. It would also highlight the opportunities museums can offer for safeguarding heritage and promoting cultural diversity, and the advantages and disadvantages of musealising ICH. However, before discussing some of the approaches to ICH safeguarding taken by museums since the appearance of the UNESCO-ICH paradigm, it is important to consider the challenges ICH would present to museums as identified by scholars during the events just examined.

4.3 The Challenges in Managing and Safeguarding ICH in the Museum

Key concerns regarding museums' role in ICH safeguarding were the potential fossilization of heritage practices and museums' top-down approach to heritage management. For instance, Kurin (2004b) suggests that their long history of dealing with material heritage might not help in approaching and working with ICH, given that, as a "thing" or "object" an ICH element is a social practice or tradition rather than a material object (p. 7). Thus, the very nature of ICH as something alive and in continuous transformation poses a major challenge to museums aiming to comply with the ICHC. The main difference between intangible and tangible heritage is its fundamental quality of vitality and, unlike, material heritage, ICH inevitably changes with time. Museums' ability to preserve things in space and time might stop the continuity of ICH expressions, leading instead to its fossilization (Pinna 2003, p. 2). Herein lies one of the paradoxes of safeguarding ICH: since what is to be safeguarded is the act of something, a process, rather than a recording or product of the action itself, museums have no way of safeguarding ICH unless it is replicated in a material form (Kurin 2007).

The concern about the transformation of ICH into tangible forms of heritage and its fossilization through museum practices has been constantly debated, particularly considering the work of ethnographic museums and the documentation of ICH as previously discussed. Recordings of "materialised" and "musealised" ICH might provide museums and communities sources for study to contextualise ICH expressions and aid in its intergenerational transmission (Bouchenaki 2004b; Fernández Cerviño 2008), but this transformation into something tangible can "freeze" and even "officialise" ICH by changing its very nature (Maranda 2004; Kurin 2004a, 2007). This artificial kind of preservation would make ICH lose its connection to the source community: by breaking its continuity, it ceases to be ICH (Pinna 2003, p. 2).

Traditional museology's top-down approach to heritage interpretation and management poses another challenge (Bouquet 2004; Stefano 2012; Bortolotto 2014). This approach limits community participation in museum work and ICH safeguarding because museum and heritage professionals are the "experts", producing and communicating knowledge in an outward direction rather than in collaboration with the community. Traditional museums' approach to community participation is timid and erratic, limited to the inclusion of the community in activities of short and medium-term duration often due to the lack of specialised or capable personnel and lack of experience engaging in dialogue with the community (DeCarli 2006, p. 45). ICH presents new challenges to museological functions, not only because of its living nature but also because ICH bearers are brought in as new actors in heritage management. Consequently, a collection of objects cannot be the focus of museum work. Instead, museums should focus on the experiences of people and their relationships with their heritage. This implies a need for a dialogical relationship where the ICH community becomes an active participant in museum processes (Bouquet 2004), something that the "Latin" New Museology had already promoted. Overcoming the traditional top-down approach can improve a museum's work and strengthen its relationship with communities through the creation of partnerships but it would require specialised training for museum staff working with ICH and capacity training for the ICH community (Kurin 2007), another challenge highlighted by experts on the field (Stefano 2012; Denes 2012).

Overall, museums' perceived unsuitability for safeguarding ICH are based on the principles of traditional museology, one which seeks to document, preserve and manage material cultural heritage. Traditional museum practices are believed to "freeze" and "decontextualise" living heritage as they are not accustomed to working with actions and processes (Bortolotto 2007). Furthermore, within traditional museology, museums are considered the authority on heritage preservation, claiming ownership of their collections. This goes against the essence of ICH whose power and authority belong to the bearer communities. Since traditionally museums have followed a top-down approach to heritage management and interpretation with museum scholars as "experts" and communities as "passive" receptors, a rebalancing and reversal of these roles is required for safeguarding ICH in the museum. The ICH community needs to be approached and included in the planning and performance of museum work as legitimate "experts" on ICH. As suggested by Kurin (2004b), for museums to become active agents in ICH safeguarding they need to re-conceive themselves and strengthen their relationships with their stakeholders, especially the ICH community.

Museum Functions	Safeguarding Measures (to ensure viability of ICH)
• Collection	• Identification and documentation
• Conservation and Preservation	• Preservation
• Research	• Research
• Interpretation	• Protection
• Exhibition	• Promotion
• Communication	• Enhancement
• Education	• Transmission (Education)
• Knowledge sharing	• Revitalisation

Fig. 3 Museum functions and ICH safeguarding measures

5 Museological Responses to the UNESCO-ICH Paradigm

As illustrated by the events following the ICHC, museum work came under scrutiny, especially regarding museums' potential for safeguarding ICH as prescribed by the UNESCO-ICH paradigm. Most concerns over museums' role in aiding in the implementation of safeguarding initiatives centred on the transformative effects of museological action that would turn ICH into a museum object, decontextualising and disconnecting it from the community to whom it belongs. However, suggesting that museums are not adequate for safeguarding ICH based only on their work documenting and reproducing material records of intangible accounts seems a narrow view of safeguarding and of museums' potential to do this, especially considering that documenting heritage is only one of many museum activities. Indeed, if we compare the standard museum functions established by ICOM[19] and reinforced by UNESCO (2015) against the safeguarding measures proposed under Article 2.3 of the ICHC, museums already perform many of these actions (Fig. 3).

For Alivizatou (2022), UNESCO's ICH safeguarding framework is essentially museological. She states, "safeguarding is a multi-dimensional, intellectual and operational, framework for managing intangible heritage with what could be described as a museological mission at its core: the task of preserving knowledges and practices and passing them on to future generations" (p. 5). However, if ICH is made up of processes and practices determined and valued by cultural bearers, working with it requires a different approach and application of methodologies to the ones used with tangible heritage. Museum practice would need to be reoriented from an interest in museum objects *per se* to the people linked to those objects (Alivizatou 2006, p. 54). In this sense, integrating ICH into the museum setting would have to go beyond including the testimonies of ICH practitioners for contextualising objects and enriching their collections.

Accordingly, as a response to the UNESCO-ICH paradigm, museums began exploring alternative museological methods that would foster the participation of

[19] Based on museum functions as described on ICOM's 2007 and 2022 museum definitions.

ICH practitioners in ICH safeguarding under the banner of participatory museology, ecomuseology and indigenous curation, a term introduced by Kreps (2009) to denote non-Western models of museums, curatorial methods, and concepts of cultural heritage preservation. These approaches would be examined by museum scholars seeking to discover whether museums could effectively engage with ICH, maintain their relationships with the ICH community and work for their benefit.

Participatory museology involves methods that include the ICH community in the documentation, curation, interpretation and presentation of exhibitions, among other activities. As previously discussed, some ethnographic museums are using these methods, but their approach is often limited. Within participatory museology, the museum is envisioned as a cultural centre, a space for dialogue and for sharing experiences reminiscent of Clifford's idea of the museum as a "contact zone" (Alivizatou 2012, p. 191; Gujadhur 2017). Underlying this argument is the understanding that safeguarding should not mean "preserving" in the sense of maintaining heritage unchanged but "ensuring the 'dynamism' of ICH (Yoshida 2004, p. 109)." Examples from Vietnam (Van Huy 2006), Laos (Gujadhur 2017), New Zealand and Greece (Alivizatou 2022) illustrate how integrating ICH bearers in the organisation and performance of diverse museum activities supports the transmission of their knowledge, the reconstruction and continuity of memories and identities and the economic development of the community.

Regional, local and community-based museums are also following participatory approaches in their attempts to safeguard ICH and promote the sustainability of communities as evidenced by examples from Spain (Fernández Cerviño 2008), Thailand (Denes 2012), New Zealand and Vanuatu (Alivizatou 2012), Hungary and Turkey (Blake 2015, 2018). Moreira (2013) suggests that by giving voice to the community, these types of museums can be used for local development. For example, the community can support the museum in assessing the surrounding environment to determine appropriate actions for safeguarding and development such as capacity training for the community and museum workers, the promotion of local tourism and the valorisation, production and consumption of local products, among other things that help disseminate heritage internally and externally and promote the socio-economic sustainability of the ICH community (ibid. pp. 11–13).

Focusing on local and community museums, Denes' (2012) work with the ICH Field School in Lamphun, Thailand[20] examined the challenges and opportunities of working with ICH in those settings and considered the best options to approach its safeguarding from a museological standpoint. The project concluded by identifying some of the challenges of attempting to use participatory approaches for safeguarding ICH—particularly the persistence of a top-down approach to heritage management and the need for capacity training for both museum professionals and ICH bearers—and recommended the use of new museological strategies that fostered

[20] This was a key event in the museum and ICH international discussion, in which many current ICH and museum scholars took part. It was co-organised by UNESCO and the Princess Maha Chakri Sirindhorn Anthropology from 2009 to 2011.

a more grounds-up approach (Denes 2012). These strategies included the previously mentioned approaches of indigenous curation and ecomuseums.

Indeed, the application of "ecomuseological principles" (Corsane et al. 2008) has been suggested as a strategy for ICH safeguarding and for strengthening the relationship between museums, ICH and communities (Corsane et al. 2008; Stefano 2012), since it is based on a grounds-up approach to heritage management as opposed to the top-down approach traditionally followed by museums. Considering that heritage is both complex and contextual it was suggested that the approach to ICH needs to be all-encompassing and holistic (Bouchenaki 2004b) and ecomuseological principles were formulated under that philosophy (Corsane 2005). Integrated and inclusive approaches to heritage management had been developed under the "Latin" New Museology with the creation of new museum formats during the 1980s, including ecomuseums. Thus, a growing interest in ecomuseology illustrates that the movement went unnoticed at the broader international level. Indeed, while community museums, ecomuseums, and other kinds of 'new museums' were already at the forefront of ICH preservation and management, the transformation of museum practice brought on by the UNESCO-ICH paradigm in the English-speaking world is mainly linked to Hooper-Greenhill's (2000) post-museum ideal and the re-evaluation of the traditional museology (Alivizatou 2012; Kreps 2009).

Nevertheless, the UNESCO-ICH paradigm brought an awakening in museological thinking and practice. It sparked interest in the museum and ICH discourse leading to academic research that emphasised the possibilities and advantages of inclusive museological practices for heritage management and presented examples of alternative approaches for safeguarding and managing ICH in the museum. Of note, are two important projects developed within the European context and emerging research on ICH museums.

5.1 Integrating ICH in Museums

The *Exploring Intangible Cultural Heritage in Museum Contexts* (2016–2017) was a collaborative pilot project between ICOMOS UK's Intangible Cultural Heritage Committee, and the Arts Council England implemented in Southeast England.[21] The project aimed to facilitate museums' exploration of ICH as defined by the ICHC, examine ICH within museum collections, enable interactions and collaboration between museum professionals and members of the ICH community to strengthen their relationships, and explore appropriate methodologies for integrating ICH (Arokiasamy 2018). Examining selected domains of ICH within participating museums,[22] the project illustrated the different, often limited, understanding of the

[21] This project was innovative in its time considering that the UK did not ratify the ICHC until March 2024.

[22] Hastings Museum and Art Gallery, Weald and Downland Living Museum, Museum of Cambridge, and Peterborough Museum and Art Gallery.

concept of ICH by museum professionals. However, it showed museums' willingness to learn and adapt to accommodate ICH and the ICH community as partners and a new audience group. Overall, the project demonstrated the importance of engagement and collaboration between actors, including the ICH community, artists and museum staff in all aspects of museum work, highlighting the importance of participatory methods.

On a slightly larger scale, the *Intangible Heritage and Museum Project* (IMP) (2017–2020) brought together museums, ICH-related NGOs and ICH practitioners from Belgium, The Netherlands, Switzerland, Italy and France in a series of meetings, forums, and workshops. Co-funded by the Creative Europe program of the European Union and supported by Flemish government and the Swiss Federal Office of Culture, the project explored how participating museums were expanding museum functions, integrating ICH into museum practice and working in collaboration with ICH practitioners in safeguarding processes, as well as the skills and competences museum professionals should have and develop to work with the ICH community. Using key UNESCO and ICOM documents[23] to analyse activities led by these museums, the project suggests that encounters between museums and ICH create a "third space",[24] where hybrid practices can emerge (Nikolić Đerić et al. 2020). IMP produced a tool kit and the book *Museums and Intangible Cultural Heritage,*[25] which summarizes key themes and case studies explored during the project. Findings from the project were also published in a special themed issue of *Volkskunde*: *'Transforming, Not Saving. Intangible Cultural Heritage, Museums and/or the World'* (2020).

Regarding ICH museums, my research investigates how ICH and its safeguarding are approached when an ICH expression and not a specific collection is the focus of museum work. ICH museums are those intentionally created for the presentation, promotion and safeguarding of a particular ICH element as defined by UNESCO (Ferrer-Yulfo 2020). Blake (2018) noticed the emergence of local more subject-specific museums as a response to the ICHC in her analysis of Periodic Reports sent to UNESCO (2003) between 2011–2013. For example, local museums in Turkey, such as the Intangible Cultural Heritage Applied Museum and the Living Museum in Beypazari Municipality, both in Ankara were created to support the implementation of safeguarding measures proposed by the Operational Directives (ibid.). She suggests that the establishment of these museums is also an important safeguarding action as these can serve as interpretation centres, information and documentation centres, spaces for ICH training, performance and exhibition spaces and workshops for artisans (ibid. pp. 25–26). These museums present an all-encompassing view of the ICH of their local/regional community and promote its safeguarding by using participatory approaches to museum work.

[23] UNESCO's Basic Texts of the ICHC, the ICHC's Operational Directives, the Ethical Principles for Safeguarding Intangible Cultural Heritage, the Seoul Declaration, UNESCO's 2015 Recommendation, ICOM's Code of Ethics for Museums and its museum definition.

[24] From Homi K. Bhaba's critical theory on hybridity. See Nikolić Đerić et al. (2020).

[25] All resources as readily available at https://www.ichandmuseums.eu/en

However, my work explored museums strongly connected to a specific ICH element, such as the Flamenco Dance Museum in Spain and the Fado Museum in Portugal, rather than ICH in general. These ICH museums were in existence before the 2008 Operational Directives.[26] In both cases, the ICH community was strongly engaged in many aspects of museum work: they were consulted as experts for curatorial purposes; they interpreted collections collaboratively with museum staff; and transmitted their ICH practices by teaching in the museum (Ferrer-Yulfo 2022). Additionally, the participation of the ICH community was highly regarded as they were part of decision-making processes either as part of an advisory committee (Fado Museum) or as part of the museum staff and management team (Flamenco Dance Museum). Both examples, demonstrate the importance of recognising the role and agency of the ICH community in determining the most appropriate ways of transmitting their knowledge and practices (ibid).

The creation of ICH museums could be considered a new phase in the development of museums' relationship with ICH and in the implementation of safeguarding strategies. However, research on how these museums and their approaches to ICH safeguarding differ from other museological institutions has just started. There are still issues to explore when examining the relationship and dynamics between museums and the ICH community, not only within ICH museums but also in other museological institutions, including art museums,[27] and from other geographical contexts. Most research has focused on the more conventional, already-established museums, mainly within the European context. However, this section shows how interest in ICH and its safeguarding is growing and how museums are actively seeking ways to answer UNESCO's call and support peoples' living heritage.

6 Safeguarding ICH: A Call to Reframe Museum Practice

This chapter examined the impact of the UNESCO-ICH paradigm on museums and museum practice starting by tracing the "unconventional" relationship between museums and ICH back to the work of ethnographic museums and their interest in preserving the knowledge, meanings and values of cultural objects. However, this relationship illustrates issues with the terminology established by UNESCO since museum professionals did not (and some still do not) comprehend the ICH safeguarding paradigm fully. ICH is more than values and meanings attached to

[26] Indeed, some ICH museums predate the ICHC, such as Antonio Pasqualino International Puppet Museum of Palermo (an example examined by IMP), which was conceived for and with the ICH practitioners and supported the proclamation of the Sicilian Opera dei Pupi as *Masterpiece of the Oral and Intangible Heritage of Humanity* in 2001 (later passed into the Representative List in 2008).

[27] Nikolić Đerić (2020), suggests that engaging with ICH might be far-fetched for art, technical and/or natural history museums, but that research shows there is space to learn from each other. Indeed, ICH can be found in all museum collections if we consider the artistic practices and technical processes that allowed these to "materialise".

objects; it is also the knowledge, practices, skills, and associated objects and spaces, that communities identify as their own (UNESCO 2003). Additionally, safeguarding should not be limited to documentation and research as had been historically done by ethnographic museums but include actions that allow the transmission and continuity of cultural expressions.

While museological approaches brought in by the "Latin" New Museology demonstrated a more holistic perspective of heritage and a broader, more participatory set of actions for safeguarding, these approaches were overlooked until the birth of the UNESCO-ICH paradigm in the early twenty-first century. The arrival of the ICHC sparked discussions on how museums could respond to UNESCO's call. Opinions regarding the suitability of museums in supporting the safeguarding of ICH are still divided, but there is only a way forward as evidenced by the different museological responses to the UNESCO-ICH paradigm that have emerged. Most criticisms against museums are based on the traditional museology that could threaten the continuity and viability of ICH by producing a "fossilised" and "official" version of itself and by separating it from the community to whom it belongs. However, as the chapter argues, these limitations can be overcome by seeking inspiration from the New Museology and critically reflecting on the "unconventional" relationship.

Participatory museology, indigenous curation, community museums, ecomuseums, and ICH museums, offer insights into how ICH safeguarding can be approached and achieved within museum contexts while considering UNESCO's parameters. These museological responses highlight the need for community involvement in museum work, the importance of collaboration and partnerships between multiple actors (ICH communities, museum professionals, related NGOs, and other relevant institutions) and the need for capacity-building for all parties: the UNESCO-ICH paradigm has changed the actors and actions within the traditional heritage protection framework. This is because, as emphasised, with ICH, it is the community, the cultural practitioners, who hold the knowledge, skills, and techniques associated with the cultural manifestations they own, value, and perform. They also know the appropriate uses and values of the objects associated with these manifestations. Accordingly, approaching ICH requires a shift in knowledge production and transmission where cultural practitioners have control over these actions: a role reversal where museum professionals take a back seat in heritage interpretation and recognise the expertise and agency of the ICH community. This offers an opportunity where all actors can learn from each other.

From this discussion, some conclusions can be drawn. First, the *participation* of ICH practitioners in museum work is essential. The ICH community is central to the UNESCO-ICH paradigm; without them, there is no ICH, and museums need to reconsider how they engage with communities. In this sense, the introduction of ICH in the heritage protection framework supports the democratisation of museum processes. Second, while it seems clear that safeguarding is a museological endeavour (Alivizatou 2022), *museological functions should be reconsidered, expanded and adapted* in response to the dynamic nature of ICH and the specific needs for its safeguarding. The inclusion of the ICH community and the reassessment of museum work, place the museum in what Nikolić Đerić (2020) calls a "third space", a hybrid space within the heritage sector born at the intersection of museum functions and ICH safeguarding measures. This space supports the development of other approaches that combine museum practices and safeguarding methods that respond to the specific needs of ICH and its community (p. 413), thus allowing museum practice to reflect, reassess, and reframe itself anew.

Overall, the UNESCO-ICH paradigm caused a reframing of museum practices as an ongoing process that still requires further exploration as the ICHC continues to develop globally. There are still many questions regarding the implementation of participatory methods and their effectiveness. Museums conceive participation in different ways; there are many types and levels and there are no mechanisms that guarantee the full and active participation of the ICH community in museum work. Additionally, many museums still do not understand "ICH" or "safeguarding", limiting the extent of their interactions. These issues can only be answered by exploring how museums deal with the politics of representation and authority within the new heritage landscape brought by the ICHC, including decolonisation agendas, cultural diversity initiatives in a cosmopolitan arena and the sustainable development goals, to mention areas for further inquiry.

References

Alivizatou M (2006) Museums and intangible heritage: the dynamics of an 'unconventional' relationship. Papers Inst Archaeol 17:47–57. https://doi.org/10.5334/pia.268

Alivizatou M (2012) Intangible heritage and the museum: new perspectives on cultural preservation. Left Coast Press, Walnut Creek

Alivizatou M (2022) Intangible heritage and participation. Routledge, Oxford

Arokiasamy C (2018) Exploring intangible cultural heritage in museum contexts: a pilot project. ICOMOS UK, London. https://icomosuk.org/wp-content/uploads/2020/07/Exploring-ICH-in-Museum-Context-report.pdf

Bae K (ed) (2013) ICOM 2004 Seoul and museum development in Korea: retrospect with global perspectives. ICOM Korea, Seoul. http://www.icomkorea.org/docs/ICOM2004_kor.PDF

Bedekar VH (2000) Problems of intangible heritage in Indian community museums. In: Vieregg H, Davis A (eds) Museology and the intangible heritage I. ICOFOM study series, vol 32. Museums-Pädagogisches Zentrum, München, pp 18–20

Blake J (2015) From global to local heritage: intangible cultural heritage and the role of the museum. Anthropol Middle East 10:22–40. https://doi.org/10.3167/ame.2015.100103

Blake J (2018) Museums and safeguarding intangible cultural heritage – facilitating participation and strengthening their function in society. Int J Intang Herit 13:18–32

Bortolotto C (2007) From objects to processes: UNESCO's 'intangible cultural heritage'. J Mus Ethnogr 19:21–33

Bortolotto C (2014) La problemática del patrimonio cultural inmaterial. Culturas. Revista de Gestión Cultural 1:1–22. https://doi.org/10.4995/cs.2014.3162

Bosch S (2000) Consideraciones teóricas para la museología, el patrimonio intangible y la identidad cultural. In: Vieregg H, Davis A (eds) Museology and the intangible heritage I. ICOFOM study series, vol 32. Museums-Pädagogisches Zentrum, München, pp 21–26

Bouchenaki M (ed) (2004a) Museum international: special edition on intangible heritage, vol 56. https://unesdoc.unesco.org/ark:/48223/pf0000135852

Bouchenaki M (ed) (2004b) Editorial. Mus Int 56:6–10

Bouquet M (2004) Report on the international expert meeting 'museums and intangible heritage', April 5–7, 2004, Oegstgeest, The Netherlands: Position paper. https://ich.unesco.org/doc/src/00085-EN.pdf
Corsane G (2005) From 'outreach' to 'inreach': how ecomuseums principles encourage community participation in museum processes. In: Junping Z (ed) Papers of the International Ecomuseum Forumi. Chinese Society of Museums, Guizhou, pp 157–171
Corsane G, Davis P, Elliott S (2008) Ecomuseology: a holistic and integrated model for safeguarding 'a spirit of place' in the North East of England. In: Finding the spirit of place: between the tangible and intangible, 16th ICOMOS General Assembly. ICOMOS, Quebec. https://www.icomos.org/quebec2008/cd/toindex/77_pdf/77-7kft-231.pdf
Davis P (2011) Ecomuseums: a sense of place. Continuum, London
DeCarli G (2006) Un museo sostenible: Museo y comunidad en la preservación activa de su patrimonio. UNESCO América Central, San José. https://archivos.juridicas.unam.mx/www/bjv/libros/6/2793/1.pdf
Decarolis N (2000) The tangible and intangible heritage. In: Vieregg H, Davis A (eds) Museology and the intangible heritage I. ICOFOM study series, vol 32. Museums-Pädagogisches Zentrum, München, pp 35–39
Denes A (2012) Acquiring the tools for safeguarding intangible heritage: lessons from an ICH field school in Lamphun, Thailand. In: Stefano M, Davis P, Corsane G (eds) Safeguarding intangible cultural heritage. The Boydell Press, Woodbridge, pp 165–176
Fernández Cerviño MX (2008) Musealizar lo intangible: El patrimonio inmaterial en el museos. In: XI Jornadas de Museología, pp 258–264. https://docplayer.es/34452461-Musealizar-lo-intangible-el-patrimonio-inmaterial-en-el-museo.html
Ferreira da Costa P (ed) (2009a) Museus e património imaterial: Agentes, fronteiras, identidade. Departamento de Património Imaterial, Instituto dos Museus e da Conservação
Ferreira da Costa P (2009b) Introdução. In: Ferreira da Costa P (ed) Museus e património imaterial: Agentes, fronteiras, identidade. Departamento de Património Imaterial, Instituto dos Museus e da Conservação, pp 15–29
Ferrer-Yulfo A (2020) Intangible cultural heritage museums: further considerations for a new museum definition. ICOFOM Study Ser 48:95–106
Ferrer-Yulfo A (2022) Transforming museum education through intangible cultural heritage. J Mus Educ 47:319–330
Fromm A (2016) Ethnographic museums and intangible cultural heritage: return to our roretrots. J Mar Isl Cult 5:89–94. https://doi.org/10.1016/j.imic.2016.10.001
Garton Smith J (2000) The impact of curation on intangible heritage: the case of Oradour-sur-Glane. In: Vieregg H, Davis A (eds) Museology and the intangible heritage I. ICOFOM study series, vol 32. Museums Pädagogisches Zentrum, München, pp 58–67
Giménez-Cassina E (2010) Who am I? An identity crisis in the new museologies and the role of the museum professional. In: dos Santos PA, Primo J (eds) To understand new museology in the XXI century. Edições Universitárias Lusófonas, Lisbon, pp 25–41
Gujadhur T (2017) A conversation with Tara Gujadhur: the Traditional Arts and Ethnology Centre in Laos (M. Stefano, Interviewer). In: Stefano M, Davis P (eds) The Routledge companion to intangible cultural heritage. Routledge, London, pp 396–401
Hooper-Greenhill E (2000) Museums and the interpretation of visual culture. Routledge, London
van Huy N (2006) The role of museums in the preservation of living heritage: experiences of the Vietnam Museum of Ethnology. Int J Intang Herit 1:36–41. https://www.ijih.org/volumes/article/13
ICOM (1984) Declaration of Quebec – basic principles of a new museology. In: dos Santos P, Primo J (eds) To think sociomuseologically. Edições Universitárias Lusófonas, Lisbon, pp 22–25
ICOM (2004) Resolutions adopted by ICOM's 21st General Assembly: Seoul declaration of ICOM on the intangible heritage. http://icom.museum/wp-content/uploads/2018/07/ICOMs-Resolutions_2004_Eng.pdf. Accessed 9 July 2024

ICOM (2009) The role of International Council of Museums for the safeguarding of intangible heritage. https://ich.unesco.org/doc/src/01367-EN.doc. Accessed 9 July 2024
ICOM (2022) Museum definition. https://icom.museum/en/resources/standards-guidelines/museum-definition/. Accessed 9 July 2024
ICOM-ASPAC (2002) Shanghai charter. Workshop on museums and intangible heritage – Asia Pacific approaches. https://icom.museum/wp-content/uploads/2018/07/Shanghay_Charter_Eng.pdf. Accessed 9 July 2024
ICOM-UNESCO (1972) Basic principles of the integral museum. In: dos Santos P, Primo J (eds) To think sociomuseologically. Edições Universitárias Lusófonas, Lisbon, pp 13–21
Kirshenblatt-Gimblett B (2004a) Intangible heritage as metacultural production. Mus Int 56:52–65. https://unesdoc.unesco.org/ark:/48223/pf0000135852
Kirshenblatt-Gimblett B (2004b) From ethnology to heritage: the role of the museum. In: 8th SIEF conference, among others: encounters and conflicts in European and Mediterranean societies. Musée national des Civilisations de l'Europe et de la Méditerranée, Marseille, pp 73–80. https://www.siefhome.org/downloads/publications/elibrary/document-cd.pdf
Kreps C (2009) Indigenous curation, museums, and intangible cultural heritage. In: Smith L, Akagawa N (eds) Intangible heritage. Routledge, London, pp 193–208
Kurin R (2004a) Safeguarding intangible cultural heritage in the 2003 UNESCO convention: a critical appraisal. Mus Int 56:66–77. https://doi.org/10.1111/j.1350-0775.2004.00459
Kurin R (2004b) Museums and intangible heritage: culture dead or alive. ICOM News 57:7–9. http://archives.icom.museum/pdf/E_news2004/p7_2004-4.pdf
Kurin R (2007) Safeguarding intangible cultural heritage: key factors in implementing the 2003 convention. Int J Intang Herit 2:10–20
López Álvarez J, Suárez López J (2009) Hacer tangible lo intangible: El patrimonio inmaterial en el Museo del Pueblo de Asturias. In: Jornadas sobre Protección del Patrimonio Inmaterial, Teruel October 14–16
Maranda L (2000) Museology and intangible heritage. In: Vieregg H, Davis A (eds) Museology and the intangible heritage I. ICOFOM study series, vol 32. Museums-Pädagogisches Zentrum, München, pp 80–83
Maranda L (2004) Museology and intangible heritage – the museum is the message. In: Vieregg H, Sgoff B, Schiller R (eds) Museology and the intangible heritage II. ICOFOM study series, vol 33. Museums-Pädagogisches Zentrum, München, pp 62–64
Maure M (1995) La nouvelle muséologie – qu'est-ce que c'est? In: Schärer M (ed) Museum and community II symposium. ICOFOM, Stavanger, pp 127–132
van Mensch P (1992) Towards a methodology of museology. University of Zagreb, Zagreb
Mingote Calderón JL (ed) (2013a) Patrimonio inmaterial, museos y sociedad. Balances y perspectivas de futuro. Madrid, Ministerio de Educación, Cultura y Deporte de España
Mingote Calderón JL (2013b) Patrimonio cultural inmaterial, museos e historia(s): Una relación antigua. In: Mingote Calderón JL (ed) Patrimonio inmaterial, museos y sociedad. Balances y perspectivas de futuro. Ministerio de Educación, Cultura y Deporte de España, Madrid, pp 13–43
Moreira FJ (2013) The creation process of a local museum. In: Bruno C, Chagas M, Moutinho M (eds) Sociomuseology 1: new focuses/new challenges. Universidad Lusófona de Humanidades e Tecnologías, Lisbon, pp 7–20
Nikolić Ðerić T (2020) Intersections: bridging the tangible and intangible cultural heritage practices. In: Jacobs M, Neyrinck J, Tsakiridis E (eds) Transforming not saving: intangible cultural heritage, museums and/or the world. Volkskunde, Brussel, pp 405–414
Nikolić Ðerić T, Neyrinck J, Seghers E, Tsakiridis E (eds) (2020) Museums and intangible cultural heritage: towards a third space in the heritage sector. Werkplaats Immaterieel Erfgoed, Bruges
Pinna G (2003) Intangible heritage and museums. ICOM News 56:2
Primo J (2013) To think museology today. In: Bruno C, Chagas M, Moutinho M (eds) Sociomuseology 1: new focuses/new challenges. Universidad Lusófona de Humanidades e Tecnologías, Lisbon, pp 45–63

dos Santos PA (2009) Museology and community development in the XXI century. Edições Universitárias Lusófonas
Smith L (2006) Uses of heritage. Routledge, London
Stam D (2005) The informed muse: the implications of 'The New Museology' for museum practice. In: Corsane G (ed) Heritage, museums and galleries: an introductory reader. Routledge, Abingdon, pp 54–70
Stefano M (2012) Reconfiguring the framework: adopting a museological approach for safeguarding intangible cultural heritage. In: Stefano M, Davis P, Corsane G (eds) Safeguarding intangible cultural heritage. The Boydell Press, Woodbridge, pp 223–238
UNESCO (1989) Recommendation on the safeguarding of traditional culture and folklore. https://unesdoc.unesco.org/ark:/48223/pf0000084696.page=242. Accessed 9 July 2024
UNESCO (2003) The convention for the safeguarding of the intangible cultural heritage. http://unesdoc.unesco.org/images/0013/001325/132540e.pdf. Accessed 9 July 2024
UNESCO (2015) Recommendation concerning the protection and promotion of museums and collections, their diversity and their role in society. https://unesdoc.unesco.org/ark:/48223/pf0000246331. Accessed 9 July 2024
UNESCO (2022) Operational directives for the implementation of the convention for the safeguarding of the intangible cultural heritage. https://ich.unesco.org/en/directives. Accessed 9 July 2024
de Varine H (2006a) The origins of the new museology concept and of the ecomuseum word and concept in the 1960s and the 1970s. In: Zhang J, Davis P, Maggi M (eds) Communication and exploration: papers of International Ecomuseum Forum 2005. Chinese Society of Museums, Guizhou, pp 75–79
de Varine H (2006b) New museology and the de-Europeanization of museology. In: Zhang J, Davis P, Maggi M (eds) Communication and exploration: papers of International Ecomuseum Forum 2005. Chinese Society of Museums, Guizhou, pp 81–82
Vergo P (1989) Introduction. In: Vergo P (ed) The new museology. Reaktion Books, London, pp 1–5
Vieregg H, Davis A (eds) (2000) Museology and the intangible heritage I. ICOFOM study series, vol 32. Museums-Pädagogisches Zentrum, München
Vieregg H, Sgoff B, Schiller R (eds) (2004) Museology and the intangible heritage II. ICOFOM study series, vol 33. Museums-Pädagogisches Zentrum, München
Yoshida K (2004) The museum and the intangible cultural heritage. Mus Int Spec Ed Intang Herit 56:1–2

Alix Ferrer-Yulfo is Professor of Practice in Museum Studies at Syracuse University. She holds a PhD in Museum and Heritage Studies from Newcastle University, an MA in South Asia Area Studies from SOAS University of London, an MA in Cultural Management from the University of Puerto Rico and a Postgraduate Certificate in Safeguarding Intangible Cultural Heritage from the Universidad de Córdoba, Argentina. Her research interests include the impact of the UNESCO-ICH paradigm on national policies and museum work, alternative museologies and the decolonization of museum and heritage studies. Her current work explores intangible cultural heritage museums (ICH museums) and how these are transforming museology through alternative museum practices, strategic partnerships, and stronger relationships with bearer communities.

Learning from Intangible Cultural Heritage in Times of Climate Change

Bart Zwegers and Karim van Knippenberg

1 Introduction

Between 13 and 15 July 2021, parts of Germany, Belgium and the Netherlands were hit by sudden heavy rainfall. The water in brooks and rivers rose at an unprecedented pace, leading to severe flooding in several areas. In the Netherlands, mainly the southern province of Limburg experienced the destructive consequences of this natural disaster, especially in the catchment basins of the rivers Geul, Meuse, Roer and Geleenbeek (Asselman et al. 2022, pp. 8–11). The total financial impairment in this region was estimated at around 433 million euros (Slager 2023). Besides human suffering and damage to homes, businesses, and personal property, the floods had significant impact on the region's heritage. In the affected area are valuable cultural landscapes, monuments, museums, archives, and other heritage institutions with vulnerable collections. Historic buildings, archaeological sites, and museum collections suffered considerable damage (RCE 2021).

This exemplifies a broader, global issue. All around the world, cultural heritage is grappling with the consequences of climate change. The impact of the climate crisis on different types of heritage varies widely. In some areas, coastal erosion and rising sea levels have already caused enormous damage to heritage. In other areas, increasing drought combined with sudden downpours proves to be devastating (Sesana et al. 2020, pp. 1–29). Additionally, less obvious effects of climate change—such as increased humidity, stronger winds, soil salinization, more fires and storms, more ultraviolet radiation, soil subsidence, new invasive animal and

B. Zwegers (✉)
Department of History, Maastricht University, Maastricht, The Netherlands
e-mail: b.zwegers@maastrichtuniversity.nl

K. van Knippenberg
Heusschen Coppier Consultancy, Gulpen, The Netherlands
e-mail: k.vanknippenberg@heusschencopier.nl

B. Zwegers and R. Vulto (eds.), *The Spillover Effect of Intangible Cultural Heritage*,
Studies in Art, Heritage, Law and the Market 13,
https://doi.org/10.1007/978-3-032-25352-1_8

plant species, and air pollution—pose serious threats to historic buildings, museums, and archives (Weststeijn 2023, pp. 25–40; Dastgerdi et al. 2019, p. 5227). Although archaeologists already warned about the consequences of climate change for cultural heritage in the early 1990s (see for example Rowland 1992, pp. 29–33), climate scientists generally pay little attention to cultural heritage. Approximately 200,000 scientific studies are published annually with the word 'climate' in the title, but the vast majority focuses on the effects of climate change on nature. Only a small portion addresses its effects on humans, with an emphasis on basic needs like food supply and housing. Although humanities and social science researchers are increasingly becoming involved in climate studies, for example in the context of environmental humanities, the relationship between heritage and climate remains largely unexplored.

This is perhaps not entirely surprising given the enormous impact of the climate crisis on various other areas. Drought and desertification complicate agriculture and threaten food security, particularly in parts of the Global South. The socially disruptive consequences of impending famine and climate migration are already visible in parts of the world (World Bank 2023). In addition, the climate crisis has major effects on nature. Biodiversity is declining rapidly, and many ecosystems are at risk of disappearing entirely. According to recent scientific findings, dozens of animal species go extinct every day (Barnosky and Matzke 2011, pp. 51–57). In light of such an overwhelming existential crisis, the threat to cultural heritage may seem like a secondary problem. As a result, heritage and climate are often seen and treated as separate issues and as separate policy areas. While this is understandable, it is unfortunate, not only because heritage should arguably be protected from the effects of climate change, but also because cultural heritage can be part of the solution for some of the challenges that the climate crisis poses.

The aim of this chapter is to show what we might learn from cultural heritage in the context of climate change, and what obstacles still stand in the way of bringing these lessons into practice. Through examples from the Dutch province of Limburg, this chapter will show how knowledge of the cultural history of our landscape and of intangible heritage practices that helped shape it, can provide valuable insights in relation to water management and land use; lessons that gain renewed relevance in the current climate crisis. Using several concrete examples of 'heritage ensembles' in Limburg, this chapter shows how heritage and cultural history can serve as sources of inspiration for climate-adaptive planning. The heritage ensemble is a relatively new approach to heritage comprising one or more built monuments and their landscape context. This includes, for example, country estates and their surroundings. The management and preservation of such ensembles is inextricably linked to intangible heritage practices regarding water management, agriculture and forestry, as well as certain governance structures and historically grown local political cultures. It is precisely these intangible aspects that make the heritage ensemble an interesting lens through which to explore the relationship between heritage and climate adaptation.

This chapter is structured in four parts. The first part outlines the current policy frameworks addressing heritage and climate change at both international and national levels. It highlights that, despite increasing global attention to the issue, meaningful integration between the heritage and climate policy domains remains limited. The second part explores the potential of intangible heritage to enhance climate resilience and examines how cultural heritage and historical knowledge can be incorporated into urban planning practices. The third part focuses on specific heritage ensembles in Limburg, identifying the challenges these ensembles face, as well as analysing how these cases can inform and inspire climate adaptation strategies. The chapter concludes by reflecting on the role of intangible heritage in landscape management amid climate challenges and proposes avenues for future research.

2 Integrating Heritage and Climate Policy: A Difficult Process

In 2005, the UNESCO World Heritage Committee warned about the potential impact of climate change on heritage. Following this warning, UNESCO analysed the extent to which its member states pay attention to the impacts of climate change on heritage (Terrill 2008). The research shows that in many countries, heritage and climate are treated as separate policy domains. There is usually no integrated approach for heritage and climate. Although most member states acknowledge the potential threat of climate change for heritage, their involvement generally remains limited to monitoring the consequences without actively taking steps to address them (Dastgerdi et al. 2019, p. 5227). UNESCO's sister organisation ICOMOS has expressed similar concerns, recognizing climate change as a significant global threat for heritage (ICOMOS 2020, p. 1). While acknowledging the global nature of this issue, the organization emphasizes the vulnerability of heritage in developing countries specifically, where limited resources hinder effective protection from the escalating impacts of the climate crisis (ICOMOS 2021, pp. 2–10; ICOMOS 2022).

Climate change and heritage also receive attention at the level of the European Union (EU). In 2021, for example, the European Parliament adopted a resolution urging the European Commission to take measures "to mitigate the effects of climate change on cultural heritage" (European Parliament 2021, p. 16). The resolution, partly the result of efforts by Europa Nostra—a federation of non-governmental heritage organizations—called for the inclusion of heritage in the European Green Deal. This led to the 2022 report *Strengthening Cultural Heritage Resilience for Climate Change: Where the European Green Deal meets Cultural Heritage* (Leissner et al. 2022). The researchers, working on behalf of the European Commission, concluded that the effects of climate change on cultural heritage are indeed significant, and that both the EU and its member states are inadequately prepared: "The information gathered is shocking: cultural heritage is under attack from climate change at an unprecedented speed and scale. Yet EU Member States do not have proper policies and action plans in place to mitigate these attacks, nor does the EU" (Leissner et al. 2022, p. 5). This report—like the UNESCO report mention before—thus highlights that many states lack integrated heritage and climate policies.

That the Netherlands is no exception in this regard is evident from the research conducted by Sandra Fatorić and Robbert Biesbroek. In their study on heritage and climate adaptation in the Netherlands, they identified several barriers that hinder efforts to make heritage climate-resilient (Fatorić and Biesbroek 2020, p. 301). Through a survey, they consulted dozens of Dutch heritage experts to gain insight into the main obstacles to climate-proofing heritage. The identified obstacles included technical, socio-cultural, and financial barriers. But according to the interviewed experts, the greatest stumbling block was a lack of institutional integration. The experts observed that although there are clear national, provincial, and local institutional policy frameworks for climate adaptation in general, there is little specific policy for dealing with different types of cultural heritage. Policy guidelines from government agencies offer insufficient support, especially when dealing with acute situations such as sudden heavy rainfall (Fatorić and Biesbroek 2020, p. 308). The interviewed experts also indicated that policymakers and politicians often struggle to assess and understand the technical and social feasibility of various climate adaptation measures. Furthermore, they stated that the protection of heritage is not sufficiently addressed in emergency scenarios (Fatorić and Biesbroek 2020, p. 309).

The picture painted by these Dutch heritage experts is confirmed when one examines the national climate adaptation policy. In recent years, policy documents and plans from the national government have barely addressed heritage. For example, in 2007, several ministries and government organizations jointly published the policy note *Make Room for Climate!* in which the national climate adaptation strategy (NAS) was explained. This document primarily focuses on spatial planning challenges in relation to economic growth and maintaining international economic competitiveness. Heritage is not mentioned. Instead, questions are posed such as: "Where will we meet the spatial needs for urbanization and economic growth? […] How will we keep our mainports (Rotterdam, Schiphol) climate-resilient? […] Where will we plan new industrial areas? [and] How can we ensure that the Netherlands remains an internationally attractive place for business?" (NAS 2007, p. 36). This not only shows how economically driven much government policy is, but also that the protection of cultural heritage is not seen as a priority.

In the years that followed, several versions of the national climate adaptation strategy were published, in which heritage was only mentioned in passing, without concrete recommendations (NAS 2016, p. 31). In 2020, a new version was released, developed by representatives of the Directorate General for Public Works and Water Management (*Rijkswaterstaat*), the Ministry of Infrastructure and Water Management, and several non-governmental organizations. Despite consultation with the Cultural Heritage Agency of the Netherlands (RCE), this version also lacks specific attention to heritage (NAS 2020). This policy document was further developed in 2023 into the national climate adaptation implementation programme (NUPKA 2023). Although the RCE contributed a chapter to this latest document, heritage is absent from the remaining chapters. Efforts have not yet succeeded "in getting heritage into those other chapters and making those cross-connections" (Ellen Vreenegoor Program Manager for Heritage, Water, and Climate at RCE, personal communication with Bart Zwegers September 8, 2023). The policy for climate change adaptation thus remains strongly sector-oriented. The following paragraph will show how this strong sectoral dichotomy could be overcome and how intangible cultural heritage can inform policy for climate adaptive landscape management.

3 Intangible Heritage and Cultural History as a Key to Integrating Heritage and Climate Policy

In the introduction of this chapter it was noted that landscape and intangible heritage are closely linked concepts. However, especially the concept of landscape is rather elusive. There exists a wide variety of epistemological and ontological meanings of this term (Turner et al. 2019, p. 155). The resulting confusion is partly due to the fact that the definitions used do not always align neatly with conventional academic disciplines. It is a transdisciplinary concept used by a growing number of disciplines and sub-disciplines, but for which no broad consensus exists. In the absence of a shared conceptual framework, the definition from the European Landscape Convention (2000) is sometimes used: "'Landscape' means an area, as perceived by people, whose character is the result of the action and interaction of natural and/or human factors" (cited in Bosma and Kolen 2010, p. 238). Just as often, however, authors use their own definitions, which frequently differ widely.

In the context of this chapter, it is especially important to historicize the relationship between humans and the landscape, and to stress the vital role of intangible heritage practices in shaping landscapes (Renes 1990). Changes in the interaction between 'natural and/or human factors' can arguably only be understood from a diachronic perspective. The relationship between humans and their environment can be seen on a scale ranging from 'humans adapt to their environment' to 'humans adapt the environment to themselves'. Although humans have always shaped their environment—through reclamation, extraction, and construction—throughout most of history it was primarily people who adapted to their environment, rather than the other way around. Since the large-scale industrialization of the second half of the nineteenth century, however, humans have increasingly reshaped the landscape with an almost hubristic confidence. Instead of being actors in a more or less static landscape setting, people became set designers, adjusting the landscape ever more forcefully to suit their needs and demands.

This development reached its peak in the decades following World War II. The post-war reconstruction period marked the height of the belief in both a socially engineered society, as well as a malleable landscape (Duyvendak 1999). The construction of post-war neighbourhoods often began with a *tabula rasa*, not only on the drawing board but also in the physical landscape itself. Like a blank sheet on the drawing board, the landscape was prepared for reconstruction. This had major consequences for water systems: brooks were straightened and covered, moats were filled in. The soil structure was disrupted by the deposition of gravel and sand layers for construction purposes. Post-war planners generally paid little attention to the existing landscape context, the historical layers or the heritage practices that helped form it. The typical uniformity of urban planning of that period reflects this (Hall 1988; Blom et al. 2004).

In recent years, partly due to climate change, there has been a growing awareness that the landscape cannot be adapted to every human desire. Rather than starting from a *tabula rasa*, planners increasingly try to take the historical layering and geomorphology of the landscape as their starting point. Not human needs, but the course of water and the composition of the soil should form the leading planning principles. In spatial planning, this principle is referred to as 'water and soil guiding' (Duijn and Pot 2023, pp. 14–18). As awareness grows that planners should take existing landscape conditions more seriously, it has also become apparent that cultural history and heritage should be more firmly embedded in spatial planning policies, and that nature, environment, and heritage should be brought together in an integral vision (Janssen et al. 2017).

The Belvedere Memorandum and more recently the Environmental Act are attempts to integrate this comprehensive view of the landscape into policy. Terms like 'environmental thinking' and 'integrated vision' typify this approach. In practice, however, getting to such an integrated vision remains difficult. Despite the shift in thinking described above, many planners and policymakers still see heritage and the environment more as obstacles that must be dealt with, rather than as opportunities to create better, more climate change resilient plans. The notion of a malleable landscape that can be adjusted to every human desire, as well as the sectoral approach that characterises this notion, continues to be a firmly embedded planning practice. This is a pity because there are many ways in which a more integral vision on the landscape would be beneficial and can result in plans that are more sustainable and climate resilient.

Archaeology, for example, is an underused source of information for urban planners. Historians and archaeologists generally study historical traces in the landscape to better understand the past, not to use this understanding for contemporary purposes. Although relatively young subdisciplines like 'disaster history' and 'environmental history' point to the relevance of historical knowledge for combating disasters in the present (Jensen 2020; McNeill 2010), explicitly drawing lessons for the future still typically falls outside the historian's remit. However, in the context of climate adaptation and spatial planning, there is a case to be made for learning from how people in the past dealt with water and drought challenges. The past can for instance teach us a lot about suitable building locations. Aerial photographs of the village of Borgharen near Limburg's capital of Maastricht (see Figs. 1, 2, and 3), which flooded in 1995, show a dry area surrounded like an island by water, standing out amidst the flooded post-war neighbourhoods. Interestingly, a Roman villa once stood on that spot. Apparently, the Romans had a better sense of where it was safe to build than post-war planners. Planners could use such information to find suitable building locations (Grond et al. 2021).

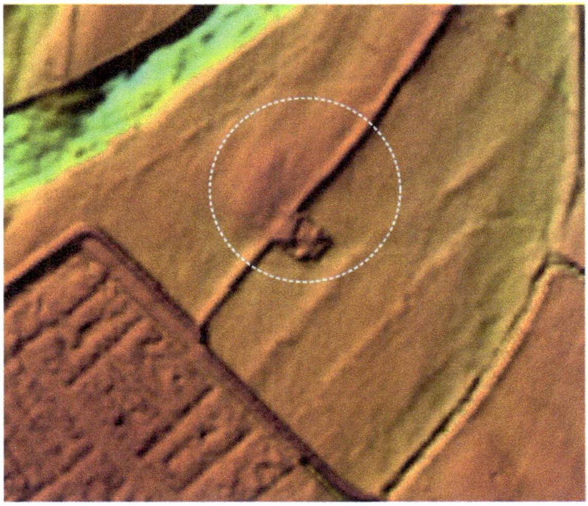

Fig. 1 Elevation map of Borgharen clearly showing the location of the main building of the Roman villa and the Merovingian cemetery. © Zwegers & van Knippenberg

Fig. 2 Aerial photograph of Borgharen showing the location of the Roman villa and the Merovingian cemetery. © Zwegers & van Knippenberg

Archaeological research, however, is not the only source of insight into suitable building locations—toponyms and historical place names are often equally telling (Paulissen 2018, pp. 21). During the 2021 floods, residents of the *Oosterbeemd* care home in Valkenburg had to be evacuated. The word *beemd* historically refers to a grassland parcel that served as a floodplain during high water. A *beemd* lies in a valley and is precisely the area where excess water from a stream would naturally flow. Therefore, you rarely find historic buildings in a *beemd*. In the past, it was well known that building in such an area was asking for trouble. Urban planners encountering place names like *beemd* on (historic) maps should seriously question

Fig. 3 Aerial photograph of Borgharen taken during the flooding of the Meuse River in 1995. The location of the main building of the Roman villa and the Merovingian cemetery remained unflooded. © Rijkswaterstaat

whether these are suitable locations for development. However, planners often ignore such information because they lack the expertise to interpret toponyms, historic place names or historic maps. Interpreting the history of a landscape in this way is therefore not common practice in planning.

In addition to archaeological and toponymic research, intangible heritage practices can be a valuable source of knowledge as well. In the hills of Limburg, for example, it is not uncommon today to plough fields in the direction of the slope. As a result, the furrows act like water slides, quickly channelling rainwater downhill where it leads to floodings of the villages in the valleys. Traditionally, farmers would plough perpendicular to the slope, reducing runoff. This method, combined with vegetation along horizontal contour lines—known as *graften*—allowed water to seep gradually into the soil. The vegetation on the *graften* was also historically used by craftsmen such as basket weavers, carpenters, and beekeepers (Huizenga 2016). With the increase in scale of agriculture, the disappearance of old crafts such as basket weaving and the associated disappearance of landscape elements that were necessary for these crafts, the landscape has become much more vulnerable to the consequences of climate change. Problems like soil erosion, rapid runoff from fields, and biodiversity loss can in part be prevented by restoring historical landscape features like *graften* and increasing knowledge about traditional farming practices and crafts (Schouten et al. 1985, pp. 118–132). Current climate adaptation policy, however, mainly focuses on finding technical, innovative planning and hydrological solutions (Déri and Sundaresan 2012). In doing so, functioning historical water systems are sometimes carelessly dismantled or disturbed. The emphasis on technical innovations seems to stem from the aforementioned belief in the malleability of our living environment. As a result, much historical knowledge of old water management systems and sustainable land use has been lost.

These examples show that (intangible) heritage can contribute to climate-adaptive planning in various ways. This requires bringing together "history and design"—as Koos Bosma and Jan Kolen argue in their book of the same name—and thus bridging two largely separate worlds (Bosma and Kolen 2010). This task is challenging for several reasons. First, there are administrative and organizational barriers that make it difficult to build bridges between these worlds. Although the concept of 'integration' has long been a feature of planning discourse, in practice, sectoral policymaking often proves hard to break through. Even though some try to develop an integrated vision, compartmentalized thinking remains persistent. "Integral is fatal" is a frequently heard phrase among spatial planning policymakers in the Netherlands (Zwegers 2024, p. 59).

Second, there are fundamental differences between the perspectives of the historian and the designer. Exaggerated: the historian looks to the past, the designer to the future. The historian wants to understand how the world was; the designer is interested in how the world could be. The historian writes, the designer draws. These differences also mean that both groups, in a sense, speak different languages or at least use different knowledge sources and methodologies. While planning design practices could benefit from historical knowledge, as the examples above show, the differing approaches and objectives of the two professions can make such cooperation difficult. Nevertheless, alongside the challenges, there are certainly opportunities to bring history and design closer together. The following sections will draw on concrete examples of Limburg heritage ensembles to show where exactly these challenges and opportunities lie.

4 Heritage Ensembles and Climate Adaptation

Ensembles are physically, functionally, and socio-culturally coherent units with a shared history (Storms-Smeets 2019, p. 24). Thinking in terms of heritage ensembles instead of individual monuments fits within the broader concept of "environmental thinking," in which broader societal values and meanings are viewed in connection with the landscape (Tennekes et al. 2022). This includes both tangible and intangible heritage. Given this integrated view of the landscape, the question arises how we can use what we know about a heritage site's origin, history, design, and transformations to address today's preservation and development challenges. This question is especially relevant for heritage ensembles in Limburg that are affected by climate change. Often, twentieth century modifications to ensembles and their surrounding landscapes have reduced their climate resilience. Such ensembles show that understanding cultural-historical developments and intangible heritage can serve as a source of inspiration for climate-adaptive planning, but also that this knowledge is still seldom taken into account.

An example of this is the *Steenen Huys* in the village of Vlodrop. This seventeenth-century castle is listed as a national monument, which means that the owners have a legal obligation to preserve and maintain is. However, due to climate change, it has become increasing difficult to do so. The castle has been affected by flooding of the river Roer on multiple occasions, notably in 2011 and 2021. In the Netherlands, the Roer traverses a broad floodplain which, near Vlodrop, extends up to the castle and the village itself. In the Dutch section of the Roer basin, interventions in the river's course have largely been limited to bank reinforcement. However, land use within the floodplain has been significantly intensified. Morphological patterns and remnants of channels have been leveled and replaced by a 'mathematical' parcelling of the land (de Mars 2013, pp. 105–110; Bleumink and Neefjes 2018). In the German section of the river basin, the Roer was extensively channelized over many kilometers during the 1970s. Both the intensification of land use and modifications to the river course have resulted in more frequent peak discharges and an increased risk of flooding. Previous measures to protect the castle and village by means of dike construction have only been partially implemented. As a result, the castle remains located outside the dike system. While this was seldom problematic in the original situation, the aforementioned landscape alterations have considerably increased the likelihood of flooding, thereby threatening the preservation of the castles' heritage values These heritage values include the seventeenth century castle building itself, some outbuildings and surrounding farms, a enclosed landscape garden, and monumental trees.

At the *Steenen Huys*, a tension arguably exists between national heritage legislation and the provincial water management policy. The castle of Vlodrop is, after all, not protected by the dike system. Its location in the meander zone of the river means that the so-called flood safety standards—that normally apply to villages and urban areas—do not apply here, leaving the monumental building vulnerably to floods (Dekker et al. 2021). One might question whether it is reasonable to keep the owners accountable for the preservation and maintenance of their property—which they formally are under the national heritage act—when the provincial government does not provide the necessary protective measures to reduce floods risk. Despite this situation, the owners of the *Steenen Huys*, driven by a strong awareness of both the material and immaterial values of the castle, have consistently endeavoured to preserve the ensemble by implementing measures to mitigate flood risks themselves. The residents of Vlodrop also play an active role in these efforts. Due to the close relationship between the village and the heritage ensemble, the villagers feel compelled to contribute to the preservation of the castle. In times of impending high water, the villagers organize a so-called 'highwater watch' (*hoogwaterwacht*). During highwater, they deploy mobile emergency barriers and sandbags to reinforce weak sections of dikes and to safeguard the cultural heritage. Based on a shared, practice of mutual assistance and a collective commitment to safeguarding the village's heritage, ensemble owners and villagers work together to protect cultural heritage, the enclosed landscape garden and the castle's surroundings. This makes it all the more concerning that existing policy measures seem to obstruct, rather than support, these locally driven heritage preservation efforts (Zwegers and van Knippenberg 2024).

A concrete example concerns insurance. Legally, owners of listed monuments are, as noted above, obliged to maintain their properties in a way that ensures their preservation. At the same time, however, the absence of flood safety standards limits an owner's ability to safeguard the monument. Indeed, due to the absence of flood safety standards, it is difficult or even impossible for the owner of a heritage ensemble to insure the monument or associated buildings against flood damage. This inability to secure insurance conflicts with the principles of the national heritage act. In the event of flooding, the owner may not be able to repair the damage, thus jeopardizing the long-term preservation of the monument.

Moreover, in line with the lack of proper flood safety standards, and as a reaction to recent floodings, monument owners in Limburg as in the rest of the Netherlands, are encouraged to take individual measures to safeguard their heritage properties. This so-called 'self-reliance' is promoted by local government policies as well as the Dutch heritage agency (*Rijksdienst voor het Cultureel Erfgoed*). Self-reliance is referred to as the notion that residents, in addition to the measures taken by the responsible authorities within the scope of their duties and responsibilities, undertake their own preventive measures to mitigate flood risks. Given the increasing urgency for owners to implement flood protection measures, there is a growing risk that interventions will be carried out which disconnect historic structures from their broader spatial and cultural context. This raises the question of whether self-reliance-based measures will, from an ensemble perspective, yield the most effective and sustainable solutions. Moreover, it remains debatable whether it is desirable for individual monument owners to act independently in addressing these challenges. The emphasis on self-reliance, and the individual responsibility it promotes, conflicts with the policy objective of managing heritage ensembles through integrated and coordinated approaches. In sum, the current promotion of self-reliance appears to reflect a policy shift in which the emphasis on ensuring flood safety is increasingly placed on the individual owner, rather than being approached as a collective or public responsibility.

Although citizens increasingly collaborate with heritage owners in efforts to protect cultural heritage, such cooperation still struggles to fit within the current policy frameworks governing monument protection and conservation—even in a context that emphasizes greater self-reliance. Does self-reliance mean no more than stacking sandbags, or can heritage owners also implement more substantial measures, even when these actions might challenge established heritage preservation norms but enhance long-term flood resilience? Cases like the *Steenen Huys* highlight more uncertainties than solutions. Yet, this example underscores the need for integrated water and heritage policies to better accommodate the perspectives and ongoing efforts of ensemble owners who are already actively engaged in both preserving and adapting their heritage sites for greater flood resilience. Crucially, this requires well-aligned policies that eliminate contradictions—such as those between flood safety regulations and heritage protection laws.

At other heritage ensembles as well, the insufficient integration of intangible heritage practices into heritage policies becomes evident. The castle of Mheer, for example, plays a central role in the small village of Mheer, located in the southern part of the Limburg province. For centuries, this castle ensemble has served as the primary venue for religious, social, and cultural gatherings within the community. As part of the ensembles' immaterial heritage practices, the current owners of the castle are deeply committed to supporting local traditions, such as processions, annual fairs, and village festivals. Their active involvement is instrumental in preserving the strong connection between the castle and the village community. In return, local residents assist in the upkeep of the estate by volunteering for minor repairs and maintenance tasks. This reciprocal relationship between the castle owners and the villagers, embodies a significant aspect of the site's intangible heritage. Yet, despite its importance, this example again highlights the broader neglect of such immaterial practices in heritage policy, as well as the persistent absence of a comprehensive approach that integrates the built ensemble with its surrounding landscape (Zwegers and van Knippenberg 2024).

In the surroundings of castle Mheer, the owner aims to restore the historical hillside forests to improve water retention and reduce surface runoff into the valley. Additionally, the owner plans to transition part of the over 90 hectares of leased farmland from conventional agriculture to agri-environmental management. This includes reintroducing small-scale landscape features that enhance ecological connectivity and reinforces the character of the local landscape (see Fig. 4). By re-introducing historic landscape elements and undoing earlier changes to the landscape, the owner tries to improve the environmental quality and contribute to broader societal goals such as water retention and climate adaptation. However, for owners, such measures are only financially viable if embedded within a long-term vision for ensemble preservation. Current financial and policy support for heritage ensembles largely concentrates on monument conservation, often neglecting issues of land use and the economic sustainability of the broader estate. Moreover, navigating this support system can be highly bureaucratic. Castle Mheer illustrates that, even when owners have a comprehensive and integrated vision and aim to restore historic landscape features, they lack the instruments and frameworks necessary to realize it. This gap must be acknowledged, particularly by local policymakers. Without an integrated approach, not only is the future resilience of individual ensembles undermined, but the broader potential of heritage ensembles to act as drivers of spatial development remains unfulfilled.

The absence of an integrated, landscape-oriented approach is also evident at the heritage ensemble of castle Nieuwenbroeck in Beesel. In recent years, several interventions have taken place in the area, including the reconfiguration of the Huilbeek stream, the construction of a dike as part of the Flood Protection Programme, and nature development projects in the nearby Beesels Broek nature reserve. However, these developments were largely driven by sectoral interests, with the preservation of the ensemble and the enhancement of its landscape value not serving as overarching goals. This piecemeal approach reflects an underlying assumption that the landscape can be engineered and controlled primarily through technical means. As a result, the current state of the Nieuwenbroeck ensemble is defined by a series of hydraulic interventions aimed at managing the water system. According to the owner, however, this situation is likely to become unsustainable. During increasingly frequent dry summers, there is a risk that the castle moat could run dry, potentially

Fig. 4 A 1947 aerial photograph of the area surrounding Mheer castle. The landscape is dominated by numerous small-scale landscape elements, particularly standard orchards. Source: © National Geographic Institute

endangering the building's foundations. Nonetheless, opportunities exist to adopt a more integrated strategy. For example, reconnecting the historical stream system to the moat, strengthening ecological links with the Beesels Broek nature reserve, or establishing designated areas for water retention could enhance both environmental resilience and heritage value. Such an approach would not only safeguard the ensemble against future climatic impacts but also restore a more holistic relationship between the castle, its landscape, and surrounding systems. This, however, would require an integral vision on the landscape that takes into account the historic landscape and explores possibilities for reconstructing it.

The core problem in this case lies primarily in the apparent lack of vision and coordination between the various stakeholders. The municipality has developed future visions for the Beesel village centre, the local water authority is implementing a stream restoration project, the province is addressing rural spatial development challenges, and nature organizations are engaged in ecological restoration efforts. Nevertheless, no integrated solution, in which cultural-historical knowledge and heritage assets could have served as valuable sources of inspiration, has been pursued. The three cases discussed all demonstrate a lack of integration of intangible heritage practices and of a holistic approach to landscape and heritage ensembles. In the case of the *Steenen Huys*, heritage practices, as embodied by the efforts of the highwater watch, play an important role in safeguarding heritage assets in times of flood risk.

Although initiatives aimed at self-reliance are encouraged in policy, the question remains to what extent they truly foster a different perspective on heritage management. The call for self-reliance and local civic engagement should be accompanied by the development of well-coordinated heritage and water policies that form the necessary preconditions sustainable heritage management. The case of castle Mheer illustrates how challenging it is to bring forward an overarching narrative for the preservation of the ensemble—including the relationship between the castle, the village, and the associated intangible practices—even though this is one of its core elements. The example of Beesel demonstrates that it is becoming increasingly difficult to bring stakeholders together around a heritage ensemble, even though such collective engagement has traditionally been a key component of the management of heritage ensembles.

5 The Past as a Guide to the Future

Having discussed the three cases, we can reflect on what cultural heritage of these sites might teach us in these times of climate change. In all three examples above, it becomes evident that a deeper understanding of the cultural history of our landscape, as well as the intangible heritage practices that have shaped it, could have contributed valuable solutions to challenges such as flood safety, heritage protection, and land use. In the case of the *Steenen Huys*, it appears that a solution to the most pressing flood threats has now been found: local villagers are actively involved in safeguarding the heritage site, and a new dike system has been constructed to protect the entire heritage ensemble. However, in the immediate vicinity of the castle, no changes in land use have been implemented. The surrounding area remains defined by rigid, mathematically parceled plots dedicated entirely to intensive agriculture. From the perspective of restoring the ensemble as a whole, it would be beneficial to adopt forms for more nature-inclusive forms agriculture that largely resemble the historic situation. This would significantly improve the land's ability to absorb (rain)water. An integrated area development process could be a way forward, allowing for dialogue and negotiation with neighboring farmers to encourage changes in land-use practices that align better with the preservation and resilience of the heritage landscape.

The example of Beesel illustrates the difficulties involved in implementing a holistic approach to the castle in relation to its landscape and surrounding systems. Although there appears to be a process of collective engagement and potential for developing an integrated vision, individual interests—such as those focused on water retention or ecological concerns—tend to dominate. As a result, rather than pursuing a truly integrated perspective, the process becomes fragmented and issue-specific (Hulst 2010). In this case, several important historical lessons were overlooked. These include the potential to reconnect the historic stream system to the castle's moat, the opportunity to strengthen ecological linkages with the nearby Beesels Broek nature reserve, and the importance of designating specific areas for water retention. At Castle Mheer, the owner already actively draws on historical inspiration to enhance the ensemble's resilience to climate change. Measures being implemented include improving water retention and reducing surface runoff, restoring the original landscape character, and planting historic fruit tree varieties in the orchard. Although challenges remain—particularly with regard to financing the measures and ensuring their long-term effectiveness—the case of Castle Mheer clearly demonstrates that the past can offer valuable solutions for future-proofing heritage ensembles.

6 Conclusion: Towards an Integrated Vision on Heritage, Landscape and Climate

Arnold van der Valk and Willem Korthals Altes argue: "Cultural heritage must maintain a strong position within the spatial planning policies of national, provincial, and municipal governments" (van der Valk and Korthals Altes 2010, p. 114). Yet, in practice—especially in planning decisions related to climate adaptation—there appears to be more of a lack of engagement with historical knowledge than an affirmation of a strong position. The heritage ensembles discussed in this chapter demonstrate that cultural-historical assets could be far more actively integrated into comprehensive landscape-based solutions. There is growing recognition that the preservation and adaptive reuse of heritage can generate added value and serve as a source of inspiration and development. This calls for a proactive attitude not only from heritage professionals, but also from planners and hydrologists—to identify key moments in planning processes where heritage perspectives can be meaningfully incorporated.

Crucially, this also requires that cultural-historical knowledge and knowledge on intangible heritage practices is well-organized and readily available when development processes in or around a heritage ensemble begin. Only then can existing structures be reinforced and the long-term preservation of ensembles be achieved. Although recent policy documents indicate that both the Cultural Heritage Agency of the Netherlands and the Province of Limburg are shifting their focus towards heritage ensembles—and intend to incorporate environmental and contemporary challenges into this perspective—the practical implementation of these policies remains limited and yields modest results.

One promising method for making cultural-historical knowledge relevant to contemporary climate adaptation challenges is 'landscape biography' (Kolen et al. 2010). Landscape biographers conceptualize the landscape as a historically evolved living environment. In this approach, landscape development is not viewed as a linear sequence of discrete phases, but—hence the analogy with a biography—as a succession of transformations, in which the past is continuously reinterpreted and re-experienced in different ways. A landscape biography makes use of cultural-historical knowledge without drawing a sharp line between past and present, making it particularly well-suited as a tool for applying heritage knowledge to current spatial planning tasks. Although the concept of landscape biography was introduced as early as the

1970s and has already been applied to many regions, its practical use in landscape/ spatial planning remains limited.

The main challenge, therefore, lies not in expanding our knowledge of the cultural history of the landscape and the intangible heritage practices that helped shape it, but in effectively integrating this knowledge into spatial policy—thereby connecting heritage, environment, and spatial planning in a coherent way. In a recent policy evaluation by the Ministry of Education, Culture and Science, the State Secretary at the time Gunay Uslu acknowledged that "heritage must be linked to major transitions such as climate adaptation and the energy transition" (Uslu 2023, p. 1). Some of the examples discussed in this chapter highlight that it is indeed worthwhile strengthening this link. The discussed case studies also illustrate, however, that there is still a long road ahead to solidify and strengthen that connection.

References

Asselman N, van Heeringen K, de Jong J, Geertsema T (2022) Juli 2021. Overstromingen en wateroverlast in Zuid-Limburg. In: Eerste bevindingen voor Valkenburg, Geulmonding, Roermonding en Eygelshoven. Deltares, Delft

Barnosky AD, Matzke N (2011) Has the earth's sixth mass extinction already arrived? Nature 471:51–57

Bleumink H, Neefjes J (2018) Handboek Beken en Erfgoed. Beeklandschappen met karakter. STOWA & RCE, Amersfoort

Blom A, Jansen B, van der Heiden M (2004) De typologie van de vroeg-naoorlogse woonwijken. Zeist, RCE

Bosma K, Kolen J (eds) (2010) Geschiedenis en ontwerp. Handboek voor de omgang met cultureel erfgoed. Vantilt, Nijmegen

Dastgerdi AS, Sargolini M, Pierantoni I (2019) Climate change challenges to existing cultural heritage policy. Sustainability 11:5227–5237

Dekker S, van Hamel GA, Kolen B, Honingh D (2021) Provinciale Normering Wateroverlast. Hoe toekomstbestending is de huidige aanpak en werkwijze? STOWA, Amersfoort

Déri A, Sundaresan J (2012) Diverse epistemic traditions in transformative climate change research and adaptation: heritage and legacy. In: Harvey D, Perry J (eds) The future of heritage as climates change: loss, adaptation and creativity. Routledge, New York, pp 78–94

Duijn M, Pot WD (2023) Goverance van water en bodem sturend. Water Gov 3:14–18

Duyvendak JW (1999) De planning van ontplooiing. Wetenschap, politiek en de maakbare samenleving. SDU, Den Haag

European Parliament (2021) Ontwerpresolutie van het Europees Parlement over de ontwikkeling van doeltreffend beleid naar aanleiding van het Europees Jaar van het Cultureel Erfgoed. https://www.europarl.europa.eu/doceo/document/A-9-2020-0210_NL.pdf. Accessed 26 June 25

Fatorić S, Biesbroek R (2020) Adapting cultural heritage to climate change impact in The Netherlands: barriers, interdependencies, and strategies for overcoming them. Climate Change 162:301–320

Grond V, Maas G, Kosian M, Vreenegoor E (2021) De stadsgenese. Cultuurhistorie en het natuurlijke systeem als gids voor klimaatadaptatie en stedelijke ontwikkeling. STOWA, Amersfoort

Hall P (1988) Cities of tomorrow. Wiley, Oxford

Huizenga H (2016) Oogst van het krijtlandschap. Cultuurhistorie en bijna vergeten beheertechnieken voor opbrengst van erf en terrein. Peredour, Maarn

Hulst R (2010) Modern erfgoedbeheer in een gefragmenteerd bestuurlijk stelsel. In: Bosma K, Kolen J (eds) Geschiedenis en ontwerp. Handboek voor de omgang met cultureel erfgoed. Vantilt, Nijmegen, pp 140–161

ICOMOS (2020) Resolution 20GA/15 – cultural heritage and the climate emergency. https://www.icomos.org/images/DOCUMENTS/Secretariat/2020/Cultural_Heritage_and_the_Climate_Emergency-Resolution_20GA_15.pdf. Accessed 26 June 2025

ICOMOS (2021) Scientific council of ICOMOS triennial scientific plan 2021–2024. Cultural heritage and climate action. https://www.icomos.org/images/DOCUMENTS/Secretariat/2022/TSP/ADCOMSC_202110_2-1_Triennial_Scientific_Plan_EN.pdf. Accessed 26 June 2025

ICOMOS (2022) Impacts, vulnerability, and understanding risks from climate change to culture and heritage. A white paper commissioned for the international co-sponsored meeting on culture, heritage and climate change. ICOMOS, Charenton-le-Pont

Janssen J, Luiten E, Renes H, Stegmeijer E (2017) Heritage as sector, factor and vector: conceptualizing the shifting relationship between heritage management and spatial planning. Eur Plan Stud 25:1654–1672

Jensen L (2020) De opmars van disaster studies. Nieuwe perspectieven in het rampenonderzoek. De Moderne Tijd. De Lage Landen, 1780–1940 4:147–164

Kolen J, Bosma K, Renes H (2010) De landschapsbiografie: instrument voor onderzoek, planning en ontwerp. In: Bosma K, Kolen J (eds) Geschiedenis en ontwerp. Handboek voor de omgang met cultureel erfgoed. Vantilt, Nijmegen, pp 212–237

Leissner J, Grady A, Maider M, Baeke F, van Cutsem A (2022) Strengtenhing cultural heritage resilience for climate change. Where the European green deal meets cultural heritage. Publications Office of the European Union, Luxemburg

de Mars H (2013) De Roer, een getemde wildebras. Natuurhistorisch Maandblad 102:105–110

McNeill JR (2010) The state of the field of environmental history. Annu Rev Environ Resour 35:345–374

NAS (2007) Maak ruimte voor klimaat! Nationale adaptatiestrategie, de beleidsnotitie. NAS, The Hague

NAS (2016) Aanpassen met ambitie. Nationale klimaatadaptatiestrategie 2016. NAS, The Hague

NAS (2020) Nationaal perspectief klimaatadaptatie. Groeiende opgave in een snel veranderende omgeving. NAS, The Hague

NUPKA (2023) Nationaal Uitvoeringsprogramma Klimaatadaptatie. Slimmer, intensiever, voor en door iedereen. NUPKA, The Hague

Paulissen M (2018) Talig erfgoed in het landschap: geografische namen als landschapshistorische bron. De Maasgouw 137:17–22

RCE (2021) Waterschade aan Limburgs erfgoed. https://www.cultureelerfgoed.nl/actueel/nieuws/2021/07/21/waterschade-aan-limburgs-erfgoed. Accessed 26 June 2025

Renes H (1990) De invloed van de mens op de zuidlimburgse beekdalen in het verleden. Natuurhistorisch Maandblad 79:80–88

Rowland MJ (1992) Climate change, sea-level rise and the archaeological record. Aust Archaeol 34:29–33

Schouten CJ, Rang MC, Huigen PMJ (1985) Erosie en wateroverlast in Zuid-Limburg. Landschap 2:118–132

Sesana E, Gagnon AS, Bonazza A, Hughes JJ (2020) An integrated approach for assessing the vulnerability of World Heritage Sites to climate change impacts. J Cult Herit 41:211–224

Slager K (2023) Gevolgen overstromingen Limburg. Inventarisatie en duiding. Deltares, Delft

Storms-Smeets EAC (2019) Erfgoedensembles in Zuid-Limburg. Leegstand en herbestemming van molens, boerderijen, kastelen en buitenplaatsen. Gelders Genootschap, Arnhem

Tennekes J et al (2022) Erfgoed als leefomgevingskwaliteit. Een referentiekader voor de dialoog over de waarde van het bestaande bij ruimtelijke ingrepen. Planbureau voor de leefomgeving, Den Haag

Terrill G (2008) Climate change: how should the world heritage convention respond? Int J Herit Stud 14:388–404

Turner S, Shillito L, Carrer F (2019) Landscape archaeology. In: Howard P, Thompson I, Waterton E (eds) The Routledge companion to landscape studies. Routledge, Londen and New York, pp 155–166

Uslu G (2023) Beleidsdoorlichting Onderwijs, Cultuur en Wetenschap. Brief van de Staatssecretaris van Onderwijs, Cultuur en Wetenschap aan de voorzitter van de Tweede Kamer der Staten-Generaal. https://www.rijksoverheid.nl/documenten/kamerstukken/2023/06/12/bijlage-1-afschrift-kamerbrief-beleidsreactie-op-beleidsdoorlichting-erfgoed. Accessed 26 June 2025

van der Valk A, Korthals Altes W (2010) Ruimtelijk ordening en cultuurhistorie: een instrumenteel en planologisch perspectief. In: Bosma K, Kolen J (eds) Geschiedenis en ontwerp. Handboek voor de omgang met cultureel erfgoed. Vantilt, Nijmegen, pp 114–138

Weststeijn T (2023) De toekomst van het verleden. Erfgoed en klimaat. Prometheus, Amsterdam

World Bank (2023) The development, climate, and nature crisis: solutions to end poverty on a livable planet. Insights from World Bank Country Climate and Development Reports covering 42 economies. World Bank Group, Washington

Zwegers B (2024) Erfgoed in zwaar weer. Limburgs erfgoed in tijden van klimaatverandering. Huis voor de Kunsten Limburg, Roermond

Zwegers B, van Knippenberg K (2024) Erfgoedensembles en klimaatadaptatie: grenzen aan de maakbaarheid. In: Randeraad N, Roosen J (eds) Studies over de sociaaleconomische geschiedenis van Limburg 69. Sociaal Historisch Centrum Limburg, Maastricht, pp 266–284

Bart Zwegers is the curator academic heritage of Maastricht University and works as a lecturer at the Faculty of Arts and Social Sciences of Maastricht University. He has an educational background in arts and culture. Between 2018 and 2021 he was a lecturer in social and political history at Radboud University Nijmegen. In 2022 he published the monograph *cultural heritage in transition. A multilevel perspective on world heritage in Germany and the United Kingdom,* 1970–2020 with Springer.

Karim van Knippenberg was trained as an urban planner and works as a heritage specialist at the consultancy firm HeusschenCopier Landschapskracht based in Gulpen, the Netherlands. Over the past years, he has helped implement the provincial program *ErfgoedLAB Limburg,* which supports owners in addressing complex issues related to the preservation of their heritage ensembles. In 2022, he obtained his PhD from Ghent University with a dissertation on the involvement of local communities in the redevelopment of vacant and underutilized historic heritage.

www.ingramcontent.com/pod-product-compliance
Ingram Content Group UK Ltd.
Pitfield, Milton Keynes, MK11 3LW, UK
UKHW020934180926
475692UK00003B/37
* 9 7 8 3 0 3 2 2 5 3 5 1 4 *